Key Concepts in
Work

The SAGE Key Concepts series provides students with accessible and authoritative knowledge of the essential topics in a variety of disciplines. Cross-referenced throughout, the format encourages critical evaluation through understanding. Written by experienced and respected academics, the books are indispensable study aids and guides to comprehension.

PAUL BLYTON AND JEAN JENKINS

Key Concepts in
Work

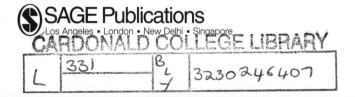

SAGE Publications
Los Angeles · London · New Delhi · Singapore

SAGE Publications Ltd
1 Oliver's Yard
55 City Road
London EC1Y 1SP

SAGE Publications Inc.
2455 Teller Road
Thousand Oaks, California 91320

SAGE Publications India Pvt Ltd
B 1/I 1 Mohan Cooperative Industrial Area
Mathura Road, New Delhi 110 044

SAGE Publications Asia-Pacific Pte Ltd
33 Pekin Street #02-01
Far East Square
Singapore 048763

Library of Congress Control Number: 2007924711

British Library Cataloguing in Publication data

A catalogue record for this book is available from the
British Library

ISBN 978-0-7619-4477-5
ISBN 978-0-7619-4478-2 (pbk)

Typeset by C&M Digitals (P) Ltd, Chennai, India
Printed in Great Britain by The Cromwell Press Ltd, Trowbridge, Wiltshire
Printed on paper from sustainable resources

contents

contents

v

Introduction

There are several good reasons why a series exploring the Key Concepts of different fields should have a volume devoted to 'work'. It is not only that work takes up an enormous quantity of time and energy in most people's lives. Nor is it simply that, for the majority, work, and the income that work generates, are the means by which people 'make ends meet'. It is also to do with the way in which many experience work as a contradictory activity, and it is these contradictions that also make work important to understand and think about. More than half a century of studies have highlighted various positive outcomes arising from work: that it plays a central role in giving many people a sense of purpose and structure in their lives; that it represents a source of accomplishment, self-worth and satisfaction; and that it is an important context for social relations and support. Yet, at the same time, work can also be a major cause of boredom, frustration and stress. Many jobs are characterized by a work routine that is monotonous or pressured (sometimes both simultaneously) and prolonged exposure to these conditions can be a serious threat to individuals' physical and psychological well-being. Even to those who gain satisfaction and fulfilment from their work, few jobs are without their monotonous or frustrating side. Indeed, for most people, work is an activity that generates both satisfaction and anxiety, fulfilment and frustration.

In addition to this contradictory nature of the work experience, there are other issues that make work a problematic activity and thereby raise important questions that need to be considered. One of these, which has important wider implications, is which various activities clearly involving work are often overlooked. In particular, work that is unpaid – notably, voluntary and household activities – tends to be neglected in many discussions on work. One effect of this is to reinforce the significance accorded to those work activities that receive payment and give much lower visibility to those work activities that are not paid. What makes this difference in attention more significant, however, is that in most societies it remains the case that women undertake a disproportionate share of unpaid household work, while men participate to a greater extent in the paid labour force. Thus the upshot of unduly concentrating on paid work is not only to neglect consideration of unpaid work, but thereby to accord a lower significance to the work that takes up a large proportion of many women's lives.

A further neglected but important consideration about work in contemporary society is that, for many workers in the paid labour market, their exact contractual status as an 'employee' is ambiguous. Depending on the national legal framework, this may mean that workers outside the primary labour market (made up of core, permanent employees) will not qualify for certain statutory rights and may receive less favourable contractual terms and treatment. Generally speaking, such workers will form part of a secondary labour market. In this volume, therefore, we refer to 'workers' and 'employees' throughout, in a conscious attempt to highlight the significance of contractual status for the working lives and wider prospects of ordinary people.

It is also important to study work because, in many respects, it is an activity that remains characterized by major shortcomings: it is not a field where the problems have been ironed out, leaving nothing that requires attention. On the contrary, it is a domain where key problems continue unresolved. Many people, for example, remain subject to working conditions that should be unacceptable in an advanced society: unsafe or unhealthy environments; workplaces where different groups are unfairly discriminated against and where bullying, harassment and unfair treatment remain everyday occurrences; work contexts where insecurity poses an ever-present threat; and organizations where those at the top award themselves huge pay increases and bonuses while neglecting to improve the pay and conditions of those lower down the hierarchy. The presence of these and other shortcomings in the way that work is organized underlines the continued importance of analysing the nature of work and the issues that need to be addressed for work to become characterized more by good, satisfying jobs, and less by bad and alienating ones.

Studying work at this time is made more significant by the scale and pace of change occurring both in the nature of work itself, and in the social, economic and political contexts in which that work is located. The growing internationalization of production of goods and services; continued developments in technology and work organization; the evolution of labour markets due to inward and outward migration flows; changes in male and female participation rates and demographic trends (particularly the ageing of populations and workforces); and shifting values regarding the balance between work and non-work lives, are all impacting on the overall nature of work. They are impacting too on the individual experience of work: the security of employment that people feel, for example, their experience of work intensity and the continued value placed on their skills and experience.

Our selection of Key Concepts tries to reflect all of these concerns. Hence, we have included, for example, discussions on domestic and voluntary work that help to define work in broader terms. The list also includes many entries that reflect both the broad character and the changing experience of work, and also the context in which work is located. Our aim has been both to convey a sense of how the experience of work is changing and how the context within which that work takes place is developing. We have attempted to take a view of work that acknowledges the importance of context and history and the way in which current developments may often be better understood with an appreciation of what has gone before. We have been mindful too that to understand fully the importance of work, we need to consider not only its presence but also its absence or threatened removal; hence we consider unemployment, redundancy and job security as further ways of reflecting on the importance of work for individuals and for society.

One of the things hardest to convey in a book of this sort is that work is a hugely diverse activity: that the nature and experience of work vary enormously between individuals and between different work settings. Further, it is often not possible to 'read off' the consequences of particular aspects of work, and thus make broad generalizations. Thus, for example, the long hours of work that many people experience (and which we consider at a number of points in the book) may be abhorred by some (those with child-care responsibilities, for example, and those with passions for different leisure activities) yet loved by others (those for whom work is their passion). Similarly, part-time working may be the way that some people positively seek a better work–life balance, while for others their part-time jobs may be the cause of their inability to secure enough income to live on. A key issue is the degree of *choice* that is available to workers within the labour market and, in this respect, the question of whether there is a suitable and acceptable alternative available to them or not may often be the determining factor. The general point here is that, while seeking patterns and explanations in the study of work, we must also exercise caution in drawing conclusions as if all work is experienced in a uniform way by all those involved.

With these points in mind, what we have sought to achieve is to give a sense of the main issues within each of the Key Concept areas, but also the questions that remain unresolved and require further attention.

The references provided at the end of each entry, together with the cross-references to other entries within the volume, shown in bold, will be of some assistance in this further exploration.

In preparing this volume we have had valuable help from several colleagues. Thanks in particular to Betsy Blunsdon, Stephen McEachern, Nicola McNeil and Ken Reed for their thoughts when we were drawing up the list of Key Concepts, and to Sue O'Brien and Penny Smith for their help in tracking down various of the sources we have drawn upon.

Absence and Turnover

Absence from work may be involuntary (due to sickness, for example) or voluntary (individuals choosing to stay away from work). Turnover refers to the termination of an employment contract, which again may be voluntary or involuntary.

As the first Key Concept in this volume on work, it might appear something of a paradox that we begin with a topic dealing with workers' absence from work and exit from their employing organizations. The fact that we begin with absence is determined by the alphabetica organization of the contents, but it is serendipitous, for in considering these two aspects of worker behaviour we begin to engage with issues of control, consent and conflict that are important to our broader analysis of work and recur as themes throughout the volume. In discussing absence, we will be considering both 'genuine' involuntary absence due to ill health and other unavoidable causes, as well as workers who absent themselves from work for other, voluntary reasons. With regard to turnover, we will examine the involuntary causes of labour turnover, such as dismissal, redundancy or retirement, as well as voluntary labour turnover, where individual workers quit their jobs.

INVOLUNTARY ABSENCE AND TURNOVER

At some time, most individuals will be forced to be absent from work due to ill health or injury. This we refer to as involuntary absence. The likelihood that workers may at times be unable to work due to ill health or injury is recognized by provision for sickness payments. These may be contractual benefits, paid by the employer, or statutory sickness benefits legislated for by the state. Where an employee has contractual entitlements to sick pay, the exact amount and duration of company sick pay entitlements will often relate to length of service and the contractual status of the worker. A significant proportion of workers, however, will not be in the fortunate position of having an employer that runs a sick pay scheme or they may have been unable to establish sufficient continuity of service or secure the type of contract that brings with it entitlements to company sick pay. Therefore, in many countries, particularly in the developed world, the state intervenes to ensure that workers who are unwell or injured have some means of financial support.

In the same way that absence may be involuntary and unavoidable for the individual worker, the termination of their employment contract may lie outside of their control. There are many scenarios where employment may be brought to an end without workers having much say in the matter. For example, the state or an employing organization, may impose a compulsory retirement age for workers – by law in the first case or through the employment contract in the second. There will also be occasions when an employing organization will seek to reduce its complement of employees and will make workers redundant (see **Redundancy**). Alternatively, the employer may seek to bring an individual employment contract to an end for a variety of other reasons, perhaps associated with the capability or conduct of an employee. For example, in terms of UK employment law, an individual's persistent absenteeism, even if genuinely related to ill health, could well be a justifiable reason for an organization to terminate their contract of employment (see **The Law and Contract of Employment**). Thus, in many cases, absence and turnover may be involuntary or imposed upon the worker. But now we turn to consider a very different situation, where it is the worker who is making choices about whether to go absent or leave the organization – voluntary absence and voluntary labour turnover.

VOLUNTARY ABSENCE AND LABOUR TURNOVER: WORKER RESPONSE TO MANAGERIAL CONTROL

Voluntary absence and voluntary turnover describe situations where individual workers make a choice. For example, workers may choose to go absent from work even though they are not genuinely ill or stay away from work longer than they need after having recovered from a genuine illness. Similarly, workers may decide to resign and to leave their employment, even though their employer would wish them to remain. This may be for better job opportunities, higher wages or self-fulfilment and this form of turnover represents a positive change for the individual concerned. But turnover may also occur in circumstances where the individual has no better job opportunity waiting for them elsewhere and this is the form of 'voluntary' turnover we are mainly concerned with here.

Voluntary absence has long been recognized as a serious organizational problem for managers. For example, early British industrialists, desperate to establish discipline and regular attendance within their factories, made efforts to influence the morals of their workers and encourage them to adopt sobriety and the Protestant 'work ethic' as a means of counteracting the tendency of workers to absent themselves from the drudgery of factory life (Pollard, 1965: 182–94). More than a century later, however, employers were still complaining of workers absenting themselves from work without good cause.

It is relatively easy to attribute such actions to a lack of 'work ethic' or motivation and many managers take this view. There is also a common perception that women are more prone to absence than men and that younger workers are more irresponsible about absence than older workers. However, research suggests that, rather than looking for easy answers in stereotypes of certain categories of worker, we also need to look to managerial control systems for the causes of voluntary absenteeism. For example, some research identifies higher levels of absence in certain areas of feminized employment, such as clothing manufacture, than in male-dominated industries, such as engineering. But the intensive controls and lack of worker bargaining power in the clothing industry have traditionally been linked to high levels of absence and quitting as an escape from the pressures of the factory floor. Thus it may be the characteristics of particular control systems within those industries that acts as the determining factor, rather than the gender of workers (Edwards and Scullion, 1982: 97–103). In order to explore this issue, we need to briefly consider the complex interaction of control, conflict and consent that is central to the employment relationship and work.

Work comes in various forms: there are countless different work activities and a range of occupations demanding different types of skills. But what all work has in common is that the tasks will need to be organized, controlled and coordinated in the interests of organizational efficiency and effectiveness. This requires management and rules governing relationships and the organization of work. The fundamental need for work as a means of gaining a livelihood is a powerful impulse for workers to cooperate and consent to managerial control, but there is also plenty of potential for conflict (see **Conflict** and **Consent**). For example, managers will enforce controls over the pace and nature of work and they will also have considerable influence in determining how much workers get paid: two areas where the interests of employers and the employed may not always coincide and where workers may wish to exert their own influence (see **Perspectives on Work**).

Hence it is important to recognize that workers are not merely passive recipients of managerial controls; they respond, react, resist even. If workers belong to a trade union, elements of their response to managerial control may be collectively organized. In some sectors such as retailing, however, a strong union voice is absent, even where levels of union membership may be relatively high: union presence does not always equate with union influence (see **Trade Unions**).

Thus, workers may face problems in exercising control over their working lives, even where collective representational mechanisms exist. In many situations the only option open to workers is that they react as individuals. Voluntary absence and turnover are most commonly examples of individualized, unorganized worker responses to managerial control systems though, more rarely, absence may also be collectively organized. We will first consider absence and turnover as an individualized phenomenon, before examining the far less common but nevertheless significant issue of absence as an organized collective action.

Much enquiry has focused on the relationship of absence levels to the strength of collective organization within a workplace, based on the premise that where collective trade union power is relatively weak, absence is an alternative way for individuals to express conflict with their working environment. But it is not a straightforward equation that a lack of collective strength leads to high levels of absence. Individualized expressions of conflict are not necessarily dependent on the lack of a strong collective voice, but in a situation where neither individual nor collective bargaining power seems likely to change one's experience of work, 'quietly to leave a situation can be an important way of expressing dissatisfaction with it' (Edwards and Scullion, 1982: 53). While the structure within which people work and bargain does not necessarily determine a specific response to managerial control, it will nevertheless have a bearing on what is possible (Edwards, 1988: 188). Thus it may be possible for different industries, occupations and workplaces to have characteristic and different patterns of absence and turnover that relate to the complex interactions of managerial control systems, custom and practice and the organization of work in different settings (Edwards and Scullion, 1982: 274–7).

The final choice exercised by the individual over whether they leave their employment once and for all or obtain a temporary respite from the pressures, drudgery or boredom of their work through absence, may depend on many external factors. For example, does the employer monitor absence and impose penalties such as the loss of entitlement to company sick pay? How easy will it be to find alternative employment? Will another job prove any better? For some workers, for whom quitting would impose a heavy cost, they may seek refuge in occasional absenteeism; if alternative employment is available and quitting is less of a risk, then that may become the preferred option. This is not a collective or 'organized' response, nor is it necessarily an action where the individual is aware of making an expression of conflict. But to avoid attending work when fit to do so, or quitting altogether, suggests at least a degree of discontent or disaffection. Thus, voluntary absence and turnover can be described as 'unorganized' and 'informal' expressions of conflict with the formal controls of the workplace.

But what happens when absence or turnover is organized? For examples of organized turnover we can look back at some of the earliest trade union strategies, while for an example of organized absence we need not go so far back in time. In times when trade union activity was outlawed in Britain, unions used a 'nameless weapon', which the historians Sidney and Beatrice Webb (1897: 168–9) called 'the "Strike in Detail"'. This practice involved the trade union organizing labour turnover, so that employers who refused to pay the union rate of pay found themselves unable to retain their workers. No actual strike was involved, but workers gave notice shortly after commencing employment and the union used its funds to support their members while out of work. The rate of turnover made it very difficult for employers to organize their production.

Fast forward to 1997 and we have a modern-day example of the use of what became termed a 'mass-sickie' at British Airways (BA). In a dispute between BA and its cabin crew, BA management used the fact that under UK employment law there is no positive legal right to strike to warn that strike action would result in serious sanctions: among other things, summary dismissals, prosecution for damages and loss of promotion. At the time, BA's actions were entirely lawful (the law on industrial action in the UK has been amended and now gives employees protection from dismissal within the first twelve weeks of a lawful, official strike). In the event, BA management threats influenced the impact of the 1997 strike as, on the day of action, fewer than 300 workers declared themselves on strike but more than 2,000 called in sick. Thus we see that, while turnover and absence may be identified in the main as individualized actions, their use as collective weapons is nevertheless possible and does indeed occur.

THE CHALLENGES OF MANAGING ABSENCE AND TURNOVER

In earlier times research suggested that managers might have complained but often did not do a great deal to tackle the problem of absence (see Behrend and Pocock, 1976: 325). At times when organizations ran their affairs with high levels of labour input, absence was indeed a problem, but it was something which was an irritant, rather than one that 'necessarily threaten[ed] the organisation of work' (Edwards, 1986: 46). However, more recent changes in the structure and nature of work, associated with the move to leaner management systems, have made voluntary absence and turnover a far more pressing problem for managers today.

The trend to so-called 'leaner', 'flexible' systems of working, which eradicate waste in terms of time, resources and manpower, is associated with more people reporting their work having 'intensified' (see **Effort and Intensity**). Leaner production systems seek to eliminate 'slack' in the system; the absence of one person is therefore quickly felt and can rapidly affect the flow of production or the quality of the service. Thus it is that contemporary managers seek more data on absence and new initiatives for its control. For example, the Chartered Institute of Personnel and Development (CIPD) in the UK, publishes detailed analyses of the cost of absence. In 2006, it recorded absence as a significant cost to 90 per cent of businesses, at an average rate, by their estimation, of £598 per employee per year. The CIPD offers employers advice on absence policies to try to bring these absence levels down. But the managerial problem remains that the pressures and controls which may be linked with more competitive and intensified working environments may also increase workers' sense of disaffection and demoralization and increase the risk of causing work-related illness. Thus, there is an increased likelihood of genuine stress-related illness as a cause of absence but there is also the probability that at least some workers will continue to choose occasionally to absent themselves, simply to gain respite from the work process (see Edwards, 1988: 189; also Edwards and Scullion, 1982: 96).

In conclusion, we can see that absence and turnover take involuntary and voluntary forms. We have considered voluntary absence and turnover as responses to the structure and organization of work and as indicators of workers' response to their working environment. Any serious analysis of absence and turnover must avoid easy generalizations about the work ethic, or lack of it, and recognize that the nature of managerial control systems will be influential factors in shaping worker response.

See also: career, management, surviving work, working time.

REFERENCES

Behrend, H. and Pocock, S. (1976) 'Absence and the individual: a six year study in one organisation', *International Labour Review*, 114 (3): 311–27.

Chartered Institute of Personnel and Development (CIPD) website: www.cipd.co.uk

Edwards, P.K. (1986) *Conflict at Work: A Materialist Analysis of Workplace Relations.* Oxford: Basil Blackwell.

Edwards, P.K. (1988) 'Patterns of conflict and accommodation', in D. Gallie (ed.), *Employment in Britain.* Oxford: Blackwell.

Edwards, P.K. and Scullion, H. (1982) *The Social Organization of Industrial Conflict: Control and Resistance in the Workplace*: Oxford: Blackwell.

Pollard, S. (1965) *The Genesis of Modern Management: A Study of the Industrial Revolution in Great Britain* (reprinted 1993). Aldershot: Gregg Revivals.

Webb, S. and Webb, B. (1897) *Industrial Democracy.* London: Longmans, Green & Co.

Alienation

Alienation refers to a sense of estrangement; the lack or loss of a close affinity with others, with activities or with oneself.

11

Alienation contrasts with several other Key Concepts discussed in this volume, such as **Job Satisfaction** and **Motivation and Commitment**, and emphasizes the way in which individuals may find work, at times or as a whole, a negative and hostile experience. We will examine alienation by considering the different approaches of two of the leading writers on the subject – Karl Marx and Robert Blauner.

MARX ON ALIENATION

In identifying the conditions under which work may be alienating for those performing it, two distinct perspectives exist, each operating at a different level of analysis. The first, developed by Karl Marx and published in *Economic and Philosophical Manuscripts of 1844* (and reproduced in Marx, 1969), locates the source of alienation within the capitalist labour process itself and the social class relations that derive from capitalist organization. By selling their labour power, workers are seen to be estranged or separated from the product of their own efforts: those labouring for a wage give up the right to control the products of their labour. Further, as a result of the division of labour, which Marx viewed as a key characteristic of the capitalist labour process, workers lose any control over the production process that they might otherwise have retained by performing a broad range of tasks.

Marx identifies four elements of alienation.

1   *Alienation from the products of labour*: workers produce not for themselves but for the employer, in return for a wage.
2   *Alienation from the process of production*: jobs are fragmented, through a division of labour, and controlled by others, resulting in workers losing any sense of performing a whole job.
3   *Alienation of workers from their 'species-being'*: for Marx, work is intrinsic to the very idea of being human. Thus, by estranging workers from the creative act of work (either by controlling what the worker produces or the way it is produced) this denies the worker an essential part of what it is to be human.
4   *Alienation from others*: the first three forms of alienation – from the product of the worker's labour, the way in which that product is produced and alienation from the very essence of what it is to be human – result in a fourth aspect of estranged labour: alienation from others. Thus, for Marx, under capitalism the worker is both self-estranged and estranged from his or her fellow workers.

In Marx's analysis, then, alienation is embedded in the very structure of capitalism: put differently, for Marx the very nature of waged labour is alienating. Given this perspective, the only way to remove alienation is to replace capitalism with a form of production where workers create and utilize the fruits of their own labour; that is, where workers are in control of their labour and the product of that labour. Thus, from a

key concepts in work

Marxian perspective, since alienation stems from the objective conditions of capitalism, any attempts to reduce or remove alienation that operate within (rather than by transforming) capitalism will simply act to mask the true conditions and consequences of capitalism.

BLAUNER ON ALIENATION

In more recent times, alternative perspectives on alienation have developed. Most notably this has involved viewing alienation not as solely an *objective* condition of capitalism as Marx did, but as also a *subjective* condition, experienced in some settings and among some workers, but not all settings or among all those working within a capitalist system. The person most identified with this view of alienation as both a subjective experience as well as an objective condition is Robert Blauner. His ideas on alienation are developed in his book *Alienation and Freedom* (1964). For Blauner, it is the nature of technology more than any other single factor that influences whether or not 'general alienating tendencies' existing within capitalism are translated into actual experiences of alienation among workers. Thus, rather than all capitalist enterprises inevitably generating alienation among the workforce (the Marxian position), Blauner is concerned with the conditions under which different technologies within those enterprises generate different degrees of alienation.

For Blauner also, alienation comprises four elements.

1   A sense of *powerlessness* – a feeling of a lack of personal autonomy or control over the work process.
2   A sense of *meaninglessness* – a result of the division of labour, with individual fragmented jobs lacking any sense of meaningful purpose.
3   A sense of *isolation* – a feeling of not being able to develop or maintain social relationships with fellow workers, due to the way that technology is utilized and work processes organized.
4   A sense of *self-estrangement* – a feeling that the worker is unable to gain fulfilment and self-expression in the job.

Blauner argues that different forms of technology make these conditions more or less likely (see **Technology**). Drawing on surveys of employees in four manufacturing industries (printing, textiles, automobile assembly and chemicals), he argues first that traditional craft-based technologies (such as in traditional print companies) that rely on individual skills

alienation

13

and judgements tend to be the least alienating. Not only do those craft employees enjoy considerable discretion and control over the way they carry out their work (thus have a low sense of powerlessness), but also craft jobs tend to be less fragmented than others (giving rise to a greater sense of meaning), are less isolating than other forms of technology (allowing a greater sense of occupational community to develop) and are less self-estranging since they allow a sense of fulfilment in the performance of the skill.

In discussing other forms of technology, Blauner identifies machine-minding (such as in the textile mill) and particularly assembly-line technologies (such as automobile assembly) as containing much greater potential for alienation. Machine-paced work (resulting in a lack of control over work pace and a lack of freedom of movement) coupled with a high division of labour (resulting in the fragmentation of jobs) are evident in traditional machine-minding jobs, but are at their most extreme in assembly-line operations where any sense of powerlessness and meaninglessness is heightened by a sense of isolation (many workers being 'tied' to a particular position on the assembly line) and a sense of self-estrangement due to the unfulfilling nature of most assembly-line jobs.

However, in discussing very highly automated work settings, Blauner ultimately provides a more optimistic analysis of alienation. For when he turns to the most advanced forms of technology (such as continuous process operations in chemical plants), he argues that these jobs are less alienating than assembly-line jobs, with many workers in such contexts enjoying more freedom of movement, lower work pressure and more responsible jobs than their counterparts in assembly-line activities. Thus, rather than viewing developments in technology as inevitably leading to greater levels of alienation, Blauner plots a non-linear, inverted 'U'-shaped relationship between technological development and alienation, with alienation first increasing as technology moves from craft-based to machine and assembly operations, but then starting to decline among those engaged with some forms of more advanced technology.

Blauner has been criticized for putting too much emphasis on technology as the explanatory variable for alienation at the expense of other possible organizational factors. Likewise, some argue that his analysis gives too little acknowledgement to the fact that workers can successfully resist alienating pressures and that different individuals working with a similar technology can experience different levels of alienation. These criticisms relate to a question of emphasis, however. For example Blauner was aware that the relationship between particular technologies and alienation is not an automatic one. As he noted (1964: 11), organizational policies, the character of the labour force and the personalities of individual employees all 'influence their subjective and behavioral responses to objectively alienating conditions'.

Finally, while Blauner held a generally positive view of automation as regards the effects on people's jobs (at least those in continuous process operations), others have argued very differently about the impact of increased automation. For example, as Braverman (1974) and others have pointed out, automation can entail a further loss of, rather than an increase in, employee control, not only as skill becomes increasingly lodged in the automated process (rather than in the worker overseeing that process) but also as the scope for monitoring worker activity is enhanced by the equipment operating in automated settings (see **Labour Process**). In addition, Blauner may have overestimated the level of interest and satisfaction in monitoring equipment that, if running smoothly, could be as interesting and stimulating as watching paint dry (see **Job Satisfaction**). However, what Blauner did importantly achieve was to conceptualize alienation as a condition that will be experienced by individuals to differing degrees, rather than that all workers under capitalism experience alienation to the same degree (for a more detailed discussion of both Marx and Blauner on alienation, see Noon and Blyton, 2007).

ALIENATION AND BUREAUCRACY

While Blauner concentrated mainly on alienation in manual worker settings such as assembly lines, later studies have considered other work contexts, for example identifying the potential link between alienation and bureaucracy and specifically the bureaucratic organization of non-manual work (for a review, see Sarros et al., 2002: 288–90; see also **Bureaucracy**). Bureaucracies are typified by a formalized hierarchy of authority, together with an extensive set of rules specifying responsibilities and governing the behaviour of employees, thereby limiting any scope for job autonomy. However, in the study by Sarros et al. (2002) of management styles in a highly bureaucratic organization, they found that the alienating effects of the organizational structure could be significantly reduced (or, in contrast, reinforced) by the leadership style adopted by the managers within the bureaucracy. In particular, in those contexts where managers adopted a more consultative style of managing and gave their subordinates a sense of involvement in decisions and more generally a greater sense of purpose in their work, lower levels of alienation were evident among the staff than among their counterparts who were subject to being managed with a greater emphasis on reinforcing the rules of the organization and the importance of employees keeping to the formal procedures. What this study indicates, therefore, is that, while bureaucratic organizations contain features that are potentially alienating (for example, by placing restrictions on the degree of job autonomy), these features can be offset by social relations established within the organization.

CONCLUSION

Though first discussed more than a century and a half ago, the concept of alienation still has relevance today. Where the emphasis has shifted during that time, however, is away from alienation as an objective condition and towards it as a subjective experience. In contemporary thinking about the causes of alienation, however, both the Marxian analysis and that of Blauner have a value: the former encourages us to think about the broad structural or societal factors giving rise to alienation, while the latter encourages a consideration of particular conditions prevailing within work organizations. More recent research on non-manual settings demonstrates the continuing importance of the concept of alienation and the problems that some face in obtaining work that is satisfying and fulfilling.

See also: *conflict, skill, surviving work.*

REFERENCES

Blauner, R. (1964) *Alienation and Freedom*. Chicago: University of Chicago Press.
Braverman, H. (1974) *Labor and Monopoly Capital*. New York: Monthly Review Press.
Marx, K. (1969) 'Alienated labour', in T. Burns (ed.), *Industrial Man: Selected Readings*. Harmondsworth: Penguin, pp. 95–109.
Noon, M. and Blyton, P. (2007) *The Realities of Work*, 3rd edn. Basingstoke: Palgrave Macmillan.
Sarros, J.C., Tanewski, G.A., Winter, R.P., Santora, J.C. and Densten, I.L. (2002) 'Work alienation and organizational leadership', *British Journal of Management*, 13: 285–304.

key concepts in work

Bureaucracy

> Bureaucracy refers to 'the control and co-ordination of work tasks through a hierarchy of appropriately qualified office holders, whose authority derives from their expertise and who rationally devise a system of rules and procedures that are calculated to provide the most appropriate means of achieving specified ends' (Watson, 2003: 86).

Bureaucracy gets a bad press. The term is seen by most as synonymous with a slow response, impersonality, inflexibility, a reliance on overly complex rules existing for their own sake and with no one able to take responsibility for decisions. Bureaucracies are portrayed as unbending, faceless, uncaring, frustrating and a means of slowing down decisions rather than an organizational system for making decisions. Likewise to acknowledge that one's job is that of a bureaucrat is seen as almost a self-disclosure as a risk-averse and rule-bound paper pusher, with little initiative, decisiveness or human emotion. To label a system as bureaucratic is an accusation of ineffective organization. Politicians secure votes by promising to tackle the problem of bureaucracy and 'red tape'. But as a result of this elision of 'bureaucracy' and 'inefficiency' we have virtually lost the ability to discuss bureaucracy objectively. Undoubtedly, some aspects of how bureaucracies work deserve all the criticism they get, but this should not be taken as a blanket rejection of bureaucracy as a form of organization (Du Gay, 2000). We need to be able to identify and recognize its shortcomings without dismissing all the precepts and values that underpin the notion of bureaucratic organization.

THE DEVELOPMENT OF BUREAUCRACY

As Albrow (1970) discusses, the term bureaucracy, as a form of government administration with authority resting in the hands of state officials, has its origins in the eighteenth century. While its merits or otherwise as an organizational system were examined by various writers in France and later in England, it was in Germany – and especially in the writings of Max

Weber – that the concept and importance of bureaucratic organization were developed. So influential was Weber's writing on bureaucracy that he has often been portrayed as the founding father of organization studies, exerting a profound influence on later writers in the field.

For Weber, the development of bureaucratic forms of authority was inextricably linked to the development of capitalism. The emergence of modern states based on market capitalism required the development of systems of government and authority founded on a rational basis of legal rules, rather than on more arbitrary systems of authority based, for example, on tradition or the power of an individual ruler. In this way, Weber identified bureaucracy as an aspect of the broader rationalization of the modern world – a rationalization required for the effective coordination and operation of large-scale market economies.

Weber viewed bureaucracy as an inevitable aspect of modernization and the means of administering large-scale institutions such as the different aspects of state machinery. But it is incorrect to see Weber as an uncritical advocate of bureaucracy. On the contrary, he recognized the dehumanizing effect of bureaucracies both on those who were subject to them and those who worked within them.

ELEMENTS OF BUREAUCRACY

To identify the essential components of bureaucracies, Weber (1968) described an 'ideal type' bureaucracy, a theoretical or 'pure' form that would never be reproduced exactly in the real world, but could act as a theoretical yardstick against which to measure the structure and functioning of actual bureaucracies. This ideal type comprised a number of defining features, the most important of these included the following:

- a bureaucracy should be based on a system of formal rules and procedures, thereby ensuring that its members do not act arbitrarily and that the rules help to maintain consistency;
- bureaucracies are arranged hierarchically, with people appointed to different positions in the hierarchy based on ability and merit (that is, appointments being based on the principle of what you know, rather than who you know);
- the bureaucracy involves extensive division of labour with each position holder having a limited area of responsibility and discretion (and thereby restricted scope for developing a power base within the bureaucracy);

- within the hierarchy, the bureaucrat is loyal to a superior position, rather than to the person that holds it (thus, relations between superiors and subordinates are based on formal rather than informal ties);
- the relationship between bureaucrats and their clients is an impersonal one; thereby, rules are applied consistently and impersonally, rather than varying from person to person.

Thus, bureaucracy was viewed by Weber as a rational administrative system, more suited to administering large-scale organizations of industrial countries than other systems. It contrasts, for example, with paternalist systems where people obtain positions either based on who, rather than what, they know or, alternatively, gain preferential treatment by virtue of who they are, who they know or how much they can pay, rather than on the merits of their case. One of the strengths of bureaucracy therefore – and one that accords well with the current emphasis on equality of opportunity and avoidance of unfair discrimination – is that bureaucracies are based on the principles of meritocracy, both in terms of how they are structured and how they dispense their function, rather than based on patronage or other non-objective systems of organization.

In practice, bureaucracies function in ways that depart significantly from the ideal type description. For example, they typically operate more flexibly than their formal characteristics would suggest. In fact, a degree of flexibility over rules is essential. A traditional form of protest in industrial disputes, for example, is to 'work to rule', involving a strict adherence to the formal rules and working procedures. What such disputes reveal is how this rigid sticking to the rules quickly gives rise to problems and hold-ups in the delivery of goods or services. More generally, studies of bureaucracies reveal the importance of informal practices in facilitating their effective operation.

CRITICISMS OF BUREAUCRACY

Evidence of this flexibility has not been sufficient, however, to prevent a growing criticism of bureaucratic forms of organization being too rigid and inflexible for the conditions of the modern world, and that bureaucracy stifles initiative and restricts the rapidity of response to changing circumstances (see **Organizations: Networks and Alliances**). The critics argue that former times in market capitalism were characterized by more stable and predictable markets and economic conditions, therefore both firms and states could afford to develop more mechanistic structures of administration that were best suited to relatively stable conditions. In increasingly globalized and technically sophisticated economies, however, levels of competition are not only more intense but those markets are also more uncertain and turbulent. These conditions are seen to require a highly flexible response from organizations, a level of flexibility that bureaucratic structures are perceived as incapable of delivering. Related to this argument is the criticism (regularly voiced by politicians) that bureaucracies are insufficiently 'entrepreneurial' or 'managerial' in their approach with too great an emphasis on 'administration'. A greater managerialism is advocated, involving, for example, making bureaucracies more open to market forces and creating devolved structures of costs and responsibility that encourage greater initiative.

In reviewing these criticisms of bureaucracy, three counter-points can usefully be made (see Du Gay, 2000, for more detailed discussion).

First, the positive attributes of bureaucracies are frequently overlooked. These include the value of neutrality, adherence to procedures, accountability and commitment to the purpose of the office. In public service, for example, this should result in bureaucracies administering state policies and decisions whatever the political shade of the government. If bureaucracies are portrayed only as slow, inefficient and anonymous, then it is not surprising that systems promoted as more flexible and more 'entrepreneurial' will appear more attractive. But this is to lose sight of the important and deeply ingrained service ethic that underlie many bureaucracies.

Second, as noted above, Weber developed an 'ideal type' bureaucracy and as later writers have shown, in reality, bureaucratic practices differ, to a lesser or greater extent, from this ideal type. We know, for example, that organizations develop informal systems of operating: bureaucracies are not as rigidly structured (not as 'bureaucratic') as often portrayed by critics. Further, while bureaucracies clearly do have faults, some of these can be seen as being addressed (though critics would say not fast enough). Important areas requiring change – and where some change is already evident – include the creation of more jargon-free paperwork in public services; improved customer/client relations including the development of 'one-stop' services rather than requiring customers/clients to navigate between several different parts of a bureaucracy; improved speed of response, including how quickly queries are dealt with, telephones answered and so on; and, more generally, an increased importance being given to the ends that the bureaucracy is designed to deliver, rather than the means (the process) of its delivery.

Finally, in criticizing bureaucracies, a frequent (though generally implicit) assumption is that the alternatives are without faults. But alternatives may offer less accountability and less consistency if devolved, independent action is encouraged. Further, there is a general assumption that a speedy, bureaucracy-free response will be the optimum one. But this is not necessarily the case.

A short example usefully illustrates this. In the 1990s, the major European airlines faced a series of problems, including a more deregulated airline market (which allowed carriers to compete on a wider range of routes) and the rise of low-cost competitors. In response, British Airways (BA), following privatization, became run increasingly in a way that gave considerable powers to the Chief Executive and weaker roles to other groups (including the Board and the employees). BA's strategy in response to increased competition was to pursue widespread cost-cutting, including a wholesale sell-off of various subsidiary activities (such as catering) and the outsourcing or franchising of other activities. The strategy didn't work – quality levels fell and passengers went elsewhere. The company plunged from a position of record profits in the mid-1990s to huge losses by the end of that decade (Turnbull et al., 2004). A replacement Chief Executive was drafted in to rebuild the company, partly by bringing important activities back in-house.

In Germany, the national airline Lufthansa faced similar competitive conditions, but is a company run more bureaucratically: the law requires a more extensive process of consultation and greater accountability. As a result, decision-making is a generally slower process. With the Lufthansa management more constrained than their counterparts in BA – including constrained by Lufthansa employee groups who opposed major cost-cutting – this forced a more considered response from the company. Instead of sell-offs, contracting out and so on, all subsidiary activities were retained within the company (catering, baggage, technical and cargo, as well as passenger operations), with no rush for cheaper alternatives. Instead the company became a lead player in the development of strategic alliances in the airline industry, resulting in the creation of the Star Alliance. More than a decade later this remains by far the most successful alliance, compared for example with the belated attempt by BA to create something similar with its OneWorld alliance.

CONCLUSION

Overall, it is important to recognize that bureaucracies are not without their problems. There remains a continuing tension to be both consistent and flexible, both neutral and human, and to have devolved responsibilities and adhere to agreed rules. But, at the same time, it is important to note that at a time when organizations are being charged with being more responsible and accountable, operating ethically and being equal opportunity employers, then elements of the ethos under-lying bureaucratic forms of organization may be seen as increasingly relevant to the twenty-first-century organization.

See also: *labour process, management, organizational culture, power and authority.*

REFERENCES

Albrow, M. (1970) *Bureaucracy*. London: Pall Mall.
Du Gay, P. (2000) *In Praise of Bureaucracy*. London: Sage.
Turnbull, P., Blyton, P. and Harvey, G. (2004) 'Cleared for take-off? Management–labour partnership in the European civil aviation industry', *European Journal of Industrial Relations*, 10 (3): 281–301.
Watson T.J. (2003) Sociology, *Work and Industry*, 4th edn. London: Routledge.
Weber, M. (1968) *Economy and Society*. New York: Free Press.

Career

In a narrow sense, career refers to a long-term sequence of jobs or positions within an occupation or organization that usually entails movement up a status and salary hierarchy. In a broader sense, however, career is a description of a person's life history.

DIFFERENT VIEWS OF CAREER

As the first part of the above definition indicates, many people think of career in terms of a planned advancement through a series of jobs within an occupation or organization, with the outcome being movement up a hierarchical ladder. However, as the second part of the definition suggests, others take a much more encompassing view of career as denoting an entire 'life history' in which the different jobs that a person undertakes to make a living may or may not relate closely to one another. Thus, while the former view emphasizes a sequence of jobs differently positioned on a ladder of hierarchical status, the latter recognizes that, for many, their career will be characterized much more by a fragmented and diverse work history. In this latter view everyone has a career – a life history – and this career may be as a housewife or a voluntary worker, not simply a career in paid work. And in the paid work sphere, while some people's work history may conform to a narrow view of career (for example, rising from a research assistant to professor), for others it will be a different sort of experience – such as a 30-year career as a school canteen assistant.

Those advocating a broad view of career criticize the narrower definition as a middle-class and elitist concept, especially a white male concept: something that those with education, qualifications and contacts have access to a much greater extent than those with fewer educational qualifications, less-recognized skills and possibly a gender or ethnic disadvantage that may have added to the difficulties of starting and building a career.

THE END OF CAREER?

For the moment, however, most discussion continues to adopt the narrower view of career as a planned progression up a hierarchy. This is certainly implicit in much of the recent debate over whether or not we are witnessing the 'end of career'. For writers such as Cappelli (1999) and Sennett (1998), factors such as less job security, the accelerated rate of technological change, the continued downsizing and flattening of organizations and the reduced emphasis on experience and loyalty as bases for promotion, are seen to have undermined traditional career paths. As a result, the notion of a career trajectory based on progressing through a series of jobs within a single company (and accompanied by progression up a salary and status hierarchy) is seen to have been replaced by less predictable, less secure and less continuous patterns of work. The economic and organizational environments in which this change is occurring are portrayed as turbulent and unreliable: in Sennett's words (1998: 22), the characteristic feature of contemporary capitalism is 'no long term'.

This assessment of the state of career, however, has been criticized as exaggerated by writers including Jacoby (1999), who argues that labour market evidence shows that long-term employment relationships remain widespread and that, while changes in both internal and external labour markets are evident, these do not (as yet, at least) amount to the 'end of career' (see also Doogan, 2001, on long-term employment patterns).

It is possible to extend this critique of the end of career thesis further. First, irrespective of certain changes occurring in labour markets, people still make broad decisions about career. These decisions are affected not only by views on the changing nature of internal and external labour markets but also by broader influences such as patterns of socialization, personal abilities and character. As a result, despite some pronouncements that 'career jobs are dead' (Cappelli, 1999), the notion of career remains important to many people. It is associated with a life plan, a goal, a path of achievement or a yardstick; for many this relates closely to their sense of identity and self-worth. These associations remain important even if the environments in which careers are pursued are less conducive than hitherto.

Second, the end of career argument also tends to overemphasize the availability and stability of careers in the past. It implies adherence to a narrow view of career (upward, predictable, hierarchical ascent). But for many, as noted above, their career – their work history – has always been characterized by insecurity, a lack of planning and a lack of control.

HOW ARE CAREERS DEVELOPING?

Increasingly for many, career is becoming comprised of diverse sets of work experiences with different employers rather than loyalty to a single employer. People are constructing their own careers by gaining a variety of experiences. This appears to be particularly the case in relation to early work history, as young entrants to the labour market acquire a number of different work experiences prior to taking any decisions on a more settled pattern of jobs. This contrasts with an earlier picture of seeking to gain experience and reputation within a single organization.

Career trajectories may be upward, downward or horizontal in direction. Where upward trajectories have halted, this is sometimes referred to as careers having 'plateaued'. There may be several reasons for this, including: individuals reaching their maximum potential or ability; a preference for the work involved at a particular point in the hierarchy; the opportunity to advance being temporarily or permanently halted; the influence of events in different parts of the life course (such as childrearing); the need to gain different skills for higher positions; the influence of declining health in later years; the impact of prejudice (such as the organization's preference for younger staff); and/or a change in values, such as valuing non-work life above the status and income attaching to greater commitment to career (see **Work–life Balance**).

Much recent discussion has been dominated by the growth in careers among women in the labour market. The widespread increase in women's educational achievement and their growing aspirations have made the possibility of career (narrowly defined), rather than just a job, increasingly available to a much greater number of women. For working couples with children, this gives rise to issues of managing two careers and family. It is far from easy for dual-career couples to resolve the different pressures of work and home life. Elloy and Smith (2003), for example, in a study of lawyers and accountants, found that dual-career couples reported more stress, more work–family conflict and greater work overload than single-career couples.

Despite the growth in the number of women in the labour market and more than a generation of legislation to eliminate discrimination, a limit on many women's careers – often referred to as the 'glass ceiling' – remains, with the result that women continue to be under-represented in senior positions (see **Discrimination**). There are various possible factors contributing to this, ranging from male prejudice to socialization: as a result of the latter, for example, many boys and girls continue to develop different expectations about their sex roles, which in turn influence career decisions. Other factors that indirectly discriminate against women's careers emphasize the way organizations are structured or how organizational cultures are socially constructed in ways that make opportunities more readily available to men (see **Organizational Culture**). An example of the latter is where there is an emphasis on staying on late at the office as an informal prerequisite for advancement and that many women with child-care responsibilities are less able to maintain this work pattern (see **Presenteeism**).

THE FUTURE

In the past, career was seen to end with retirement. However, increasing life expectancy and better health in later life, coupled with the prospects of financial shortfalls in many pension schemes and the need to fund a longer retirement period, have all contributed to a growth in post-retirement careers. A growing number of people now retire from one organization and embark on additional economic activity elsewhere. Singh and Verma (2003), for example, in a study of over 1,800 retirees in Canada found that two out of five returned to work, either part-time, full-time or as self-employed. Those most likely to return to work were ones who had previously had a high attachment to work, were more likely to have been in managerial positions and more likely to have experienced upward career mobility in their work history.

For others, however, the issue will not be extending career past normal retirement age, but the opportunity to move out of a career trajectory earlier in order to gain a different balance between work and non-work life. For some, therefore, the issue may not be the threat posed to career by short-term jobs and insecurity, but rather a more active rejection of the values that have traditionally been placed on pursuing a career, that in practice often entails progressively greater responsibilities and higher work demands.

See also: *job security, knowledge work, pay and performance, skill.*

REFERENCES

Cappelli, P. (1999) 'Career jobs are dead', *California Management Review*, 42: 146–67.

Doogan, K. (2001) 'Insecurity and long-term employment', *Work, Employment and Society*, 15 (3): 419–41.

Elloy, D.F. and Smith, C.R. (2003) 'Patterns of stress, work–family conflict, role conflict, role ambiguity and overload among dual-career and single-career couples: an Australian study', *Cross Cultural Management*, 10 (1): 55–66.

Jacoby, S.M. (1999) 'Are career jobs heading for extinction?', *California Management Review*, 42: 123–45.

Sennett, R. (1998) *The Corrosion of Character*. New York: Norton.

Singh, G. and Verma, A. (2003) 'Work history and later-life labour force participation: evidence from a large telecommunications firm', *Industrial and Labor Relations Review*, 56 (4): 699–716.

key concepts
in work

Collective Bargaining

> Collective bargaining is the process by which 'a trade union bargains with an employer, or a group of employers, over the pay and other conditions of employment of its members' (Edwards, 2003: 4).

The term 'collective bargaining' is credited as having first been coined by Beatrice Webb who, with her husband, Sidney Webb, were eminent British trade union historians writing in the late nineteenth and early twentieth centuries (see Webb and Webb, 1897: 173). In their description of collective bargaining, the Webbs first explained the process by distinguishing it from 'individual' bargaining. This account will follow their example and begin in the same way, before examining the structure of bargaining and changes in the context and style of negotiations.

THE BALANCE OF POWER AND THE REGULATORY FUNCTION OF COLLECTIVE BARGAINING

If an individual employee were to enter into a contract of employment with an employer purely on the basis of his/her individual circumstances, on what the employer was prepared to offer and making no reference to contractual conditions applying to other employees, then this would be an 'individual' bargain. But the dynamics of the employment relationship are such that an individual employee is unlikely to be equally matched to bargain with his/her employer. The employer has greater economic power and, as Webb and Webb (ibid.: 217) pointed out, 'wherever the economic conditions of the parties are unequal, legal freedom of contract merely enables the superior in strategic strength to dictate the terms'. The effects of this power will be most apparent in conditions of monopsony, where an employer or group of employers, has a monopoly of control over the demand for labour, for example, where there is just one main form of employment within a particular locality. The power of the employer will also be enhanced in conditions of unemployment, where there is a large pool of labour competing for a limited number of jobs.

Thus the employment relationship between an employer and an individual worker is fundamentally unbalanced, or asymmetrical, in terms of economic power and this situation is compounded by a competitive labour market, where workers compete against one another and may be forced into accepting lower wages and conditions of employment by their need for work. By the conditions of a person's employment we mainly mean substantive matters relating to, for example, wages, hours of work, sick pay entitlements, holiday entitlements, and the like; in other words, the *market relations* of the contract. Collective bargaining is a process which seeks to influence market relations, and will also focus on procedural issues, by which we mean the regulation of the use of power and authority in the employment relationship. Thus, for example, there will be agreements on procedures to be adopted in the event of a dispute or misconduct; in other words, the *managerial relations* of the contract (see Flanders, 1970: 86–8).

There are different perspectives on how the imbalance of power in the employment relationship is regarded and accommodated. The entry on **Perspectives on Work** considers the debate in more detail and will not be repeated in full here, but it is important to understand the significance of ideological perspectives for the role of collective bargaining in the employment relationship. From a unitary perspective, the employer's economic power conveys rights to control and manage the employment relationship and these rights should operate free of interference save for the forces of competition, the premise being that managers will manage in the best interests of all. The pluralist perspective also acknowledges the right of managers to manage, but further acknowledges that there will be times when the respective interests of the employing organization and workers will not coincide and in these circumstances the economic power of the employer may be used coercively. Therefore, from the pluralist perspective, the role of collective unity through trade union organization is a valid and necessary means to mitigate, though not eradicate, the effects of the power imbalance between workers and employers. Put simply, where workers were 'willing and able to combine, they preferred it to bargaining as individuals with their employer because it enabled them to secure better terms of employment' (ibid.: 215).

Collective bargaining, therefore, involves workers acting together, through their trade union, which bargains over terms and conditions of employment on their behalf. However, the process is dependent on the employer recognizing the trade union as the employees' representative for bargaining purposes (see **Trade Unions**). Once this is agreed, collective bargaining may proceed.

While collective bargaining has been much associated with bargaining over pay, it is not simply an economic activity; it is also fulfils a wider regulatory, or 'rule-making' function (ibid.: 216). Employment may be regulated by the state, via laws; it may be regulated by individual agreements between the employer and one employee; or it may be regulated by collective agreements, where representatives of employers and employees jointly author rules on employment conditions, through the collective bargaining process. Thus, collective bargaining is a process of joint decision-making on substantive and procedural issues related to the contract of employment. It has been described as a means of establishing greater industrial democracy in that the employees' voice is represented in decisions that affect their working lives.

THE STRUCTURE OF COLLECTIVE BARGAINING: THE BARGAINING UNIT, THE COLLECTIVE AGREEMENT AND BARGAINING SCOPE

A work group that is represented by a trade union will normally be referred to as the 'bargaining unit'. A bargaining unit might be small and specific, for example, a group of workers at a particular workplace, or it might be a wider occupational group, for example, university lecturers or postal workers. It follows that bargaining will take place at different levels: at the individual workplace; at company level; or at the level of the industry, encompassing workers in the same occupation who may be employed by different employers, as in the case of firefighters in the UK, for example.

The collective bargaining process involves negotiation between representatives of a trade union and the employer and, if agreement is reached, there will be a 'collective agreement' that applies to all workers in the bargaining unit. The coverage of a collective agreement, that is how many and what type of workers it covers, will relate to the level at which bargaining takes place and the size and nature of the bargaining unit. The nature and influence of the rules established by means of collective bargaining will vary according to the scope of bargaining. The scope refers to the range of matters that managers are prepared to see as negotiable, in contrast to matters over which they retain rights of unilateral decision-making.

However, as in all bargaining processes, there may be occasions when agreement cannot be reached and the parties have a 'failure to agree'. At this point, either employers or trade unions may impose sanctions to exert leverage on the bargaining process: for example, trade unions may ballot their members on whether or not to engage in industrial action, or employers may threaten to lock out the workforce (that is, prevent access to the workplace) or to remove the opportunity for work by moving production elsewhere. Industrial action by unions and their members may take a variety of forms, but the complete withdrawal of labour, or 'strike', represents perhaps the most visible and most contentious expression of industrial conflict (see **Conflict**).

CONTEXT AND CHANGE IN COLLECTIVE BARGAINING AND THE STYLE OF NEGOTIATION

In more recent years the context for collective bargaining has changed. In the UK, for example, collective bargaining in the 1960s and 1970s was characterized by a dominant pluralist perspective and a political context where voluntary collective bargaining was regarded as 'the best method of conducting industrial relations' (Donovan, 1968: paragraph 203). However, in the 1980s and against a background of industrial restructuring, recession and neo-liberal economic policies, the incidence of collective bargaining fell. Its decline, and the declining influence of trade unions, have continued since that time. This trend has been particularly noticeable in the UK and the USA but is not restricted to these countries. Furthermore, research in the UK has suggested that even where unions have retained a presence, their declining power has often meant the scope of collective bargaining has narrowed. This has been termed the 'individualization' of the employment relationship, but does not mean that employers are now negotiating with individual employees. Rather, it seems that where collective bargaining has fallen into abeyance, it is increasingly the case that employers do not negotiate with anyone, but instead unilaterally determine rates of pay (Brown et al., 1999). This said, large groups of workers, particularly in the public sector and in manufacturing in the UK and beyond, continue to rely heavily on collective bargaining as the means of securing improvements in their wages and conditions. The fortunes of trade unions have in the past been cyclical in terms of influence and activity, and there is no reason to assume that collective bargaining will not survive into the future, as a force for joint regulation in the employment relationship.

But there is considerable pressure on trade unions, in a period of reduced power, to adopt different bargaining styles in order to gain influence with employers. The process of negotiation is more complex than may first appear and much attention has been directed to that part of the bargaining process which represents a 'trial of strength' between employers and trade unions, each seeking an outcome that is more beneficial to the party it represents. This is an adversarial, zero-sum view of bargaining, where opposing parties seek a division of rewards that most benefits their own side. Yet, as Walton and McKersie (1965) pointed out several decades ago, this represents only one part of the negotiation process and does not reflect the different activities that occur within negotiations. In fact, Walton and McKersie characterize negotiations as embracing four interrelated processes. They label adversarial bargaining, noted above, as 'distributive bargaining', where the parties seek to influence the distribution of a fixed set of rewards in a zero-sum way (a gain for one side representing a loss for the other). In addition, however, negotiations also contain more 'integrative' processes where the parties jointly seek solutions to problems. Walton and McKersie saw these two processes co-existing within negotiation activity, with the parties engaging both in joint problem-solving activity (integrative bargaining) as well as more adversarial negotiations over the division of rewards (distributive bargaining).

Walton and McKersie also identify two further negotiation activities. The first they term 'attitudinal structuring' and this relates to one party seeking to persuade the other to view a situation in a particular way – that is, structuring the attitudinal context in which the negotiations are taking place. An example of this would be management embarking on a set of negotiations by first explaining to the trade union's negotiators the state of the business or developments in the market or among competitors that they view as influencing the context of the negotiations. A corresponding union effort at attitudinal structuring would be to explain to management the mood of the membership, their priorities for the negotiations and/or the union's own information of what agreements have been reached elsewhere.

The fourth component of negotiations Walton and McKersie term 'intraorganizational bargaining'. This is a recognition that negotiations do not necessarily occur simply *between* two parties, each of which is internally united over the negotiations. In practice, each party will frequently contain divergent views regarding the main objectives of the negotiations and the appropriate tactics for their party to follow. The latter may be seen in examples of tensions within the British trade union movement, as certain unions adopt a more partnership approach with management. While some union representatives and commentators see this as a means of ensuring unions retain a foothold in organizations and maintain a collective bargaining presence, there are strongly held opposing views from within the unions themselves that, by engaging in partnership, unions risk losing their independence and may consequently lose credibility in the eyes of their members. The argument is one that is fiercely contested (see Kelly, 1996) and only time will tell the implications for the future of collective bargaining.

In summary, collective bargaining is a process of joint regulation of the employment relationship by employers or managers and trade unions. The incidence of collective bargaining has fallen in recent decades and styles of negotiation have changed, but it continues to be the method of determining pay and conditions for large groups of employees.

See also: *the law and contract of employment, power and authority.*

REFERENCES

Brown, W., Deakin, S., Hudson, M., Pratten, C. and Ryan, P. (1999) *The Individualisation of Employment Contracts in Britain*, DTI Employment Relations Research Series 4. London: Department of Trade and Industry.

Donovan, Lord (1968) *Royal Commission on Trade Unions and Employers' Associations 1965–1968*, Cmnd. 3623. London: HMSO.

Edwards, P. (2003) 'The employment relationship', in P. Edwards (ed.) *Industrial Relations: Theory and Practice*, 2nd edn. Oxford: Blackwell, pp. 1–36.

Flanders, A. (1970) *Management and Unions: The Theory and Reform of Industrial Relations*. London: Faber and Faber.

Kelly, J. (1996) 'Union militancy and social partnership', in P. Ackers, C. Smith and P. Smith (eds) *The New Workplace and Trade Unionism: Critical Perspectives on Work and Organization*. London: Routledge, pp. 77–109.

Walton, R.E. and McKersie, R.B. (1965) *A Behavioral Theory of Labor Negotiations*. New York: McGraw-Hill.

Webb, S. and Webb, B. (1897) *Industrial Democracy*. London: Longmans, Green & Co.

key concepts in work

Conflict

> Conflict at work results from a perceived opposition of goals between two or more parties or a sense of grievance or injustice by one party in its relations with others.

Workplaces are characterized by both cooperation and conflict. The latter can occur at a number of levels within work organizations: between individuals, within and between work groups or between larger collectives such as management and trade unions. An important source of conflict is when one party feels a sense of injustice. This injustice may be felt over substantive issues such as: the terms and conditions of employment; how much work employees are expected to complete; or the conditions provided for undertaking that work. Injustice may also be felt over procedural issues: how one is being treated at work; how decisions are made; how much one's opinions are listened to and so on.

CONFLICT, CAPITALISM AND CONTROL

At the workplace, the issue of conflict is brought centre-stage by a capitalist context that means workers' effort is devoted to producing profits in which they will not have an equal share. Indeed, most of any surplus value that workers produce will probably go to another social group, comprising employers and/or shareholders. This gives rise to what Edwards (1986: 5) has termed 'structured antagonism', or conflict, right at the heart of the work process.

But the issue of profit is not the whole story, nor is it straightforward, for even if all profits were to be shared out equally or there were to be no profit motive whatsoever (for example, in a public-sector organization), the issue of the control of work remains. The control and organization of work are subject to the authority of management. Most commonly, this authority will be exercised in accordance with the principles of a capitalist market even if there is no *direct* link with the generation of surplus profit; as a result, there is potential for conflict over how work is done and how much effort is to be expended (see **Power and Authority**). Here, again, we have to pause in our discussion of 'what conflict is' because, depending on the circumstances, it may or may not find expression in worker behaviour. There will be occasions when workers will group together to express their conflict with the structure and/or processes of their work. In different circumstances, however, workers may respond to such pressures as individuals, by isolated acts of resistance. Alternatively, workers may see no opportunity to allow the conflict they feel to find expression. In this latter case it is important to recognize that this does not mean the conflict is not felt, simply that it is not expressed, perhaps because there is no perceived possibility of an improvement in the situation. In such circumstances it can happen that an apparently minor incident gives rise to a spontaneous and bitter dispute with management, as long-suppressed resentment rises to the surface. But it may just as easily be the case that conflict remains latent and finds expression only in a lack of worker motivation. Thus, it is helpful to think of the potential for conflict as existing at different levels: first, there is the 'structured antagonism' associated with the capitalist context for work; second, there is the organization and control of work; and finally, there is the issue of how conflict is expressed in worker behaviour (Edwards, 1986: 5–10).

EXPRESSIONS OF CONFLICT

The way that conflict is demonstrated can take a variety of forms. To list only some of the most common manifestations, workers can express conflict by taking strike action, refusing to work overtime, going absent or quitting their job, sabotaging equipment, working slowly or, more generally, minimizing their compliance and cooperation with the work process. What this list underlines is that conflict can be expressed not only through conflict behaviours (such as going on strike) but also through attitudes (such as adopting a non-cooperative approach to work). In addition, conflict can be organized or unorganized. Organized conflict will involve groups rather than individuals and requires a degree of coordination. Examples of organized forms of conflict include strikes, overtime bans and orchestrated (and large-scale) absenteeism. The organization required to mobilize a workforce for such action to occur is normally provided by a trade union. Unorganized conflict, on the other hand, involves individuals acting alone, such as by quitting their job.

Many of the different forms of conflict are not exclusively organized or unorganized in their nature but could fall into either category depending on how the conflict is manifested in particular circumstances. Going absent, for example, may be the means whereby an employee expresses her or his individual discontent with the workplace (i.e. a form of unorganized conflict) or it could take the form of mass absence, coordinated by a group or trade union, to express more general opposition to some aspect of work (see **Absence and Turnover**). Forms of conflict such as working slowly and sabotage likewise could represent either unorganized or organized forms of conflict, depending on the specific form they take.

In thinking about why conflict can be expressed in such a wide variety of ways, one consideration is the extent to which these different forms may represent alternatives, with some being more suitable or acceptable in certain situations than others. For example, employees in certain occupations, such as many working in the health professions, may find it unacceptable to express conflict through strike action if they perceive it as endangering the lives of the patients in their care. However, in these situations, action short of a strike, such as a refusal to work overtime, may be more acceptable, given the lower impact this is likely to have on health-care recipients. In other situations, a lack of a coordinating body such as a trade union may make expressing conflict through organized forms very difficult, resulting in a reliance on unorganized expressions of conflict such as individual absence and quitting.

CONFLICT AND FRAMES OF REFERENCE

The frame of reference, or view of the workplace, that one adopts exerts a profound influence on how one perceives the issue of workplace conflict. Some conflict could be said to stem from poor communications, giving rise to rumours and misunderstandings. Over a long period, Human Relations views of the workplace have emphasized the importance of good communications in reducing conflict, highlighting, for example, the pivotal role played by those holding supervisory positions, who act as conduits for passing information both upwards to management and downwards to the office or shop-floor. This view of the causes of conflict has a partial validity: in some situations, conflicts would not arise or, if they did, be less acute, if communications were better. However, to put too great an emphasis on this as the main source of any conflict is to hold a highly unitary view of the workplace.

The unitary view of conflict is that it is wholly dysfunctional, that interests of all parties in the workplace are essentially identical and, if these interests were communicated by managers more effectively and there were no agitating agents such as trade unions stirring up dissent, there would be no grounds for conflict. The assumption this contains, however, is that the content of any communication is fundamentally non-conflictual. This position is in sharp contrast with a more Marxist perspective, which holds that conflict is an inherent part of the capitalist work process; it may be expressed or be latent depending on circumstances and opportunity, but it is always present. From this perspective, conflict cannot be 'managed' away.

The 'pluralist' view of work, on the other hand, holds that the workplace comprises parties who have separate interests as well as ones that overlap or coincide. In common with the Marxist critique, pluralism sees the areas where interests between parties differ as a potential source of conflict, but it does not agree that this need be a permanent or continual state of affairs. Within this pluralist perspective, conflict is seen as normal and to be expected. For the organization to function successfully in these circumstances, there is a need for effective negotiation and grievance-handling to address conflictual issues. From the pluralist perspective, this is the job of managers. Thus, though the unitary and pluralist views take different positions in the analysis of conflict, they have in common their rejection of the Marxist view of conflict as a constant (and, under capitalism, irreconcilable) factor of work. Both pluralism (which envisages working compromises) and the unitary frame of reference (which envisages harmony) see the resolution of conflict as possible through managerial intervention (see **Perspectives on Work**).

Underpinning much of the managerial view of workplace conflict is the notion that most conflict is dysfunctional both for work organizations and individuals. However, Lewis Coser several decades ago made the case that conflict can in practice yield various positive outcomes for the parties involved. Building on the work of Simmel (1955), Coser (1956) emphasized the contribution that conflict can make to the maintenance and adaptation of social relationships and social structures. Several of Coser's arguments relate to the ability of conflict to strengthen intra-group identity and cohesion. Other comments concern inter-group relations, including the proposition that conflict 'makes group members more conscious of their group bonds and increases their participation' (ibid.: 90). From Coser, we derive such ideas as that adversarial or conflictual relations will potentially yield: a clearer definition of different options, positions and key interests; an avoidance of one party dominating the agenda; a more active engagement in the negotiation process; and the adaptive use of trade-offs and concessions that allow both sides to secure their highest priorities.

THE FUTURE

Over the past generation, one of the most evident changes in the pattern of conflict in many countries has been a dramatic decline in strike action, both in terms of the number of strikes occurring and their scale (in the UK, for example, the annual numbers of strikes occurring has fallen by over 90 per cent since the 1970s; for more details, see Blyton and Turnbull, 2004). Among other things, this reflects not only the marked reduction in trade union membership and a growth in legislation restricting lawful industrial action but also the decline in numbers employed in industries such as coal-mining that were formerly highly strike-prone. In coal, this strike-proneness reflected a variety of factors, not least the physical and dangerous nature of the work task, together with the geographical isolation of much of the work, that contributed to a heightened sense of solidarity among mine workers and a willingness to support one another in any grievance with employers.

Despite a reduction in the number and scale of strikes taking place, strike action has not 'withered away', as some writers in the past predicted, but remains a significant and dramatic form of conflict expression. Further, given the pluralist argument that conflict is probably best viewed not as an issue that can be permanently 'solved' but something that is latent within the nature of the employment relationship and requiring regular negotiation and accommodation, one outcome of a fall in strike levels is an increased potential for conflict to emerge in more covert, individualized forms such as individual acts of sabotage or, more mundanely, working without enthusiasm. A problem this in turn generates for management is that these more hidden aspects of conflict behaviour may be far more difficult to identify and effectively manage than the highly visible forms of conflict (strikes, refusals to work overtime and so on) more typical in earlier periods.

See also: collective bargaining, labour process, trade unions.

conflict

REFERENCES

Blyton, P. and Turnbull, P. (2004) *The Dynamics of Employee Relations*, 3rd edn. Basingstoke: Palgrave Macmillan.

Coser, L. (1956) *The Functions of Social Conflict*. New York: Free Press.
Edwards, P.K. (1986) *Conflict at Work: A Materialist Analysis of Workplace Relations*. Oxford: Basil Blackwell.
Simmel, G. (1955) *Conflict*. Glencoe, IL: The Free Press.

Consent

> *Consent refers to agreeing to, or supporting a proposal or course of action.*

How management seek to control the work process, and in turn how this can generate conflict and resistance by employees, have attracted much attention. Yet in practice, what is striking about worker behaviour is not that workers object to so much in organizations but that they object to so little. In most work situations for most of the time, workers actively cooperate with the work process; the typical behaviour pattern is one of consent and cooperation, rather than conflict. So, while the issue of management's control over the labour process is important to study, so too is the workers' consent to that labour process (see **Labour Process**). Indeed, the existence of consent is crucial for management. Because of it, management control strategies can afford to be more distant and less visible than would be the case if workers' consent was less in evidence. More importantly, the difficulties that management face if relying on control measures to secure commitment and discretionary labour from workers – that extra labour on which organizations crucially depend – make this consent by labour to work particularly significant.

SOURCES OF CONSENT

There are many sources of workers' consent, some of which have been subjected to greater investigation than others. At one level, the contract of employment itself, in that it is freely entered into by the employee as well as the employer, is an important basis of worker consent regarding the nature of the job that the individual has agreed to undertake (see **The Law and Contract of Employment**). But there are factors relating to the contract of employment that complicate the issue of worker freedom and consent. First, we can question the very notion of a contract of employment being 'freely' entered into by a worker. By focusing on the 'freedom of the individual' it becomes possible to dismiss the fact that for many workers 'market freedom' does not allow them to enter work of their choice. Workers encounter the problem that Cohen (1988: 243) has defined as the difference between 'being free to do something' and 'doing something freely'. For if there is no alternative (for example, only one employer in a locality) the opportunities for workers to *choose* their work may be very limited. Thus, being free to take a job will depend on there being a '*reasonable* or *acceptable* alternative course' (ibid.: 245, emphases in original). While acknowledging these complicating factors, it is nonetheless the case that the employment contract signals a basis for consenting to expend effort in return for a wage.

In practice, the generation of consent is multi-faceted and, in addition to the contract, there are a number of other sources of employee consent to the labour process, not least the influence of society and the community outside the workplace, which fosters particular attitudes towards work and employment. Within the workplace, there are also organizational hierarchies that act as a further powerful agent in the generation of consent to managerial power and authority. If management has secured legitimacy in the eyes of lower-ranking employees, then workers' consent to managerial decisions over their work may be given willingly (Fox, 1971: 14). If not, then their *compliance* may be something that has to be enforced through coercive workplace discipline (Edwards, 1986: 47–9). However, the increasing focus on managerial skills of leadership and communication emphasizes management styles that seek to foster and promote worker consent by means other than overt control.

CONSENT AND INTRINSIC ASPECTS OF THE JOB

Having an enjoyable job, a good working environment and a personal sense of responsibility for clients or customers, are all likely to stimulate active consent towards, rather than resistance to, a work process. So, too, is a sense of identification with the company, a feeling of team-spirit shared with work colleagues and a sense of self-discipline or moral attitude of what constitutes a 'fair day's work'. The existence of an internal promotion hierarchy is also likely to act as an important basis for consent: workers showing to management their suitability for promotion by their active engagement with, and competence in, their present job (Burawoy, 1979: 106–8). In this way, internal labour markets and workers competing for job openings at higher levels, act as a source of discipline on worker behaviour, encouraging support for management's rules, at least among those who desire upward progression to better-rewarded jobs. In looking to advance in the internal labour market, worker conflict – or certainly the outward expression of conflict – is reduced as workers seek the approval of those in charge of the promotion process.

On the other hand, internal labour markets can also generate significant peer conflict as workers vie for promotion openings. Over a long period, one way of minimizing this conflict and creating an ordered internal labour market system has been through the use of 'seniority' as a principle for advancement, whereby promotion is based on the amount of individual experience or length of service. Seniority systems are not without their shortcomings and tensions (particularly among talented younger workers) but overall act to generate consent and co-operation with the labour process as workers 'wait their turn' in an ordered progression up a work hierarchy.

Consent may also follow from the worker's identification with the employer and a desire to contribute to the success of the organization. This is likely to be more true in smaller than larger organizations and also in work processes where there is strong identification with the nature of the product or service being generated. It is therefore important to see work itself as a socializing process that generates worker consent. Extrinsic rewards such as pay and other benefits are supplemented by the intrinsic rewards of job satisfaction and self-fulfilment and wider societal influences that value the work ethic (see **Job Satisfaction**). In general, the intrinsic rewards most likely to satisfy the individual's social and psychological needs and generate high levels of consent to the work process relate to workers being given responsibility, independence, knowledge, opportunity and challenge. But while such elements may be integral to higher-skilled or managerial jobs, they are not normally present, to any significant degree, in lower-level jobs (Fox, 1971: 12–14). In lower-skilled or intensive, automated working environments, the main factors generating consent may relate more to extrinsic rewards or the threat of unemployment.

INSECURITY, COPING AND CONSENT

Consent may also result from work pressures such as job insecurity, short-term employment contracts and heavy workloads. In situations of insecurity, for example, consent may be gained by workers demonstrating their commitment in an effort to secure greater security and/or contract renewal. In addition, many employees consent to the work process simply to cope with their workload. Where such workload levels coincide with, for example, feelings of responsibility for clients, this can encourage high levels of engagement with the work process simply to get through the amount of work. Yet, how is it that such apparently negative factors can result in worker consent and active cooperation? Where there is no suitable alternative, some workers will effectively decide to 'make the best of things' and consent in order to cope with life and to avoid being miserable, in the knowledge that a search for another job will involve personal disruption, inconvenience and financial risk (see Argyris, 1964: 70).

EXTRINSIC FACTORS AND CONSENT

The payment system, particularly incentive schemes, can also play an important part in generating consent – workers recognizing the financial benefits of maintaining or increasing their work effort. The influence of financial incentives is very evident in the text that has looked most closely at the issue of consent: Michael Burawoy's *Manufacturing Consent* (1979). This work is based on a factory study that focuses on how workers behave. What Burawoy emphasizes is the extent to which workers consent to the labour process in order to pursue two objectives: maximizing their earnings and getting through their workday in as agreeable a way as possible.

In particular, the piece-rate pay system in operation encouraged workers to act in such a way as to maximize their earnings under the rules of the piecework arrangement, without producing in excess of agreed work norms (see **Pay and Performance**). Work groups competed with one another to achieve the optimum quota of work to maximize earnings and engaged in game-playing as part of the competition. All

consent

41

this achieved the twin objectives of maximizing earnings and helping the time pass quickly. The game to 'make out' or achieve the necessary output thus represented an important part of the working environment, a means of making money and passing the time.

As Burawoy points out, the indirect effects of this pattern of behaviour are significant. First, by creating games and competition over achieving the optimum output, workers are effectively agreeing (consenting) to the broader labour process: they are working voluntarily without the need for more direct management control. In this way, the games represent not a challenge to management but a fundamental *acceptance* of the terms of the employment relationship. In this case, the piece work system was key to generating consent. Contemporary equivalents of the piece-rate system – different forms of bonus scheme and performance-related pay, for example – represent similar encouragements to maximize work effort.

In summary, there are various sources of worker consent to the labour process. These include the influence of wider societal values and the individual's desire to gain some sense of value from work; the influence of power, authority and status that exists within organizations; the intrinsic aspects of jobs that contribute to a sense of job satisfaction; and, finally, extrinsic rewards, including financial incentives. It is clear that worker consent cannot be reduced to any single explanation, but is a product of influences both outside and within the workplace. What is equally clear is that this consent plays a vital role in the management of work and in management's ability to secure continuing performance from its workforce.

See also: conflict, management, power and authority.

REFERENCES

Argyris, C. (1964) *Integrating the Individual and the Organization*. New York: John Wiley.

Burawoy, M. (1979) *Manufacturing Consent: Changes in the Labour Process under Monopoly Capitalism*. Chicago: The University of Chicago Press.

Cohen, G.A. (1988) *History, Labour, and Freedom: Themes from Marx* (reprinted 2003). Oxford: Oxford University Press.

Edwards, P.K. (1986) *Conflict at Work: A Materialist Analysis of Workplace Relations*. Oxford: Basil Blackwell.

Fox, A. (1971) *A Sociology of Work and Industry*. London: Collier Macmillan.

key concepts in work

Customers

Customers are individuals, groups or organizations who purchase goods or services from a supplier.

In recent years, recipients of a wide range of services – hospital patients, students and rate-payers, among others – have been re-designated in much political and economic discourse as customers of health facilities, educational establishments, local authority services and the like. Likewise, within organizations, employers increasingly use the concept of the 'value chain' in an attempt to connect each aspect of the work process with a designated 'internal customer' at the next stage of the process. This happens particularly in private-sector firms, but in recent times has also become more evident in the public sector, where an 'internal market' has been artificially created within, for example, the UK National Health Service (NHS), as a means of injecting competitive, private-sector values into provision of the service. The premise is that a more market-focused approach inside the organization will result in a better, more cost-efficient service for the end 'customer', namely the public. This is a hotly disputed assumption, however, and is quoted here only as an indication of how the 'customer' has come to the fore across all types of organizations.

In workplaces, authority relations are normally viewed as flowing from management to employees. Managers act as the representatives of the employer (that is, owners or shareholders in the private sector and the local, regional or national state in the public sector) and this role underpins managerial claims to authority over the workforce (see **Power and Authority**). As part of this authority relationship, it has long been customary for managers to make reference to the market for the organization's goods or services as a means of further bolstering their claim to authority. Specifically, the market in general, and competitive pressures in particular, are used to legitimize managerial actions such as demands for greater productivity or refusals to grant higher wage rises. In recent years, this reference to the market has been a particular characteristic of the pursuit of higher-quality output: in this endeavour, the

customers

43

importance of meeting customers' expectations over quality is typically adduced by management to reinforce demands for improved employee performance.

THE INCREASED SIGNIFICANCE OF THE CUSTOMER IN THE WORKPLACE

A growing number of researchers argue that this generalized presence of the market and the customer in the workplace has grown into a more explicit presence. What Chomsky (1999) has termed the 'passion for free markets' has characterized the decades since the 1980s, in the context of a growing dominance of neo-liberal ideology across the globe. Neo-liberalism is a new version of the classical liberal economics of Adam Smith: in essence, the market is regarded as the best mechanism for the distribution of society's resources. Associated with this focus on entrepreneurship and competition is a new focus on the customer; the customer is 'king'. This has had profound effects on the working lives of ordinary people across the world: for example, the customer demands lower prices, so cheaper methods and locations must be found for production; the customer demands higher quality, so improved technology and new forms of work organization must be implemented. The situation has been compounded by the continued growth of service-sector activities; as a result, the importance of the customer has been brought centre-stage.

In the service sector, customers have a more direct relationship with those employed by the provider of the service. Writers in what has been called the 'New Service Management' (NSM) school, have therefore asserted that, as we shift from making 'things' to delivering 'services', the behaviour of workers towards customers is increasingly the factor that will differentiate the service and secure competitive advantage (see **Emotional Labour**). Thus, from this perspective, service-sector workers should be carefully selected for specific attitudes and attributes and should be provided with sufficient training in communication, teamwork and interpersonal skills to allow them to develop an effective interface between the organization and the customer. Workers should therefore be developed and managed in a way that increases their sense of job satisfaction, for NSM writers assume the existence of a 'satisfaction mirror'. They draw a causal link between job satisfaction and customer satisfaction, in the sense that if workers have a sense of job satisfaction, it will be reflected in the quality of service they provide; it

key concepts in work

is argued that this will lead in turn to greater customer satisfaction and vice versa.

The arguments of the NSM writers are underpinned by a unitary frame of reference that interprets the employer, worker and customer as having shared interests and assumes that, if customers are satisfied, workers will be satisfied, and so on, in some sort of virtuous circle of satisfaction. This interpretation has been criticized for not reflecting reality (see **Perspectives on Work**). Further, empirical research has failed to find evidence of any clear relationship between job satisfaction and customer service or, indeed, any serious widespread attempts by employers to invest in high-quality training in order to empower service-sector workers, who are generally low-paid and low-skilled (see Korczynski, 2002: 19–28). What empirical research *has* found, in contrast, is that service-sector workers receive minimal training, relatively poor contracts and encounter a high level of surveillance, frequently through technology, in the form of cameras or computerized tracking systems, but also through customer feedback in all its forms. So powerful is this new dimension of customer influence that for writers such as Korczynski (2003), the significance of customers in the workplace is now such that they represent a source of authority distinct from management, largely (though not wholly) acting as a further constraint on employee behaviour. For Korczynski (2003), this reflects a broader move away from production and increasingly towards consumption as the key dynamic in society – a development that is frequently characterized as the growth of 'consumer capitalism'. In turn, this diminishes the status of the producer and advances the status of the consumer and the voice and interests of the customer within contemporary society. One manifestation of this is the increasingly important role accorded to customers in both private and public spheres.

This growing role of the customer in the workplace takes a number of forms in practice. First, the increased significance of the customer potentially provides management with further legitimacy to exercise power in the workplace. As Korczynski (ibid.: 269–70) puts it, 'management call on an active concept of the consumer in constructing authority within organizations'. In this way, management bolsters its authority by adopting the role of interpreter of customer demands. This is further facilitated by the redefining of disparate groups (passengers, patients, ratepayers, students and so on) as customers.

The second role of customers is as evaluators of employee performance – what Fuller and Smith (1991: 3) refer to as 'consumer control or management by customers'. Through the use of consumer feedback via surveys, focus groups, monitoring of complaints and so on, management gain additional information regarding employee behaviour. The fact that much of this feedback can be linked to specific situations and interactions means that it can be identified directly with specific employees. This extra source of evaluation of employee behaviour can also extend beyond the normal purview of management. For example, the growth of 'How am I driving?' advertisements on the back of transport vehicles, with a freephone number for other road users to pass on comments, gives the managers of those transport drivers an opportunity for additional surveillance of a group that previously had a greater degree of independence. The outcome of eliciting customer feedback is, as Fuller and Smith (ibid.: 11) put it, 'in essence, workers gain an additional boss'.

An extension of this use of customers as a source of information is companies' use of 'pseudo-customers' in the form of 'mystery shoppers' of one kind or another. These are individuals, either members of management or employed specifically by the company, whose task is to pose as genuine customers while simultaneously undertaking covert surveillance of how a service is performed. This can provide management with information relating to different elements of the service interaction.

CUSTOMERS AS A SOURCE OF EMPLOYEE POWER

The growing prominence of customers as a source of authority, however, does not necessarily act wholly in the single direction of bolstering managerial power and weakening employees' positions in the workplace. As Korczynski et al. (2000) discuss, in front-line service work in particular, employees' knowledge of their customers can bolster efforts to resist some aspects of managerial power. For example, in call centre operations, a common managerial objective is to maintain a high target in respect of the number of calls completed, thereby potentially putting pressure on employees to foreclose interactions with customers speedily in order to meet the target. However, where employees report customers expressing greater satisfaction with the service because they felt they were not rushed or they considered that they had received personal treatment or where their enquiry had been handled thoroughly, this in turn provides employees with a counter-argument to resist managerial attempts to impose more stringent targets. Thus, in these situations, knowledge of customers may be invoked by employees as an argument for more lenient targets than management might otherwise seek to impose. This is all the more significant where interaction with customers – and particularly the gratitude of satisfied customers – represents an important source of job satisfaction for employees.

A second source of customer influence not necessarily acting to support managerial authority can be identified in relation to the role of public opinion during industrial disputes. It has become increasingly recognized by both management and trade union representatives that public opinion can have a direct bearing on the outcome of disputes. Since strikes and other forms of industrial action, in the public sector in particular, often disrupt services and create inconvenience for the users of those services (indeed, are potentially life-threatening where emergency services are involved), public opinion will often a priori be in favour of terminating the dispute and may be unsympathetic to those employees withholding their labour. However, various disputes show the ability of employees and their representatives to gain public support, despite the inconvenience created. In the early period of the 2002–2003 UK firefighters' strike, for example, both opinion polls and many newspaper editorials supported an end to the strike via a large pay settlement for the firefighters, in recognition of this dangerous occupation (Blyton and Turnbull, 2004: 317–25).

CONCLUSION

Overall, the greater prominence given to consumption in contemporary society, coupled with the growing proportion of economic activity that involves employees providing services directly to customers, is increasing the power of customers in the workplace. Much of this power is consistent with managerial authority and represents a further basis on which control is exercised over employees. However, not all customer power acts to weaken the employees' position vis-à-vis management. Employees' direct access to customers, their ability to champion the interests of the individual customer and the potential for acquiring public sympathy for their demands, provide some opportunities for employees to harness, rather than simply be subject to, the growing presence of customer power.

See also: *employment patterns, labour process, perspectives on work, surviving work.*

REFERENCES

Blyton, P. and Turnbull, P. (2004) *The Dynamics of Employee Relations*, 3rd edn. Basingstoke: Palgrave Macmillan.

Chomsky, N. (1999) *Profit Over People: Neoliberalism and Global Order.* New York: Seven Stories Press.

Fuller, L. and Smith, V. (1991) 'Consumers' reports: management by customers in a changing economy', *Work, Employment and Society*, 5 (1): 1–16.

Korczynski, M. (2002) *Human Resource Management in Service Work.* Basingstoke: Palgrave Macmillan.

Korczynski, M. (2003) 'Consumer capitalism and industrial relations', in P. Ackers and A. Wilkinson (eds), *Understanding Work and Employment: Industrial Relations in Transition.* Oxford: Oxford University Press, pp. 265–77.

Korczynski, M., Shire, K., Frenkel, S. and Tam, M. (2000) 'Service work in consumer capitalism: customers, control and contradictions', *Work Employment and Society*, 14 (4): 669–87.

Discrimination

In its most literal sense, discrimination simply means to differentiate between people or things. In the context of work, however, discrimination is most commonly used to refer to unfair discrimination (see Jenkins, 1988: 311).

key concepts in work

48

DIRECT, INDIRECT, INSTITUTIONALIZED AND POSITIVE DISCRIMINATION

Such is the ubiquitous nature of unfair discrimination in the labour market that, in 1997, the European Union (EU) made anti-discrimination a founding principle of the Union, under Article 13 of the Treaty of Amsterdam. Associated EU Directives required member states to outlaw discrimination on the grounds of sex, race, religion or belief, disability, age or sexual orientation. Several member states have had their own anti-discrimination laws for decades, though they may not have been so wide-ranging in their coverage. The UK, for example, passed an Equal Pay Act in 1970, the Sex Discrimination Act in 1975 and the Race Relations Act in 1976. The latter two statutes brought the concepts of 'direct' and 'indirect' discrimination on grounds of sex or race into British law. It is useful to begin our discussion by considering these distinctions and variations of discriminatory practice.

Direct discrimination is best defined as a situation where the intent to discriminate is clear, for example where an employer advertises a job and states in the advertisement that only white candidates or men need apply, as black applicants or women will not be considered for selection. Indirect discrimination, on the other hand, is not overt, but, rather, is more subtle and hence more difficult to prove in terms of clear intent. Essentially indirect discrimination may involve a situation where a 'provision, criterion or practice' is applied to a job that is more difficult for a certain category of workers to satisfy and as a result that group is indirectly disadvantaged (Jenkins, 1988: 323). For example, if an employer made it a condition for consideration for promotion that employees worked regular overtime, one likely effect of such a condition would be that female employees would suffer a detriment in relation to their male colleagues, because women's patterns of work generally do not allow as many overtime hours as men's due to their greater involvement in child-care (see **Domestic Work** and **Presenteeism**). Thus, the condition would indirectly discriminate against women.

Institutional racism may be another source of indirect discrimination, where discriminatory criteria, practices and attitudes can be described as being embedded in the norms and institutions of an organization. In terms of institutionalized and indirect discrimination, it is important to recognize that a lack of understanding, awareness or even intent on the part of the perpetrator is no defence; both direct and indirect discrimination in employment are equally unlawful. The only defence an employer can make against accusations of direct or indirect discrimination, apart from not having done it, is to say that there was a 'genuine occupational qualification' for having employed a particular category of worker.

Positive, or reverse, discrimination in favour of disadvantaged groups is also unlawful as, by definition, if one discriminates positively in favour of one group, one discriminates *against* another. Positive action, in the form of the encouragement of certain under-represented groups to enter into particular areas of employment, for example, women and ethnic minorities in the UK police force, is, however, lawful.

discrimination

Despite a fairly widespread international acceptance that unfair discrimination is unjustifiable, when we consider different aspects of the labour market, we see discrimination and inequalities persisting. For example, on the international stage, though female participation in the labour market has increased in middle- and high-income countries, such countries still exhibit gaps between female and male participation and earnings and these gaps get larger in many less wealthy economies. If we take a closer look at the UK, women and ethnic minorities continue to earn less and have more limited employment prospects than their male, white counterparts. In addition, people with disabilities are disproportionately likely to find difficulty in gaining employment and many older and younger workers are discriminated against in terms of employment opportunities and earnings. For example, in the UK in 2005, though the gender pay gap had narrowed by 12 per cent since 1975, full-time women's average hourly earnings were still more than 17 per cent less than those of men and white women and ethnic minority men and women remain more concentrated in low-paid jobs (EOC, 2006).

In addition, once *in* employment, individuals falling within such groups may have to contend with a 'glass ceiling' on their prospects for advancement. The glass ceiling is a term used to describe an intangible, but nevertheless very real, barrier to progression within an organization, industry or profession. It denotes an obstacle to advancement and fulfilment of potential posed by the attitudes, expectations and stereotypes that are encountered by certain groups of workers in their working lives. Such factors form an unseen barrier, or 'glass- ceiling', that may be so much part of the institutional framework of work, certain categories of the labour force find it very difficult to escape the lower or middle-ranking positions within an organization or industry. It is possible to see the effects of the glass ceiling, despite its lack of visibility. For example, even in organizations where women dominate the workforce, they may be under-represented in managerial positions and the block to progression for women in certain professions cannot be adequately explained by factors such as different life choices or educational attainment as compared with men (see Grint, 2005: 211–17). These issues of inequality persist, even in countries such as the UK, where there has been equal opportunity legislation of one form or another for more than 30 years.

If the law does not guarantee equal opportunity, how do we explain what is happening? Economic models of discrimination in the labour

key concepts in work

market offer several possible explanations. First, there is the classical economic position, of discrimination being the straightforward consequence of competition between workers within a context of employers, trade unions and customers, who each bring some pressure to bear on the available levels of wages and opportunity. In part, the argument here is that to some extent workers are exercising preference in the jobs they compete for. Second, human capital theory presents an alternative explanation, which focuses on the investment that individuals make in their own development in terms of skill, education and training during their working lifetimes. Discrimination may then be viewed as the consequence of individuals having made different choices over their life-long 'investment'. For example, compared with men, women might choose to make different investments in their human capital due to their expectations of a break in their working lifetimes for child-bearing and rearing. A third model suggests that discrimination is the product of employers' imperfect knowledge of the labour market. This approach suggests that employers' imperfect knowledge of the *actual* potential productivity and performance of particular types of workers, for example, women, leads them to rely on stereotypical evaluations of worker characteristics as the basis for employment decisions. The result is more limited job prospects for some categories of workers (Mayhew and Addison, 1983: 313–17).

Theories of labour market segmentation have augmented and criticized elements of the economic models already discussed. Since the mid-1970s when Piore (1975) proposed that the labour market was divided into two main segments – primary and secondary sectors – interpretations of labour market segmentation have developed. In summary, in Piore's definition, the primary sector offers good job tenure, chances for progression and relatively high wages. The primary labour market is associated with the core internal labour market of an organization. The secondary labour market, in contrast, is characterized by low-paying jobs, poorer conditions, few prospects for career progression and job instability (ibid.; Dex, 1988). Women and ethnic minorities were, and remain, generally more likely to populate the secondary sector. The argument runs that, under conditions of instability and lower wages, the chances for investment in human capital are more limited. Thus, participants in the secondary labour market typically become trapped by poorer employment conditions and are denied the chance of breaking free from these constraints by being excluded from the employment opportunities associated with firms' internal labour markets (Dex, 1988:

286–7). But these theories can themselves be criticized for, for example, failing to take account of the socio-economic roles and positions of men, women and ethnic minority workers.

Individually, none of these models seems wholly adequate as an explanation of unfair discrimination in the labour market. There is insufficient discussion of the effects of power, class, poverty, educational attainment and social norms that define opportunity and mould the expectations an individual brings to the labour market in the first place. These may be influenced by long-held conceptions and ideological viewpoints of, for example, male and female work. In turn, these may be reflected in gendered occupations and different levels of participation in the labour market among different ethnic groups. Expectations may also be influenced by levels of educational attainment and aspirations, factors that again are not neutral in terms of gender, race, disability or age. It is, in any case, erroneous to discuss women or workers with disabilities, older workers or ethnic minorities as though they are homogeneous groups with uniform sets of preferences for work. Further, one has to take account of straightforward employer prejudice leading to discriminatory employment practices, as well as the actions of workers as they seek to protect their position within the labour market against, for example, the influx of migrant workers. Employees may themselves perpetuate discrimination by seeking to exclude new categories of workers from joining their ranks. Thus, the presence of discrimination may best be explained in terms of a complex interaction of several factors within the labour market. Economic models contribute to the explanation, but these must be used and evaluated within a context that takes account of wider social pressures and the power relations in the employment relationship.

THE FUTURE OF ANTI-DISCRIMINATION – MANAGING DIVERSITY?

The labour market is changing and in some countries with mature and developed economies there is increasing pressure for work–life balance as well as fairness in employment (Blyton and Dastmalchian, 2006; see also **Work–life Balance**). One of the managerial initiatives associated with the 'business case' for combating discrimination is that of 'managing diversity'. This business case for anti-discrimination is focused on the human resource management (HRM) approach to equal opportunity, which proposes that managers should go beyond legal regulation and adopt policies celebrating difference and distinctiveness within the organization's internal labour market. There is a strong link here with the HRM view that competitive success can be achieved through people and their creativity. Yet employers' practices, in contrast to policies, still seem to be characterized by apathy. Policy statements on diversity may be undermined by poor implementation of policy and inconsistent practice and empirical research has generally failed to establish a clear link between diversity and the bottom line or to find evidence of any significant level of greater equality in the labour market (Cassell, 2006). Overall, despite legal intervention, unfair discrimination continues to be a feature of many workers' experience of the labour market. Legislation makes clear the state's view of discrimination, but has not yet succeeded in eradicating a phenomenon that has deep roots in socio-economic factors, including class, power and patterns of work and employment across the globe.

See also: career, employment patterns, the law and contract of employment.

REFERENCES

Blyton, P. and Dastmalchian, A. (2006) 'Work-life integration and the changing context of work', in P. Blyton, B. Blunsdon, K. Reed and A. Dastmalchian (eds), *Work-Life Integration: International Perspectives on the Balancing of Multiple Roles*. Basingstoke: Palgrave Macmillan, pp. 17–27.

Cassell, C. (2006) 'Managing diversity', in T. Redman and A. Wilkinson (eds), *Contemporary Human Resource Management: Text and Cases*. Harlow: Pearson Education, pp. 306–30.

Dex, S. (1988) 'Gender and the labour market', in D. Gallie (ed.), *Employment in Britain*. Oxford: Basil Blackwell, pp. 281–309.

Equal Opportunities Commission (EOC) (2006) *Facts about Men and Women in Great Britain*. Manchester: EOC.

Grint, K. (2005) *The Sociology of Work*, 3rd edn. Cambridge: Polity Press.

Jenkins, R. (1988) 'Discrimination and equal opportunity in employment: ethnicity and race in the United Kingdom', in D. Gallie (ed.), *Employment in Britain*. Oxford: Basil Blackwell, pp. 310–43.

Mayhew, K. and Addison, J. (1983) 'Discrimination in the labour market', in G.S. Bain (ed.), *Industrial Relations in Britain*. Oxford: Basil Blackwell, pp. 311–38.

Piore, M. J. (1975) 'Notes for a theory of labour market segmentation', in R. Edwards, M. Reich and D. Gordon (eds), *Labour Market Segmentation*. Lexington, MA: D.C. Heath.

discrimination

> *Domestic work refers to the unpaid work activities undertaken within the home, including housework and child-care.*

Most of the discussion in this volume is focused on different aspects of paid work. Yet major areas of work activity fall outside the paid work sphere, notably voluntary work and domestic work (see **Voluntary Work**). The fact that these work activities do not receive payment acts to lower their visibility as work; indeed, in many discussions about work, they vanish altogether. Yet they are not only major areas of work in their own right (for example, in terms of the amount of time and effort devoted to them and their equivalent monetary value) but also in terms of their importance for, and influence on, the paid work sector. Thus, by reviewing the changing (and not so changing) nature of domestic work, this also sheds additional light on a number of areas of paid work activity.

Our discussion proceeds as follows. First, we examine briefly the nature of the domestic work sphere and its links with paid work, together with some methods used to quantify the overall size of domestic work – in particular, how to attribute a monetary value and thereby compare the size of domestic work with the paid work sector. We also consider the gender distribution of domestic work. What makes this a particularly important issue is the fact that most domestic work – particularly routine housework, such as cleaning and cooking, and child-care – continues to be undertaken disproportionately by women. We need to explore this and its consequences and consider the evidence for how much this picture is changing, given the rise of women's participation in the paid labour force. Finally, we will speculate on the future direction of domestic work in the light of current changes in demographic patterns, as well as changes evident in the nature of paid and unpaid work.

THE NATURE AND SIZE OF DOMESTIC WORK

Domestic work covers a variety of unpaid activities in the home: routine housework activities such as cleaning, cooking and shopping; less routine activities such as garden maintenance, DIY and home repairs; and child-care. In various ways, domestic work plays a key – though largely unrecognized – role in the effective functioning of the paid work sector. Among the main aspects for this role, Noon and Blyton (2007) point, for example, to: the importance of the domestic sphere for childhood socialization, including the development of work values; the significance of the domestic sphere for producing labour that is fit for work – clothed, fed and rested; its role as a source of psychological support, where those in paid work can relax away from the pressures of the job; and the way that consumption in the domestic sphere acts as a motivator for continuing commitment to paid work activity.

In combination, the activities comprising domestic work represent an enormous quantity of work undertaken, both in the amount of time expended and in the equivalent monetary value of the work produced. However, assigning that monetary value is problematic, for there are two distinct ways this can be calculated. On the one hand, it is possible to estimate the cost of purchasing the different individual work tasks from outside providers (gardeners, cooks, cleaners, child carers and so on). Chadeau (1985) and others refer to this as measuring the foregone expense – the costs that otherwise would be incurred if not carried out as unpaid domestic work. On the other hand, one can measure the monetary value of the person's time within the household undertaking the unpaid domestic work – how much income that person would acquire by spending their time in paid work, rather than on unpaid domestic work. This latter approach is known as measuring the foregone wage.

These two measures will give rise to somewhat different monetary estimates of the value of domestic work (typically the foregone expense will generate a higher estimate). Yet, whichever method is chosen, one thing is clear: the monetary value of unpaid domestic work activities is very high. Chadeau's (1985) meta-analysis of over 30-studies, for example, yielded a combined average estimate of the value of domestic work as equivalent to over one-third of Gross National Product (GNP).

WHO DOES THE DOMESTIC WORK?

The scale of domestic work and its overlooked nature as 'real' work are made much more significant by the fact that it is work undertaken disproportionately by women, rather than shared equally between men and women. In a recent *Social Trends* report, for example, women in the UK were recorded as spending, on average, almost twice the amount of

domestic work

time each day on housework and child-care activities than men (an average of over four hours per day for women, compared to approximately two and a quarter hours for men) (Office for National Statistics, 2005: 174). This difference raises a number of important and wide-ranging issues, for example, about the fairness of the division of labour within households; the impact on women's role and status in society; and the implications for women's activity in the paid labour sphere. We will briefly consider some of these issues here.

First, however, we need to look at the distribution of time in a little more detail. Some areas of time use reported in the same *Social Trends* report cited above reveal comparatively little difference between the sexes: for example, men and women both spend roughly the same amount of time each day sleeping, travelling and undertaking personal care activities (such as eating, drinking, washing and dressing). However, while women spend much longer, on average, on domestic work, men spend more time than women in paid employment. Indeed, if time spent on paid work and unpaid housework and child-care are combined, the differences between men and women are markedly reduced. Further, Sullivan (2000) notes that in surveys spanning more than two decades, this approximate parity in overall work time between men and women has remained evident since the mid-1970s. But at the same time, the significance of the distribution of paid and unpaid work remains – men remain disproportionately engaged in paid work activities, women in unpaid domestic work.

Yet, as we discuss elsewhere in this volume, the traditional picture of male breadwinner, female homemaker is undergoing significant change due to the rise in female paid work activity, particularly the rise of women engaging in part-time paid work (see **Employment Patterns**). An important question this raises is whether entry into paid work results in a redistribution of domestic work activities or women experience a 'dual burden' of paid and unpaid work. Early analyses following the increase in paid work among women tended to detect only very slow change occurring in the distribution of unpaid work roles (and especially the overall responsibility for those activities). However, more recent survey evidence and comparisons over time suggest that change is becoming more evident. This suggests there may have been a delayed effect – what Gershuny and colleagues (1994) term a 'lagged adaptation' – in regard to the distribution of domestic tasks: change is occurring but more slowly than changes in female labour market participation.

In a 20-year comparison of how people spend their time, Sullivan (2000) concludes that the increase in male involvement in domestic tasks between the mid-1970s and later 1990s was 'significant' and that this was apparent not only where women were in full- or part-time employment, but also where they were not involved in paid work. Overall, the proportion of couples' domestic work time contributed by women fell by 14 percentage points between 1975 and 1997: in 1975, women on average accounted for 77 per cent of total time spent on domestic work; by 1997 this had fallen to 63 per cent (ibid.: 442). However, important elements of inequality in the distribution of domestic work remain clear. In particular, where both adults were working full-time in 1997, women on average still accounted for 60 per cent of the total time spent on domestic work (though this was down from 68 per cent in 1975) (ibid.: 443).

THE FUTURE

Various factors could influence the future pattern of domestic work. These include the possibility that more of that work (for example, gardening and cleaning) may be contracted out to paid service providers or to unpaid members of extended families (for example, grandparents undertaking child-care for dual-earner couples). In addition, the total time spent on child-care may fall as a consequence of any continued decline in birth rates and household sizes. In terms of who undertakes the domestic work, it is possible that the trend towards men undertaking a greater share of household activities will continue, particularly if women's participation in the labour force remains on the increase. However, a three-country study by Crompton, Brockmann and Lyonette (2005) suggests that the growth in male participation in domestic work may have become stalled in recent years. One possible explanation offered for this relates to the widespread experience of increased work pressure that has been reported (see **Effort and Intensity**). The authors argue that increased work pressure (leading for some to increased working hours) will disproportionately affect those in 'career' jobs and the holders of those positions remain disproportionately male. Hence, should work demands continue to intensify, this could significantly impede any further redistribution of domestic work activities. However, the current attention being given to the importance of securing improved work–life balance may act to mitigate (at least to some extent) the pressure towards work intensification, particularly for more powerful groups within the workforce (see **Work–life Balance**). In turn, this could contribute to further moves towards a more equitable distribution of work and non-work responsibilities.

See also: *career, informal work, working time.*

REFERENCES

Chadeau, A. (1985) 'Measuring household activities: some international comparisons', *Review of Income and Wealth*, 31 (3): 237–53.

Crompton, R., Brockmann, M. and Lyonette, C. (2005) 'Attitudes, women's employment and the domestic division of labour: a cross-national analysis in two waves', *Work, Employment and Society*, 19 (2): 213–33.

Gershuny, J., Godwin, M. and Jones, S. (1994) 'The domestic labour revolution: a process of lagged adaptation', in M. Anderson, F. Bechhofer and J. Gershuny (eds), *The Social and Political Economy of the Household*. Oxford: Oxford University Press, pp. 151–97.

Noon, M. and Blyton, P. (2007) *The Realities of Work*, 3rd edn. Basingstoke: Palgrave Macmillan.

Office for National Statistics (2005) *Social Trends 35: 2005 edition*. London: Office for National Statistics.

Sullivan, O. (2000) 'The division of domestic labour: twenty years of change?', *Sociology*, 34 (3): 437–56.

key concepts in work

Effort and Intensity

> *Work effort is the overall amount of physical and/or mental energy that is devoted to a work task. Work intensity relates to the pace or pressure of work activity.*

58

How hard people work, if those in some jobs work harder than others and if workers work harder now than in the past (and, if so, why) are important questions for those interested in understanding the changing nature of work. In turn, these questions relate to broader issues such as the productivity of different economies: to what extent do productivity gaps between countries, for example, reflect that people in some countries work harder than in others (rather than, for instance, different levels of investment in capital equipment)? Also relevant are issues concerning job stress and satisfaction: to what extent are the amount and pace that people are working affecting their level of psychological well-being? Important too are questions pertaining to work–life balance – to what extent is society getting the balance right (or wrong) between how hard its citizens work and the rest of their lives (see **Work–life Balance**)?

MEASURING EFFORT AND INTENSITY

Questions such as the ones outlined above, probably like all important questions, are much easier to pose than to answer. Consider for a moment how we might go about trying to research and measure changes in how hard people are working. An immediate problem in obtaining an objective measure for individuals is that in many jobs the outputs are not precisely or fully quantifiable. The work effort of school teachers, for example, could be measured in terms of the time they spend on their work or the 'output' of their students' exam results. But much more difficult is measuring how much they have inspired their students and given them an enthusiasm for learning that will last into later life. Further, if we attempt to measure the labour productivity of an individual or a group (that is, the amount of output as a proportion of the number of individuals contributing to that output), any measure is complicated by the several factors that can impact on how productive an individual or group might be – the extent and quality of capital equipment being used, for example, or the efficiency of management in organizing and coordinating the work process.

Given the difficulty of obtaining objective measures in most situations, an alternative is to seek a subjective assessment of how hard people are working and compare these assessments over time. A number of studies have asked people at work how hard they feel they are working. In the 2004 Workplace Employment Relations Survey (WERS), for example, over three-quarters (76 per cent) of employees either agreed or strongly agreed with the statement 'My job requires that I work very hard' (Kersley et al., 2006: 100). Other studies contain questions relating to the experienced level of work intensity or work pressure. Seeking responses to statements such as 'I work under a great deal of pressure', 'I am working at a high speed' or 'I never have enough time to get my job done' (often using response scales ranging from Never to Always) are typical approaches used in surveys to gauge workers' subjective sense of their work pressure.

There are problems with using self-assessment questions such as these, however. First, there is likely to be an understandable reluctance on the part of employees to report that they are not working hard; they may feel this runs the risk of them being given a lot more work to do or even that their job is unnecessary. The approach of asking identical questions over a long time period seeks to control for this bias. The assumption here is that the level of reluctance to report low work pressure will remain reasonably constant over time; therefore any changes in proportions recording high or very high levels of work pressure are likely still to be meaningful.

Another problem is that the overall nature of work is changing – for example, many jobs now require less physical and more mental activity – so if individuals are being asked if they are working harder now than in the past, this may be a request to compare two quite different types of effort (manual and mental). This is problematic enough, but we are also asking people simultaneously to juggle other things in their heads when answering such questions. For example, in many countries weekly hours of work have declined since the early 1980s; in such cases employers are likely to have sought to offset any reductions in hours with increases in productivity (see **Working Time**). So, if people are working harder but for shorter hours, does this translate into more intensity, but overall less effort or is the experience one of both greater intensity and more effort? In thinking about this, it is important to bear in mind that work effort and work intensity are not the same thing. While the former may be thought of as an 'extensive' measure – overall how much effort is expended during the work period – the latter is more a measure of work pressure: the level of intensity under which the effort is performed.

INCREASED LEVELS OF WORK PRESSURE

Notwithstanding these difficulties surrounding measurement, however, in general what the measures show is that, over time and across a variety of countries, people record higher levels of work pressure now than they did 25 years ago. Green (2001, 2004; see also Green and McIntosh, 2001) in comparing national and cross-national surveys since the early

1980s, shows that an increased proportion of employees report that they are working under greater pressure, compared to their counterparts in the earlier period. This is reflected, for example, in the growing proportion of people reporting that they 'mostly' or 'always' work 'under a great deal of pressure', that their job involves 'working at high speed' or 'working to tight deadlines'. A significant proportion of the workforce now report that they experience considerable work pressure. In the WERS 2004 survey, two-fifths (40 per cent) of employees agreed or strongly agreed with the statement 'I never seem to have enough time to get my work done'. This proportion rose to over half (51 per cent) among those working more than 48 hours a week, indicating for that group both high levels of work effort and high work intensity (Kersley et al., 2006: 100–1).

INFLUENCING FACTORS

What accounts for this reported increase in effort over the past generation? We can point to a number of factors that seem to have a bearing on this. In Green's (2004) study, for example, he found that those reporting greatest work pressure were more likely to be those working with technology (those working with computers being more likely to report growing intensity) and those experiencing major work reorganization. On the former, many aspects of communication and computer use appear to have increased expectations of work effort, including increased availability when away from the workplace by remaining connected to work through mobile phones, the Internet, e-mails and so on (see **Technology**). Also important in many work contexts is that information and communications technology can be used by supervisors and others to monitor employee work rates more closely than in the past (for example, the ability of computer-based technologies to track how many calls are completed by call centre employees, how many key strokes made by data entry workers or the number of items read by barcode equipment used by supermarket check-out staff).

In terms of the influence of work reorganization, much recent work restructuring has been accompanied by reductions in workforce levels, as firms seek to cut costs as part of their reorganization of operations. A common result is that a smaller number of remaining workers are required to cover more tasks, thus resulting in more intensified work regimes. One way of achieving this broader coverage of jobs by fewer workers has been to increase the level of labour flexibility within work organizations by training workers to undertake a broader range of functions within the workplace (see **Flexibility**). In the WERS 2004 survey, for example, two-thirds of workplaces reported that they had trained at least some of their staff to be functionally flexible and over four out of five employees trained in this way were undertaking jobs other than their own at least once a week (Kersley et al., 2006). The increased ability to switch from one task to another creates scope for management to increase the overall level of labour utilization and thus potentially the overall level of worker effort.

Another development to increase labour utilization (specifically, how much of the work period is actually spent working) has been management practices designed to define the working period exclusive, rather than inclusive, of preparatory activities such as walking to and from the actual work area. Efforts to tighten the definition of the working period have included the introduction of 'bell to bell' working, which refers to the bells or buzzers announcing the start and finish of working periods and the start and finish of break times, with employees required to be in position to commence working when the bell for the start of the shift sounds and only terminating work after the bell signalling the end of the shift. Such managerial attempts to minimize non-productive time have long featured in relations between employers and employees. In the nineteenth century, for example, Karl Marx remarked on employers' continual efforts to minimize the 'porosity' of the working day: the number of holes or 'pores' in the working period when workers are not actually working. Marx (1976: 352) characterized employers as continually 'nibbling and cribbling' at workers' meal times and other breaks in an attempt to maximize the quantity of labour effort in the working day (see **Working Time**).

Other factors that may help to explain overall increases in reported work effort include developments in process controls that have enabled the spread of just-in-time (JIT) and 'lean' production systems. JIT systems emphasize work 'flowing' steadily and continuously through the different stages of production, with components arriving 'just-in-time' to be incorporated into the manufacturing process and with only minimum stocks held of materials, work-in-progress and finished articles. Among other implications, this method of organizing production potentially undermines the ability of employees to build up 'banks' of finished or part-finished work that could then be used to create an additional break or an easier work pace.

In addition, the spread of various human resource management practices may have contributed to increased levels of reported effort and intensity. These practices range from the introduction of performance targets and more widespread use of performance appraisals to the greater prevalence of performance-related pay systems and employee involvement schemes, designed to enhance levels of employee motivation and commitment. Further, these practices have expanded at a time of weakened trade unionism, creating, for example, easier conditions for managers to eliminate job boundaries without meeting large-scale union opposition. In the past many trade unions staunchly defended job boundaries as a way of maintaining power within the workplace. Such resistance has become more difficult to organize and sustain as trade union membership levels in many sectors, and across a large number of countries, have fallen (see **Trade Unions**).

One final factor that may be contributing to increased levels of effort relates not to pressures emanating from employers, but employees themselves choosing to work harder, not least to increase their financial rewards from work. As we noted in the Introduction to this volume, work cannot be considered separately from other aspects of society and many commentators have noted that, in society at large, there has been an increased emphasis on consumption as a source of individual identity and satisfaction. Consumption requires sufficient income and, as consumption expectations rise, for many the only way to secure the necessary income is by working harder (either to achieve promotion to a higher and better-rewarded position or to increase earnings through performance-related bonuses, overtime payments and the like). Further, as levels of personal debt continue to rise – a direct reflection of the desire to maintain high levels of personal consumption – increased work effort may also be a sign of the increased pressure that many may feel under to reduce their levels of debt.

Hence, there are both employer- and employee-based factors that may help to account for more people reporting not only that they are working harder but also that the work is more intensive than a generation ago. While more individuals appear to be recognizing that this potentially creates greater problems for achieving work–life balance and while there is a growing recognition that consumption levels are unsustainable in the longer term because of associated environmental damage, in the shorter term there is little sign that reported workloads and work pressures are likely to fall and could well register further rises for many in coming years.

See also: *consent, labour process, management, pay and performance, presenteeism.*

REFERENCES

Green, F. (2001) 'It's been a hard day's night: the concentration and intensification of work in late twentieth-century Britain', *British Journal of Industrial Relations*, 39 (1): 53–80.

Green, F. (2004) 'Why has work effort become more intense?', *Industrial Relations*, 43 (4): 709–41.

Green, F. and McIntosh, S. (2001) 'The intensification of work in Europe', *Labour Economics*, 8: 291–308.

Kersley, B., Alpin, C., Forth, J., Bryson, A., Bewley, H., Dix, G. and Oxenbridge, S. (2006) *Inside the Workplace: Findings from the 2004 Employment Relations Survey*. Abingdon: Routledge.

Marx, K. (1976) *Capital*, vol. 1. Harmondsworth: Penguin.

Emotional Labour

> Emotional labour involves 'the act of expressing organizationally desired emotions during service transactions' (Morris and Feldman, 1996: 987).

As consumers of an ever-widening range of services and thus as participants in an ever-growing number of service encounters, all of us are increasingly the object of other people's emotional labour. For those working in the service sector – be they telephone call centre workers, bank cashiers, restaurant waiters or airline check-in staff – part of their task involves not only the system requirements of their job (to complete the telephone call, handle the transaction, serve the meals or assign the airline seats) but also to perform those tasks in a way that emphasizes the value the organization places on that customer's business. Thus, the *way* a service is provided represents part of the service itself. The required behaviour: 'the ever-present smile, the cheery voice, the politeness when under pressure, the enthusiasm for the task or product, the suppression of annoyance or fatigue, the willingness to please' (Fineman, 2003: 35), are all designed to convey a sense of personalized service in which respect for the customer is a prominent message. In this way, emotional labour has come to represent an essential component of customer service, involving the display of emotions that has the aim of engendering a particular response: the response of a 'satisfied customer'; and thus a customer more likely to return with repeat business in the future.

The recognized value of being respectful and friendly to potential customers is, of course, nothing new. The adages of 'service with a smile' and 'the customer is always right', go back a long way. What has changed in recent years, however, is the growing use of emotional labour in an ever-increasing array of situations; the use of more elaborated forms of emotional labour; and increased attempts by management to ensure a consistency in the delivery of the required emotional style.

THE GROWTH OF EMOTIONAL LABOUR

The main factors that explain the growth in emotional labour include an increase in levels of competition in most service industries, together with employers seeking to differentiate their product by the quality of the service (and thus the level of customer satisfaction) that their employees provide. This has combined with an overall growth in service-sector employment; over seven out of every ten employees in most industrial societies now work in service-sector jobs, many of these in 'customer-facing' positions (see **Employment Patterns**). The result is, first, a growing proportion of the labour force now undertakes emotional labour as part of their job and, second, that this aspect of work has come to be seen as increasingly important by employers who, as a result, are taking various steps to ensure its consistent and 'authentic' delivery. Such consistency is sought by various means, including careful selection, recruitment and induction procedures; direct supervision of employees' verbal and non-verbal behaviour; and various other ways of monitoring employees actions. The latter include supervisors listening in to telephone conversations in call centres, the use of 'mystery shoppers' hired by companies to report on service encounters and customer feedback surveys on specific service interactions (see **Customers**). Systems of punishment (such as disciplinary action) and reward (for example, 'employee of the month' awards) are also used to reinforce the message of the 'correct' way to perform the job.

Several areas of debate have developed around emotional labour. These include identifying the different dimensions of emotional labour that exist; assessing the extent to which (and the conditions under which) the performing of emotional labour is a problematic activity;

emotional labour

considering the extent to which emotional labour has particular gender implications; and exploring the ways that workers respond to emotional labour (both positively and negatively), including the coping strategies used to reduce the strain of performing emotional labour under difficult conditions.

DIMENSIONS OF EMOTIONAL LABOUR

Morris and Feldman (1996) distinguish different aspects of emotional labour in terms of:

- *frequency*: some jobs (such as check-out operator in a busy supermarket, for example) entail a higher frequency of emotional labour encounters than others;
- *duration*: in some activities, such as a fast food outlet, emotional labour is performed for very short periods, in other situations, for longer spells;
- the degree of *emotional dissonance* involved.

Emotional dissonance refers to the gap that individual employees experience between their real and their displayed emotions, which is likely to vary not only between individuals but between jobs, as well as between different customer interactions in relation to a single job. For example, the person at the airline service desk required to deal in a friendly and polite way with irate customers reporting lost bags, may experience more emotional dissonance (not feeling friendly if being verbally attacked for the lost bag) than his or her counterpart at the nearby service desk explaining to customers how to check in their bikes and hang-gliding equipment.

It is this dimension of emotional labour – the gap between real and displayed feelings – that was a major focus of the landmark research in the area of emotional labour by Hochschild (1983). Studying airline flight attendants, Hochschild was highly critical of the requirements for, and effects of, emotional labour, identifying an overwhelmingly harmful impact of performing such labour among the female attendants she studied. Hochschild's concerns centred on the alienating effects of being required, over long periods, to display emotions that were organizationally required rather than genuinely felt. More broadly, and given the tendency for many of the jobs requiring emotional labour to be filled by women, Hochschild was critical of the impact of emotional labour on women's overall position within the labour force. She argues that emotional labour tasks act to further reinforce stereotypes of women as being better suited to 'caring' roles – the dispensing of emotional support – rather than higher-status (and much better rewarded) occupations where rational or technical skills are uppermost. This early study by Hochschild set much of the tone for initial thinking and writing on emotional labour, which emphasized, for example, the way that certain situations (such as long-haul airline flights or angry or abusive customers) made emotional labour particularly problematic and the ways that individuals coped with this 'burden' of performing emotional labour.

In more recent years, however, various studies have adopted a some-what more neutral tone, identifying the different degrees of emotional labour required by different jobs; the different ways of performing that labour; and the conditions under which emotional labour can create positive, satisfying outcomes, rather than be associated with negative consequences. Researchers such as Wharton (1993), for example, have identified the importance of job autonomy modifying the impact of emotional labour. In those jobs in Wharton's study where the workers performing emotional labour felt that they had a measure of autonomy and control, the emotional labour aspect of the job was more likely to be associated with positive job satisfaction. Other studies have also identified the importance of management's attitude to problematic emotional labour situations. Where employees feel supported by the organization – for example, in situations where customers are behaving unreasonably – employees report more satisfaction with their emotional labour role.

Another factor relates to the meaning of the emotional labour for the employee. Those individuals who fully identify with their role and view it as their vocation or 'calling' – many in the health and social welfare professions, for example – are likely to find fewer problems arising from performing emotional labour than those for whom the job has less intrinsic meaning.

COPING STRATEGIES

Many of the early studies of emotional labour and its potentially negative impact on employees appear to have underestimated the ability of employees successfully to reduce the pressures arising by various coping strategies. At their simplest, these strategies involve such behaviours as going somewhere ('off-stage') to let off steam or alternatively 'switching off' – that is, outwardly adhering to the display rules but engaging in an inward mental escape. Writers such as Korczynski (2003) have also demonstrated the importance of collective 'communities of coping' in call centres where employees share with one another particularly bad experiences with angry or abusive customers and thus reduce the tendency to take such abuse personally (see also **Surviving Work**).

Further, in practice, workers perform emotional labour to different degrees. Some have drawn a contrast between 'surface' and 'deep' acting. Surface acting involves a compliance with the display rules (expression, verbal comments and so on), while deep acting involves fully internalizing the display rules and developing a set of feelings that values the emotional behaviour. In some difficult situations, a further coping strategy by employees may be to reduce their level of compliance with the display rules, for example, by covertly reducing the emotional 'script' that they are formally required by management to adhere to.

Yet, whatever the problems that might arise from performing emotional labour in certain situations, there are various reasons for customer-facing staff to perform their emotional labour tasks effectively. Not only is this likely to meet with management approval (or at least the absence of disapproval) but it can also have benefits in other tangible ways. Smiling at people is more likely to elicit a friendly and more positive interaction in return; satisfied customers are more likely to increase employees' own sense of job satisfaction. And, as studies of waiters and waitresses have found, those who smile more tend to do better at attracting larger tips from customers than those smiling less (see Noon and Blyton, 2007, for more detailed discussion of the various aspects of emotional labour).

THE FUTURE

As regards the future development of emotional labour, various signs point to this becoming a progressively more important aspect of the ever-widening range of service delivery. As customers, our expectations appear to be ever increasing in relation to the form and manner in which services are offered. As a result of this growth, the gender aspects of emotional labour are likely to diminish as more men working in service-sector activities take on additional emotional labour functions. Whether increased customer expectations mean that emotional labour tasks will become more onerous and problematic for those undertaking them, however, remains to be seen.

See also: *alienation, skill.*

REFERENCES

Fineman, S. (2003) *Understanding Emotion at Work.* London: Sage.
Hochschild, A.R. (1983) *The Managed Heart: Commercialization of Human Feeling.* Berkeley, CA: University of California Press.
Korczynski, M. (2003) 'Communities of coping: collective emotional labour in service work', *Organization,* 10 (1): 55–79.
Morris, J.A. and Feldman, D.C. (1996) 'The dimensions, antecedents and consequences of emotional labor', *Academy of Management Review,* 21 (4): 986–1010.
Noon, M. and Blyton, P. (2007) *The Realities of Work,* 3rd edn. Basingstoke: Palgrave Macmillan.
Wharton, A. (1993) 'The affective consequences of service work: managing emotions on the job', *Work and Occupations,* 20 (2): 205–32.

Employment Patterns

Employment patterns refers to the characteristics of employment, including the location, structure and composition of the workforce.

Many of the key developments in the nature of work and employment over the past generation have been shaped by a fundamental structural change that has been occurring in advanced economies, as the proportion of the working population engaged in service activities has increased and the proportion employed in manufacturing has declined. Across the industrial economies as a whole, seven out of ten employees now work in the service sector: in several countries (including Canada, the United States and a number of European countries) over three-quarters of employees now work in services. Back in 1971, the proportion of employees in industrial countries working in the service sector was five out of ten and, in 1961, the proportion was just over four out of ten. The result has been that, in the UK since the early 1970s for example, while the number employed in the service sector has risen by almost four-fifths, the total employed in manufacturing has fallen by three-fifths. As a result, by 2005, more than seven times as many people (almost 22 million) in the UK were employed in service industries as in manufacturing (just over 3 million).

MEN AND WOMEN IN EMPLOYMENT

This growing prominence of service-sector employment is reflected in several other workforce developments, in particular, the changing proportions of male and female and full- and part-time workers. First, the period since the 1970s has witnessed a marked growth in the proportion of the workforce that is female. Several supply-side factors help to account for this change, including the growth in educational qualifications among women, rising aspirations, the influence of economic factors and changes in attitudes towards paid work and child-rearing. On the demand side, the most important factor accounting for the rise in women's economic activity is the growth in service-sector employment as a whole and the increased opportunities for women's employment within service industries. As a result of these influences, in the second half of the twentieth century, the level of economic activity of women in Britain (that is, those of working age active in the labour market) increased from just over two in five (43 per cent) to almost three in four (74 per cent), with much of this increase concentrated in the second half of that period (Hakim, 2004: 60). Overall between 1979 and 2004, the growth of women in paid employment in Britain rose two and a half times faster than the equivalent figure for men. This pattern is repeated, to a greater or lesser extent, across most industrial countries and, as a result of both this trend and in many instances a stable or slightly declining level of male labour force participation, a growing proportion of the overall labour force is female.

PART-TIME WORKING

Much of the net increase in women's employment activity rates is accounted for by a rise in part-time working. Though there has been some increase in recent years in men working part-time – not least due to a growth in the number of male students with part-time jobs – women comprise the majority of part-time job holders. On average in industrial countries, three-quarters of part-time jobs are held by women. Within this overall rise in part-time working, however, the proportion of the labour force working part-time varies considerably from country to country. Among European Union members, for example, while just over one in twenty workers in Greece works part-time, almost one in three workers in the Netherlands is part-time. Several factors help to account for such wide variation. These include national differences in the structure of employers' non-wage payments: in particular, whether the costs to employers of hiring part-time workers are *pro rata* their full-time equivalents (that is, costs varying according to the number of hours worked) or whether national insurance and equivalent payments are levied *per capita* (that is, employers are required to make the same payment irrespective of number of hours worked). While the former encourages an expansion of part-time schedules, the latter acts as a financial disincentive and significant obstacle to any such expansion. Also relevant in accounting for variations in levels of part-time working is the comparative size (and rate of growth) of the service sector in different economies, as most part-time jobs are located within service activities (in the UK, over nine out of ten part-time jobs are in the service sector). Industries particularly reliant on part-time working include retail distribution, hotels and restaurants, health and social work and education.

Over half the women engaged in part-time work in the UK have a dependent child, compared to just over one-quarter of women in full-time work. It is significant that in those countries (particularly in Scandinavia) with a more extensive range of 'family friendly' work practices and statutory welfare provisions (such as state nursery facilities) that facilitate the combining of full-time jobs and child rearing, the incidence of part-time working among women has fallen in recent years while the proportion of women working full-time has increased. In the UK and many other industrial countries, however, part-time working continues to a greater extent to represent a means for women to combine paid work and family responsibilities.

In a number of countries, the distribution of part-time work hours is highly diverse. This is particularly the case in Britain and the USA and is most marked in terms of the large numbers of part-timers engaged on very short hours schedules. For example, around two in five female part-time workers in Britain (and approaching half of male part-time workers) work sixteen hours a week or less, while one in eight female part-timers (and a fifth of male part-timers) work eight hours or fewer each week. This variation in part-time schedules adds significantly to the diversity evident in working time patterns as a whole, both in terms of the number of hours that people work and the timing of those work hours (see **Working Time**).

In addition to contracts specifying a fixed number of hours, two further ways in which short schedules have been introduced are through 'minimum hours' and 'zero hours' contracts. The former typically specify a guaranteed minimum number of weekly hours to be worked with the employee undertaking to work more hours when the need arises. Zero-hour contracts, on the other hand, offer no minimum guaranteed duration, but contract workers to be 'on call', with work offered (usually at short notice) to cover absence or other circumstances that cause regular employees to be away from their workplace. As a proportion of the overall workforce, the numbers of people working these on call arrangements remains small but their greater presence in some countries (such as the Netherlands and Sweden) coupled with the considerable flexibility they offer employers, may foreshadow a more general increase in the future, particularly where their costs of employment are significantly lower than the amount required to engage staff from temporary work agencies. In the UK around 5 per cent of workplaces were using some zero hours contracts in 2004 (Kersley et al., 2006).

To date, much part-time work has been characterized by being disproportionately concentrated in lower-level positions and with less favourable access to training and promotion. Part-time jobs have, on average, also been characterized by poorer terms and conditions compared to their full-time counterparts. In Europe in recent years this has been addressed partly through the European Union's Part-time Workers Directive and in the UK, the ensuing legislation – the Part-Time Workers (Prevention of Less Favourable Treatment) Regulations – that came into force in 2000, gives part-time workers the right to be treated no less favourably than equivalent full-time workers, to receive the same hourly rate of pay, the same access to pension and sick pay schemes, pro rata annual and parental leave and no less favourable treatment as regards access to training (Gennard and Judge, 2005).

CONTINGENT WORK

The rise of part-time working is only one way in which the labour force is developing away from what became viewed in the second half of the twentieth century as 'standard' employment (full-time employees engaged on indefinite contracts). Other developments away from this standard employment model include the growing use of what some refer to as 'contingent' workers (their engagement more directly contingent on the immediate market circumstances of the organization). Types of employees that comprise the contingent workforce include agency workers and those working for other types of contractor (or independently as self-employed), those on casual or fixed-term contracts, and – in some discussions of contingent workers – those working from home. While some of these categories demonstrate remarkable growth, others are more variable or stable in scale. In the UK, for example, while the number of employees contracted to agencies has shown a marked growth over the recent period, the number of temporary workers has fallen back slightly in the recent period (from over 7 per cent of all employees in 1996 to 6 per cent in 2005) (for more detailed discussion, see Blyton and Turnbull, 2004: 60–79).

FUTURE PATTERNS OF WORK

While several of the trends discussed above are likely to continue in the coming period (the growing proportion of employees located in the service sector, for example, and the growing activity rates of women) possibly the most far-reaching overall trend will prove to be the progressive ageing of populations in the industrial world, as birth rates continue to fall or stabilize and death rates carry on declining. As a consequence, the average age of populations is rising, the average age of many workforces is increasing and the population of working age in developed countries continues to shrink relative to those over pensionable age (currently between 60 and 65 years). In Germany, the continuing fall in birth rates has resulted in forecasts for the next half century of very significant falls in the population in general and in the number of employees in particular. The latter has been forecast to fall by as much as 33 per cent between 2010 and 2050; see Trinczek (2006).

This trend, which is evident not only in Germany but in a large number of industrial countries, raises important questions for both societies as a whole (such as the age at which old age pensions should become payable and the funding of both those pension entitlements and elderly welfare provision more generally) and work organizations (for example, concerning the recruitment of older workers, the increased significance of pensions for both employees and employers and the growing need for provisions for employees to care for elderly dependants). Thus, while discussion of employment patterns over the past generation has been dominated by issues surrounding women's increased economic activity, the next generation is likely to see far greater prominence being given to the economic activity of older workers, both male and female.

See also: career, domestic work, flexibility, globalization and labour migration, work–life balance.

REFERENCES

Blyton, P. and Turnbull, P. (2004) *The Dynamics of Employee Relations*, 3rd edn. Basingstoke: Palgrave Macmillan.

Gennard, J. and Judge, G. (2005) *Employee Relations*, 4th edn. London: Chartered Institute of Personnel and Development.

Hakim, C. (2004) *Key Issues in Women's Work*, 2nd edn. London: Glasshouse Press.

Kersley, B., Alpin, C., Forth, J., Bryson, A., Bewley, H., Dix, G. and Oxenbridge, S. (2006) *Inside the Workplace: Findings from the 2004 Employment Relations Survey*. London: Routledge.

Trinczek, R. (2006) 'Work-life balance and flexible work hours – the German experience', in P. Blyton, B. Blunsdon, K. Reed and A. Dastmalchian (eds,) *Work-Life Integration: International Perspectives on the Balancing of Multiple Roles*. Basingstoke: Palgrave Macmillan, pp. 113–34.

Flexibility

For employers, workforce flexibility refers to the ability to use labour in a more adaptable and variable way. For employees, flexibility refers particularly to the degree of choice available in their work arrangements.

No assessment of the changing nature and experience of work would be complete without an examination of the growth in workforce flexibility. Its increasing prominence from the early 1980s onwards tells us much about the changing nature of work and employment relationships, as well as the greater importance that employers have attached to adjusting the labour input as a source of lower costs and increased competitiveness and profitability. In more recent years, employee concerns to secure greater flexibility over their work arrangements has also become more prominent.

The heightened attention towards labour flexibility has occasioned a corresponding growth in research and writing on the subject. To give an overview of this literature and enquiry, the discussion below explores a number of the main themes. First, we review why flexibility is important to employers and how workforce flexibility forms part of a broader pursuit of more flexible organization. Following this we consider the main sources of workforce flexibility; the traditional approaches to workforce flexibility and the factors that have brought about changes in those approaches; the main trajectories of flexibility development and why variations occur between countries; the effects of flexibility on employees' experience of work; and the employee agenda in relation to achieving greater flexibility.

FACTORS ENCOURAGING GREATER INTEREST IN FLEXIBILITY

It is relevant at the outset of discussing why flexibility is of growing importance to employers to make two general points. First, it is important to remember that, for employers, flexibility is not an end in itself but a means to other ends, such as lower costs or higher profitability. Acting more flexibly is an indication of adaptability and agility, but not an agility for its own sake – it is to achieve continued market success. Second, changes in the nature of competition have made many markets less certain and more short term, thus increasing the requirement for organizations to be able to respond effectively to the more turbulent market conditions. Coupled with this market uncertainty, other changes such as developments in technology (particularly the adaptability of microelectronics) have provided the scope for more rapid changes, as well as creating a requirement for organizations to be sufficiently flexible to capitalize on the versatility and potential of new technologies (see **Technology**). The upshot of these forces has been an increased emphasis on organizations achieving greater flexibility in all their aspects: in the manner that labour performs its tasks, in the way that organizations are structured and in the relationships that organizations have with one another (Procter, 2005). In this way, workforce flexibility can be seen as nested within a broader flexibility agenda that includes the questioning of pre-existing organizational structures and the potential for the development of more versatile organizational forms (see **Organizations: Networks and Alliances**).

SOURCES OF WORKFORCE FLEXIBILITY

As Procter (2005) points out, despite the many levels and identified sources of organizational flexibility, disproportionate attention has been paid to the flexibility that employers can secure from their workforce. In the debates that surfaced in the 1980s, two main sources of workforce flexibility were identified: *functional flexibility*, which refers to the range of activities that individual workers perform; and *numerical flexibility*, which relates to employers' ability to adjust the volume or timing of labour to match fluctuations in output demand. These two main sources of flexibility have been further subdivided in subsequent discussions. Studies of functional flexibility, for example, have distinguished between skilled workers being trained to perform work in other skilled areas (referred to as multiskilling) and expanding the number of jobs performed by unskilled and semi-skilled workers (multitasking). Similarly, numerical flexibility can be secured by several means, for example, altering the headcount (such as by the use of short-term contracts); modifying working time patterns (sometimes termed temporal flexibility) by, for example, the temporary introduction of shift working, extended hours or short-time working; and utilizing contract labour, such as agency staff, to meet fluctuations in output demand or temporary labour shortages (for a more detailed discussion, see Blyton, 1996).

In his early contribution to the flexibility debate, Atkinson (1984) elaborated a model of the 'flexible firm', anticipating the development of both functional and numerical forms of flexibility. He depicted an organization's labour force as comprising both a 'core' of workers, whose skills represented a vital contribution to the continuation of the business, and a 'periphery' of other workers, undertaking necessary, but secondary, activities within the workplace. Atkinson identified functional flexibility as particularly important for the core workforce, with firms gaining important capability by maintaining a key group of adaptable and multiskilled workers. In contrast, numerical flexibility – secured through such means as short-term and part-time contracts and the use of subcontractors and self-employed workers – was seen to be associated more with the 'periphery' workforce, whose role was perceived in part as bearing the brunt of any fluctuations in output demand.

In the event, however, this depiction of the flexible firm has not become the norm that some a generation ago anticipated. Both the distinction between core and periphery, and the application of different forms of flexibility to different groups, have proved difficult to substantiate (see, for example, the critique by Pollert, 1988). Different studies, for example, have identified 'core' functions being undertaken by supposedly 'peripheral' part-time staff, while other studies have identified both functional and numerical forms of flexibility being applied to all sections of the workforce. As a result, few researchers have been able to identify explicit and differentiated flexibility strategies that equate even approximately to Atkinson's original 'flexible firm' model.

THE DEVELOPMENT OF FLEXIBILITY

For many, what the discussion generated by Atkinson's model did underline, however, was the growing attention being paid to flexibility by employers. Before the 1980s, flexibility was already (and always has been) important to employers. For example, casual forms of employment by the hour or the day typified many industries in the past, providing employers with the means to match the volume of labour with demand. In traditional dock work, for example, where the pattern of work demand was subject to the tides and vagaries of the weather, men were engaged to load or unload a ship and were likely to be laid off when the task was completed. Overtime and short-time working are other long-established sources of flexibility enabling employers to expand or contract the labour input as fluctuations in demand warranted. However, while these practices indicate the long-standing importance of flexibility to employers, the recent period has seen further emphasis being given to securing greater levels of labour flexibility.

Several factors account for this. For example, the development of new technologies has undermined many previous ways of separating jobs and defining work roles (see **Technology**). As formerly distinct tasks such as typing and clerical work or design and manufacture have become increasingly integrated by computer-based equipment, job boundaries have become less clear-cut. Traditionally, many of those boundaries, particularly in larger manufacturing organizations, acted as an important basis of trade union influence. Maintaining customary job demarcations was particularly important to those unions, the source of power of which rested on the representation of individual crafts or occupations (see **Trade Unions**). A similar influence was evident in relation to the use of temporary workers or contract staff, with trade unions generally seeking to enforce a policy of work being undertaken in-house by regular, permanent employees.

flexibility

It is thus no coincidence that the accelerated development of workforce flexibility coincided with a weakening of trade union power in the UK and elsewhere in the 1980s and 1990s. In the UK in particular, the state played an important role in this development, both championing the importance of labour flexibility and actively facilitating this through legislation that not only maintained comparatively low levels of employment protection but also reduced union influence by imposing greater restrictions on trade union activities. These statutory interventions provided the conditions for employers to pursue flexibility primarily as a means of increasing labour utilization and reducing unit labour costs. What gave this pursuit added impetus was the major economic recession in the early 1980s to which many organizations responded by reducing workforce levels. The situation this left in many work settings was one of smaller workforces tasked to fulfil the various functions previously carried out by a larger workforce. A key way of achieving this was to increase the level of that workforce's flexibility (and often their overall work effort; see **Effort and Intensity**).

From the 1980s onwards, there was a simultaneous growth of numerical and functional flexibislity. In terms of the former, common developments included more widespread use of agency workers and other outsourcing and subcontracting arrangements, coupled with a greater use of different working time arrangements to shadow fluctuations in demand (see **Working Time**).

NATIONAL VARIATIONS

Recent trajectories of workforce flexibility vary between countries, influenced in part by the aspects of flexibility that employers have been restricted from advancing in the past. In turn, these restrictions may reflect such factors as the focus of trade union influence, as outlined above, or other constraints such as statutory restrictions on employers' freedom to deploy labour. In Germany, for example, functional flexibility has developed extensively over a long period, partly due to the country's established provisions for vocational training and partly reflecting the low level of union influence over shop-floor organization in German enterprises. In the recent period, the key flexibility development in Germany has been increased working time flexibility. German employers have prioritized this as a means to overcome both the 'restriction' of a comparatively short working week and the past reluctance among German workers for weekend working. At the same time, statutory restrictions on German employers, in respect to offering temporary rather than permanent contracts, have restricted the development of other forms of numerical flexibility.

In Spain, on the other hand, an important restriction on employers' freedom to deploy labour has been the statutory protections gained by workers holding permanent contracts. This has led to a considerable growth in the use of temporary contracts in Spain as employers have sought greater flexibility by avoiding offering permanent contracts to employees. As a result, over the past two decades, Spain has maintained the highest proportion of its workforce on temporary contracts in Europe (Blyton and Martinez Lucio, 1995).

By whichever means greater workforce flexibility has been sought, however, the overall outcome has been a substantial growth in flexibility throughout industrial economies. An important question arising from this is: what have been the effects of this increased flexibility on employees? In practice, these effects will vary depending on the type of flexibility and the nature of different organizational and national contexts, but a number of general points can be made (each of which connects with other Key Concepts discussed elsewhere in this volume). First, flexibility appears to have been an important contributor to the reported increases in work pressure (see **Effort and Intensity**). Flexibility is designed to increase labour utilization by enabling employees to work more consistently on tasks where demand is greatest. One outcome of this is likely to be a reduction in the amount of time that employees spend not working.

Second, the growing use of agency staff, subcontractors and other forms of temporary work may have contributed to a perceived increase in job insecurity, particularly in periods of heightened unemployment and redundancy levels (see **Job Security**). Third, the growth of more variable working time arrangements potentially increases the difficulty of maintaining a satisfactory balance between work and non-work life if unpredictable work patterns hinder the planning of non-work activities (see **Work-life Balance**). Finally, developments in flexibility can be seen to have reduced the standardization of the work experience and contributed to a greater individualization of work, with employees subject to a variety of work times, contractual conditions and so on. Among other things, this potentially increases the difficulties faced by trade unions who seek to recruit members partly on the basis of a sense of workers' shared interests (see **Trade Unions**).

EMPLOYEES' GROWING INTEREST IN FLEXIBILITY

In the extensive discussions that have taken place, most attention has been paid to the employer's search for flexibility. But employees too have an interest in achieving greater flexibility, particularly if this means gaining additional skills and variety in their job. In addition, many studies have shown the value that employees place on having some discretion or choice over their working time pattern, either through formal systems such as flexible working hours or informal arrangements they establish with their co-workers or supervisors (see, for example, Berg, 1999). Flexible working hours systems normally define a core time in the workday when all employees are required to be at work; however, either side of that core time, employees can exercise choice over their starting and finishing times, provided that over an agreed period the contractual number of hours are worked. Flexible working hours systems receive widespread support from employees. To date, however, flexitime systems remain more common in some occupations than others (in non-manual rather than manual worker contexts) and in some countries more than others (far more prevalent in Germany than the UK).

Overall, flexibility responds to both key employer and employee objectives and as a consequence is likely to remain a major issue in contemporary organizations for the foreseeable future. For employers, flexibility addresses their concerns for adaptability and optimizing labour utilization at times and in areas where demand is greatest. For employees, flexibility represents greater choice to match work and non-work lives. In the recent past, it has been the employer's agenda on flexibility that has been dominant, not least as a result of widespread state support for enhancing flexibility and trade union weakness to resist unwanted developments. However, we can anticipate employee interests becoming rather more prominent in the coming period as labour market developments such as the continued rise is dual-earner households – and the non-work pressures that this generates – become increasingly apparent.

See also: *job design, management, organizations: networks and alliances, skill, teamworking, working time, work–life balance.*

REFERENCES

Atkinson, J. (1984) 'Manpower strategies for flexible organisations', *Personnel Management*, August: 28–31.

Berg, P. (1999) 'The effects of high performance work practices on job satisfaction in the United States' steel industry', *Relations Industrielles*, 54 (1): 111–35.

Blyton, P. (1996) 'Workforce flexibility', in B. Towers (ed.), *The Handbook of Human Resource Management*, 2nd edn. Oxford: Blackwell, pp. 259–82.

Blyton, P. and Martinez Lucio, M. (1995) 'Industrial relations and the management of flexibility: factors shaping developments in Spain and the United Kingdom', *International Journal of Human Resource Management*, 6 (2): 271–91.

Pollert, A. (1988) 'The "flexible firm": fixation or fact?', *Work, Employment and Society*, 2 (3): 281–316.

Procter, S. (2005) 'Organizations and organized systems: from direct control to flexibility', in S. Ackroyd, R. Batt, P. Thompson and P.S. Tolbert (eds), *The Oxford Handbook of Work and Organization*. Oxford: Oxford University Press, pp. 462–84.

Fordism

> *Fordism refers to the era of mass production that is said to have characterized industrial economies for a large part of the twentieth century. It was originally associated with the organization of vehicle production by Henry Ford in the USA.*

In our discussion, we need to consider Fordism on several different levels, because not only is it a term that describes a particular pattern of industrial organization and means of mass production but it is also identified with a style of management and regulation of work, as well as with wider economic and social norms associated with a particular period in the development of capitalism. This period was largely contained by the decades between 1920 and 1970 (Amin, 1994: 7–11). Thus the Fordist era, some would argue, ended in the early 1970s and since that time we have been in a post-Fordist era. The phrase 'some would argue' is used deliberately, because not everyone is convinced that Fordism accurately describes a period that clearly 'existed' and has now somehow 'ended'. In this Key Concept we will unravel the strands of this debate: first, we consider Fordism as a labour process, that is, as a system of work which converts workers' labour power into an end product (see **Labour**

Process); we then proceed to examining the issues raised by its application as a label for an era of capitalist development.

FORDISM AS A LABOUR PROCESS

The history of work has seen different prescriptions, at different times, for methods of control to reduce the unpredictability of human labour and increase its productivity and reliability. As we discuss in more detail elsewhere (see **Scientific Management**) one of the major influences on the organization of work at the beginning of the twentieth century, was F.W. Taylor, the pioneer of this approach. Taylor began from the assumption that maximum output could be accomplished by the separation of the planning of work (a managerial responsibility), from its execution (by the worker). Managers were needed to determine the 'one best way' that tasks should be done, by 'scientifically' analysing a job, breaking it down into its constituent elements and then assigning each of these to different workers, with payment calculated on the basis of a monetary and time value for each 'piece' completed by the worker – hence, piece rates or piecework payment systems – as the prime incentive for high-volume task completion (see **Pay and Performance**).

Taylor's principles were taken up by Henry Ford, the founder of the Ford Motor Company, with some key differences though in many respects there was no major innovation within Ford's methods. Workers performed distinct tasks, according to the principles of Taylor's 'one best way' and Ford used long-established mechanical techniques. However, Ford *was* innovative in the way he addressed principles of 'human organization for work' (Drucker, 1950: 19). First, instead of monetary bonuses recommended by Taylor, Ford never paid piecework, which he regarded as 'endless bother'; rather, he paid a standardized daily rate, which we discuss below. Second, Ford introduced the 'moving assembly line' to his Highland Park plant in Detroit in 1913 (Beynon, 1973: 18–20). The moving line ensured that the pace of work was determined by the speed at which managers set the production line, in accordance with managerially determined rules and targets. Ford held that 'the man … must have every second necessary but not a single unnecessary second' for the performance of his tasks (Ford, 1922: 85, cited in Beynon, 1973: 19). Ford's methods were highly successful in increasing the volume of production in his factories and heralded an era of mass production of standardized products for mass markets.

A further, very important feature of Fordist production was not simply the standardization of the final product but also the standardization of the individual parts and components that went to make up that end product (Blauner, 1964: 90). In this regard, technological advances and mechanization facilitated the increased division of labour, work intensification and higher levels of productivity. Workers thus had little or no control over the method or pace of work and there was far less need for them to possess the skills or exercise the autonomy that had been identified with earlier, pre-Fordist production methods, which had been centred on more specialist skills, associated with the work of craft workers, before mass industrialization (Noon and Blyton, 2007: 175). This last point is often held up to question, in the sense that it is disputed how much autonomy the craft worker ever had in reality and therefore to idealize the life of skilled artisans in the pre-industrial age may be inaccurate and somewhat misleading (Grint, 2005: 180). We do not have to concern ourselves with the details of that debate here, but what we do need to note is that, indisputably, Ford's methods of control incorporated a significant managerial dilemma: namely the fact that workers became disaffected, or *alienated*, by the increasingly meaningless nature of their work (see **Alienation**).

In Ford's manufacturing plants, monotony and 'the iron hand and arbitrary justice of the foreman' characterized the working environment and many people found it difficult to work there for any length of time. In 1913, for example, 'Ford required between 13,000 and 14,000 workers to run his plants at any one time, and in that year over 50,000 workers quit' (Beynon, 1973: 19). In a significant intervention in 1914, designed to address some of these issues, Ford increased the daily wage from $2.30 per day to what became known as the 'Five Dollar Day'. This high, standardized daily wage rate was intended by Ford to give greater managerial control over the flow of work by mitigating the effects of workers' alienation and the incidence of absenteeism, lateness and turnover that had characterized their response to the intense pressure of their working environment (ibid.: 20–1). While the Five Dollar Day was initially highly attractive for workers and did have a positive impact in improving factory discipline relating to lateness, absence and turnover, it did not resolve all employment relations problems. Discontent persisted but it was difficult for workers to be heard: it was a fundamental tenet of Ford's regulation of factory life that he was unambiguously opposed to trade unions and tried to ensure their exclusion by means of factory police and elaborate internal networks of 'spies'.

Fordist principles of work organization were exported around the world and were prevalent in car manufacture and other industries such as electrical engineering and chemicals (Noon and Blyton, 2007: 152). They formed a highly influential template for mass production in many other industrial nations. But the Fordist model developed to the greatest extent within the economic and institutional framework of the United States and, when it was taken up by other corporations and in different national contexts, it was applied within varying institutional systems and disparate social and cultural norms. Thus, there is debate over how uniformly it was implemented, in practice, elsewhere. There is also disagreement over the extent to which mass production, Fordist-style, could be said ever to have truly characterized an era, for twentieth-century industry was not, in fact, dominated by moving assembly-line factory production. However, it is inescapable that the Fordist model 'greatly influenced all forms of work organisation' (Blauner, 1964: 91). It certainly influenced manufacturing industry for much of the twentieth century, but there was a time, in the early 1970s, when analysts began to say that Fordism was passé.

THE POST-FORDIST DEBATE

The essence of the post-Fordist argument is that the period of mass production, in which Fordism was centrally located, has been overtaken by a 'post-Fordist' era. But the concept of a post-Fordist era is itself challenged and it is therefore better to regard post-Fordism as a 'debate' that encompasses strongly held, different points of argument, rather than something which is easily defined. In essence, it is a debate about the 'transition from one dominant phase of capitalism in the post-war period to another thirty to fifty year cycle of development based upon very different economic, societal and political norms' (Amin, 1994: 3). For the purposes of the present brief explanation, we can pinpoint certain characteristics that are said to be central to an understanding of post-Fordism, but readers should be aware that this is a brief summary of a much wider and multilayered debate.

Capitalism is an economic system that is subject to periodic instability, crisis and change, but it is also the case that markets can enjoy relatively long cycles of stability. Commentators seek ways to explain the instability of markets and of the capitalist system and also seek a means of predicting what the future holds. Fordism, as a system of work organization and a source of mass production that fuelled mass consumption in the twentieth century, was heralded by some analysts as a distinct phase in the development of capitalism. This phase is argued to have extended from around 1920 to the early 1970s, when, in line with the varying fortunes of the capitalist system, the world economy became characterized by crisis, recession and stagnation. Thus analysts who favoured the argument that capitalist economies were shifting into a different phase identified a 'post-Fordist' (or *after* Fordist) era. Fordism's characteristic mass production of standardized goods was said to be exhausted; markets were judged to be saturated with such products. Some economists argued that markets needed to be revitalized by the stimulation of more variable demand and that the Fordist era had given way to a post-Fordist era of 'flexible specialization'. The shift towards greater flexibility in production of non-standardized, better-quality goods was argued to be a new paradigm for this new phase in capitalism. Characteristic features included the adaptability of productive processes, institutions and people, in the face of volatile markets, with the prime objective of satisfying customer demand for higher quality and greater individuality (Amin, 1994: 13–15). The era of the flexible specialist thus has some resonance with the picture painted of the craft worker, pre-Fordism, when goods were said to be more reliant on the skills and expertise of the individual worker.

But this post-Fordist analysis has not gone unchallenged. For example, from a radical or Marxist viewpoint, it is argued that, in trying to divide capitalism into a series of artificially distinct epochs, there is a failure to acknowledge the more fundamental nature of historical change (ibid.: 3). From this perspective there has been no paradigm shift between the old industrial, social and economic order of Fordism to a changed post-Fordist model. Rather, it is argued that there are essential continuities from one period of history to another. Furthermore, we have noted that there are questions over the autonomy of craft workers before Fordism; that Fordism itself did not universally characterize the nature of work in the decades up to 1970; and also that mass production of standardized goods has not disappeared since that time. It is also the case that, in contrast to the image of the modern-day worker as a flexible specialist, many workers continue to report their experience of intensified work, characterized by the monotony, limited skill content and strict managerial control long identified with Fordism (Pollert, 1991; see also **Surviving Work**). Indeed, it has been strongly argued that managerial initiatives masked under the name of 'flexibility' increase insecurity of employment and intensify rather than diminish the pressure on workers (Hyman, 1988: 55–7; see also **Flexibility**).

A further aspect of the post-Fordist debate is an alternative analysis, namely, neo-Fordism – or '*new* Fordism'. Neo-Fordism is a term coined to describe production systems that have maintained the strong managerial controls associated with Fordism, while introducing some flexibility and variation in the design of products and work organization, mainly through innovative technology (Grint, 2005: 301). Thus, neo-Fordism accepts that Fordism *per se* is passed, but points to continuities with the past. It suggests that flexible initiatives have been added to Fordist techniques in terms of work organization, the use of people and the nature of more variable products. Neo-Fordism thus allows for an understanding of continuity between the present and the period when Fordism was at its height, while the post-Fordist position suggests that there has been a fundamental break with the era of standardized mass production.

In summary, Fordism is a term that describes the style of mass production and work organization pioneered by Henry Ford in his factories in the early twentieth century. The post-Fordist debate focuses on the changes in the world economy and what it sees as a transition from one phase in capitalism to another. In this debate, Fordism, as the symbol of a particular approach to industrial organization, mass production and the consumption of standardized goods, is alleged to be a phase of capitalist development that has now been displaced by an era of flexible specialization – the post-Fordist era. The neo-Fordist position in this debate is that there is continuity between the present day and the Fordist era, but that technological innovations and organizational developments have brought new flexibilities to a new form of Fordism for the modern age. Critics of the post-Fordist debate, from a Marxist or radical perspective, argue that it is unsatisfactory and misleading to try to artificially impose historical guillotines to particular periods of industrialization and market change and argue that we are witnessing – and participating in – the onward march and evolution of work in the capitalist system, pure and simple.

See also: conflict, effort and intensity, job design, labour process, scientific management.

REFERENCES

Amin, A. (1994) *Post-Fordism: A Reader*. Oxford: Blackwell.

Beynon, H. (1973) *Working for Ford*. Harmondsworth: Penguin.

Blauner, R. (1964) *Alienation and Freedom*. Chicago: The University of Chicago Press.

Drucker, P.F. (1950) *The New Society*. New York: Harper & Row.

Grint, K. (2005) *The Sociology of Work*, 3rd edn. Cambridge: Polity Press.

Hyman, R. (1988) 'Flexible specialization: miracle or myth?', in R. Hyman and W. Streeck (eds), *New Technology and Industrial Relations*. Oxford: Blackwell, pp. 48–59.

Noon, M. and Blyton, P. (2007) *The Realities of Work*, 3rd edn. Basingstoke: Palgrave Macmillan.

Pollert, A. (ed.) (1991) *Farewell to Flexibility?* Oxford: Blackwell.

Globalization and Labour Migration

> Globalization refers to 'the integration of spatially separate locations into a single international market' (Blyton et al., 2001: 447).

In this Key Concept we are looking to broaden the focus on work by recognizing its increasingly globalized character and the ways that work-forces within single countries are becoming more diverse as a result of continuing cross-national labour migration. Our particular interest is the implications for patterns of work and employment, rather than the many broader social, economic and political questions raised by globalization and international migration (for a general introduction to globalization, see Grint, 2005: 355–84, also Waters, 2001). Our discussion falls into two main areas: (1) the employment and related issues raised by the increasing international division of labour; and (2) those issues generated by recent trends in cross-national labour migration.

THE GROWING INTERNATIONALIZATION OF LABOUR

The expression 'globalization' is now in everyday use, reflecting in part the growing variety of goods and service activities that have become more cross-national in their production and distribution. What this means in practice is that firms increasingly operate across national boundaries to produce and sell their products and services either directly or through third parties. Various factors have encouraged this development. These include political decisions to deregulate industries and open more markets to competition, for example, in finance, telecommunications and transport. Also central have been technical developments in information and communications technologies that enable much greater and faster coordination of activities that may be geographically separated by large distances.

However, at the core of the globalization of production trend lie large (and many smaller) corporations seeking competitive advantage from lower-cost labour processes available in different parts of the world. Access to these lower costs can be achieved either directly by corporations establishing production and service facilities in low-cost countries or indirectly by those firms purchasing goods and services from suppliers located in those countries. Either way, a key driver to the globalization of production is the large differential that exists between labour costs in developed and developing economies. Moreover, it is not only wage levels that vary between the developed and developing worlds. In many other respects, too, terms and conditions of employment in developing countries are often vastly inferior to those operating in the developed world: hours of work are longer, job security lower and pensions, sick pay and social security systems much less available (Castles and Miller, 1998). In combination, this gulf in terms and conditions represents what Pocock (forthcoming) describes as 'an important fault line of inequality' between workers in developed and developing economies. And for those studying the changing nature of work, this fault line is a key point of comparison between work in different countries.

Further, this inequality is not a problem solely for those experiencing the poorer terms and conditions in low labour cost countries. Many commentators, for example, have raised concerns that globalization has the potential to fuel a more general international 'race to the bottom' on workers' pay and conditions. That is, the potential availability of low labour cost alternatives for transnational corporations exerts pressure on workers in higher-cost, developed economies to compete for their own jobs and accept lower terms and conditions to reduce the threat of work being transferred to other parts of the world. Pressure to concede terms and conditions in order to retain jobs can be exerted not only at workplace and firm levels but also at national level. Governments may be subject to pressures from employers' organizations, for example, to reduce the costs of employment (such as employers' social security contributions) and provide greater labour market flexibility (by reducing employment protection legislation, for example) more characteristic of many low labour cost economies.

Yet in practice, it has so far proved to be the case that any race to the bottom on social standards or basic conditions of employment cannot simply be assumed as an inevitable effect of globalization. It is certainly true that some employment groups, including less skilled workers in labour-intensive industries such as textiles, have been adversely affected. In other sectors, however, there is as yet no systematic evidence of this negative effect. This may partly reflect the fact that developed economies retain a number of advantages for companies located there, including better transport and infrastructure, availability of high-value markets and access to greater employee skills, as well as the reality of the sunk capital costs. In combination these factors hinder companies from acting as 'footloose' organizations regarding where to locate and relocate their activities. Having said this, it remains the case that the threat of relocation is one further pressure on trade unions and others representing employee interests to concede to employer demands for higher performance and lower-cost operations. And in terms of opening up new facilities, it is a growing reality for many organizations in western countries that they have the option to take work offshore, be that locating manufacturing operations in China or Vietnam, call centre functions in India or the Philippines or assembly activities in Mexico or Brazil.

In challenging low pay and poor working conditions, labour retains some scope for action. Groups including international trade union organizations and others campaigning to reduce levels of international worker inequality, and in particular to remove excesses of long hours, low pay and poor protection, have used a variety of tactics in efforts to achieve fair treatment and improved labour standards. These include taking industrial action in developed economies on behalf of workers in less developed contexts, coordinating simultaneous protest action that spans national boundaries and pressing for collective agreements with employers that cover the company's workforce, irrespective of the country of operation.

However, probably most effective to date have been publicity campaigns targeting companies sourcing many of their goods and services from the developing world to ensure minimum standards in their subsidiaries and supplier companies or run the risk of their brand being associated with exploitative practices, such as the use of illegal child labour or unsafe working conditions. The importance of brand image and the vulnerability of brands to bad publicity may in the long term prove a more effective means of improving standards than more traditional pressures applied by trade unions, governments and other bodies (see **Customers**).

LABOUR MIGRATION

Migration has always been closely connected with economic development. An issue facing both individual localities where new industrial growth is taking place and entire countries embarking on economic development, is often a shortage of available labour and thus a reliance on people migrating to areas where labour is required. Typically in the past, this has involved large-scale movements from rural areas into towns and cities, as well as emigrations from one country to another, to take advantage of new work opportunities. This pattern remains in evidence today. Patterns and flows of migration are rarely simple and unidirectional, however. In addition to within-country movements and migration to countries with a labour shortage, there are also reverse movements, for example, as migrants return to their country or locality of origin.

Some countries, such as Australia and Canada, continue to encourage inward migration to support their economic growth. And within countries such as the UK, economic development continues to be affected by a lack of labour migration from areas of labour surplus to ones of shortage. This lack is in part due to many people being understandably reluctant to move away from their locality, their family and friends. In this respect, labour markets are 'sticky' – there are obstacles and resistance to labour markets smoothly mirroring the growth and decline of particular sectors and regions.

Of the different migration patterns, it is international migration that tends to gain more attention than within-country movements of labour or reverse migration. Care needs to be exercised when looking at migration statistics, however. For example, the change in migration in the UK between 2000 and 2004 was a net inward migration of just over a quarter of a million people (Salt and Millar, 2006: 336). However, this figure was comprised of a net inflow of more than four times that amount (over 1.2 million) and a net outflow of just under one million (ibid.). Overall in the UK, there were 1.5 million foreign migrants working in the UK in 2005, representing 5.4 per cent of the UK employed population.

The pattern of cross-national migration has varied at different times. In Europe for example, while the second half of the twentieth century was characterized by both within-continent and trans-continental movements (particularly to North America and Australia), currently one of the most visible patterns involves workers from countries that have joined the European Union (EU) in recent years taking advantage of freedom of movement provision to move to other EU states where wage levels are considerably higher. In the two years after Poland and several other countries joined the EU in 2004, for example, approaching half a million Eastern Europeans registered for work in Britain. In many cases this migration will be temporary, with many workers returning to their home country following a period of working abroad.

Migrant workers are a highly diverse group. Some, for example, are professional workers operating within a global labour market. This is the case with professional occupations such as oil production engineers and certain areas of medical and scientific research. However, many migrants are workers with much less labour power, seeking a better income than is available within their domestic labour market. Among these groups, there is a clear tendency to figure disproportionately in certain sectors and poorer jobs – those involving manual work with low wages, longer hours and with little job security. Of those finding jobs in Britain from Eastern Europe between 2004 and 2006, for example, almost half (49 per cent) were in temporary jobs, many of them engaged in work such as box packers, kitchen assistants, cleaners and farm workers (Travis, 2006: 4–5). Elsewhere, in countries such as the USA, entire sectors of low-paid service work, including domestic work and office cleaning, have become heavily reliant on migrant labour. Factors that force many migrant workers, initially at least, into lower-paying jobs include quali-fications and experience that do not always match the requirements of the receiving labour market, a weaker grasp of the host country's lan-guage and the presence of employment discrimination (OECD, 2001: 167; see also **Discrimination**).

The poor bargaining position of many incoming workers in turn can undermine the position of many existing workers as wage levels adjust to reflect the growing supply of migrant labour in particular sectors, regions and localities. In addition, for those migrants entering countries illegally or while seeking asylum are not awarded work permits, many enter paid work clandestinely. This leaves such workers open to exploitation and vulnerable to low wages, long hours, poor job security and hazardous work conditions (see **Informal Work**).

CONCLUSION

While labour is less mobile than capital in a progressively globalized economy, it is evident that workers' lives are increasingly intertwined at an international level. This interconnection may be direct, through the migration of some groups to work in other settings, or indirect, via the impact of unequal terms and conditions not only on the individuals directly subject to them but also their counterparts in more developed economies. One upshot of these developments is that, through migration and the location (and relocation) of transnational corporations, in various respects labour is becoming global in character. Labour has some agency within this globalizing process – some means to influence the wage–effort bargain, for example – but the continued existence of vastly different terms and conditions of employment in the developed and developing worlds creates significant leverage for capital in its various relations with labour.

See also: employment patterns, flexibility, job security.

REFERENCES

Blyton, P., Martinez Lucio, M., McGurk, J. and Turnbull, P. (2001) 'Globalization and trade union strategy: industrial restructuring and human resource management in the international civil aviation industry', *International Journal of Human Resource Management*, 12 (3): 445–63.
Castles, S. and Miller, M. (1998) *The Age of Migration: International Population Movements in the Modern World*. London: Macmillan.
Grint, K. (2005) *The Sociology of Work*, 3rd edn. Cambridge: Polity Press.
OECD (Organisation for Economic Cooperation and Development) (2001) 'The employment of foreigners: outlook and issues in OECD countries', *Employment Outlook*, Paris: OECD, pp. 168–89.
Pocock, B. (forthcoming) 'Equality at work', in P. Blyton, N. Bacon, J. Fiorito and E. Heery (eds), *The SAGE Handbook of Industrial Relations*. London: Sage.
Salt, J. and Millar, J. (2006) 'Foreign labour in the United Kingdom: current patterns and trends', *Labour Market Trends*, October: 335–55.
Travis, A. (2006) 'New in the UK: the "guest" workforce who don't stay long', *The Guardian*, 23 August: 4–5.
Waters, M. (2001) *Globalisation*. London: Routledge.

key concepts in work

Human Relations

The human relations movement emphasized the importance of managers paying attention to workers' intrinsic social needs from work, for example, for personal interaction and communication, as much as to their extrinsic need for pay.

HUMAN RELATIONS AND SCIENTIFIC MANAGEMENT

The principles and practices of both scientific management and Fordism, which together were highly influential in the organization of work from the early twentieth century onwards, were instrumental in increasing levels of worker productivity (see **Fordism** and **Scientific Management**). But such methods of control incorporated a significant managerial dilemma: namely, the risk that workers would become disaffected, or alienated, by the increasingly meaningless nature of their work (see **Alienation**). The technocratic assumptions of scientific management, which effectively saw the worker as part of the wider machine of work, assumed that organizational efficiency would be secured, and workers' motivation guaranteed, by means of monetary rewards alone. Thus, it was held by Taylor, the pioneer of scientific management, that the interests of the 'rational economic man', would centre on the size of the wage packet and this would influence and control worker behaviour. This assumption was not wholly borne out in practice, however. Tayloristic organization of work encountered worker opposition despite monetary rewards for higher levels of performance (Grint, 2005: 119). For example, workers might try to find ways to restrict their output as their only means of exercising some control over their working day; alternatively, labour turnover, absenteeism or industrial disruption might occur as workers responded to the demands of their working conditions.

Research undertaken at the Hawthorne Plant of the Western Electric Company of Chicago, USA (Roethlisberger and Dickson, 1966) was to be of central importance in putting forward an alternative to Taylor's 'economic man' as the focus for securing greater organizational efficiency. The research extended, in total, over a period of 12 years. Studies into worker behaviour began as early as 1924 and started out as an enquiry into the 'incidence of fatigue and monotony among employees', focusing on physical conditions of work such as temperature and humidity (ibid.: 3). But the results of the initial research were 'unexpected' and led to an expansion and extension of the research, such that it continued for several years and during certain phases expanded to include investigation of around 20,000 employees (ibid.). The name of Elton Mayo became synonymous with these studies, though more for publicizing the results than for conducting the research investigations (see Rose, 1988).

The findings of what came to be known as the 'Hawthorne Studies' contradicted assumptions about the 'rational' economic interests of workers and highlighted their social needs. Thus, it was that, from the late 1930s onwards, an emerging 'human relations' movement appeared. But, as with most other developments in work, this movement had its antecedents: the '"social man" of the human relations movement originated in the theories of the great nineteenth century sociologists Pareto and Durkheim' (ibid.: 112).

As we go on to discuss the human relations school in more detail, it is important to recognize that, while it identified alternative means of securing motivation, it did not challenge the division of labour and the principles of scientific management *per se*. It largely accepted the technocratic orientation of Taylorism, but was distinct in addressing alienation through meeting the intrinsic needs of workers for social interaction and self-fulfilment, as opposed to scientific management's focus on extrinsic needs for financial reward as the sole means to secure worker compliance (Grint, 2005: 119). Thus, as we consider the Hawthorne Studies and the human relations movement in general, it is important to not only recognize their contribution to managerial thought and practice but also to realize that what they put forward is just one interpretation of the manager's role in the workplace. In later years, other enquiries, such as a UK group of studies known as the Manchester Studies (see Lupton, 1963), failed to support all the findings and conclusions put forward by the Hawthorne experiments. Thus, though we do not have space to explore fully the debate here, we need to recognize that the conclusions drawn by the Hawthorne researchers are themselves contested. In particular, from a radical perspective, they are criticized for putting forward a somewhat limited, unitary, managerially focused perception of the dynamics of working relationships that fails to recognize conflicts of interest between employers and employees by assuming that attending to workers' social needs is the essential recipe for harmony and productivity in work (for further reading, see Rose, 1988; see also **Perspectives on Work**).

THE HAWTHORNE STUDIES

This research became particularly famous for a series of experiments undertaken with workers in the Hawthorne plant's Bank Wiring Room, and for the prescription offered for the better management of enterprises. Researchers conducted experiments with the physical working environment by, for example, altering lighting; they also enquired into the role of supervision. They examined the effects of fatigue and monotony on output and found that their expectations of variations in output relating to changes in the physical environment were confounded. They concluded that the group of workers was reacting more to the nature of supervision and the experience of being studied than they were to the actual physical environment of their work (Grint, 2005: 120–1).

The Hawthorne researchers also found that the internal social organization of work groups was highly influential. They distinguished between the 'formal organization' of an enterprise, corresponding to the formal hierarchy of responsibility and authority and the functions, rules, regulations and systems that make a firm viable, and the 'informal organization' of social relationships existing within working groups. Such informal relationships were identified as potentially important for collaboration within and between work groups, in the interests of organizational efficiency. In this way the informal organization 'facilitates the functioning of the formal organization' (Roethlisberger and Dickson, 1966: 558–9). Yet at the same time, the researchers also highlighted the fact that the informal organization might just as easily develop 'in opposition to the formal organization' (ibid.). In their studies the researchers found that 'men had elaborated, spontaneously and quite unconsciously, an intricate social organisation around their collective beliefs and sentiments' (ibid.: 524). These beliefs were not necessarily accurate, nor 'logical' (Grint, 2005: 122), but were nevertheless powerful and might lead workers to behave in a way that did not conform to a straightforward analysis of their individual economic interests. For example, the informal organization of a work group might exert collective controls over individual members' outputs, in order to prevent 'rate-busting'.

(Rate-busting escribes a situation where a rate of pay for a particular job is set by management according to an assumed level of output that the worker will be capable of. If some workers exceed that output by an appreciable amount, then the rate would be likely to be re-evaluated, new and higher targets for output would be set and thus the rate would be 'busted' for all workers in that group.) Hence, the informal organization could exert internal group controls to mould individual members' behaviour in the interests of the group as a whole, but against the interests of the firm in gaining maximum productivity.

Thus the Hawthorne Studies looked at 'industrial organization' on two planes: the technical organization and the human organization. They defined the technical organization as 'the physical environment of work', while the human organization comprised not only the workers as individuals but also the 'social organization' resulting from the interaction and patterns of relationships between those individuals within the organization (Roethlisberger and Dickson, 1966: 553–8). The researchers concluded that, rather than being separate and distinct from one another, the technical organization and human organization were 'interrelated and interdependent … [t]he human organization is constantly molding and re-creating the technical organization … [l]ikewise changes in the technical organization require an adaptation on the part of the human organization' (ibid.: 553). The Hawthorne researchers concluded that the nature of the technical organization and the patterns of supervision and control had an impact on workers' productivity and therefore a focus on purely extrinsic, monetary motivations of workers neglected the significance of their social needs for organizational efficiency. While adequate financial reward was necessary, the researchers argued that their findings showed this was not sufficient to secure workers' full engagement with their work. They also found that workers did not always appear to behave in their rational economic interest; they concluded that 'social interaction, not money, was the prime motivator at work' (Grint, 2005: 119).

In conclusion, the human relations movement suggested that managers should pay attention to workers' social needs for, for example, personal interaction and communication. Furthermore, it was argued that managerial control systems and supervision should take account of the effects of fatigue, monotony and repetition when designing jobs (see **Job Design**). The Hawthorne researchers also drew attention to the existence of the 'informal organization' of social relations that exist within groups of workers and highlighted the possibility that such informal systems might conflict with the values and norms sought by the 'formal organization', that is, the employing organization. Their analysis emphasized the need for managers to bring these informal social values and norms into line with organizational objectives by means of, among other things, better communication strategies. Such strategies would aim to explain the rationale for managerial decisions and emphasize the harmony of interests between the employing organization and the worker and that managers were acting in the interests of workers (see **Perspectives on Work**). The assumed harmony of interests was based on the premise that workers' aspirations could be realized, and their interests best served, through the success of their employing organization. To this end it was important that managerial communication should emphasize the importance of workers following the managerial lead, and devote effort and commitment to their work (Roethlisberger and Dickson, 1966: 569–89).

The early human relations movement thus gave rise to a distinct approach to analysis of the behaviour of workers within organizations. As time progressed, its prescription of communication as the main method of controlling worker morale and performance was augmented by the work of motivational theorists such as Maslow and Herzberg, among many others, who offered new explanations and various prescriptions for securing motivation and commitment to the process of work (see **Motivation and Commitment**).

See also: *management, participation and involvement.*

REFERENCES

Grint, K. (2005) *The Sociology of Work*, 3rd edn. Oxford: Blackwell.
Lupton, T. (1963) *On the Shop-floor: Two Studies of Workshop Organisation and Output*. Oxford: Pergamon Press.
Roethlisberger, F.J. and Dickson, W.J. (1966) *Management and the Worker*. Cambridge, MA: Harvard University Press.
Rose, M. (1988) *Industrial Behaviour*. Harmondsworth: Penguin.

human relations

> Informal work refers here to paid work that is undeclared and thus falls outside the scope of taxation, social insurance and other regulations. Other, unpaid aspects of informal work are dealt with elsewhere (see Domestic Work and Voluntary Work).

Much of the discussion in this volume focuses on activities in what we might term the 'formal' work sector – that is, where the goods and services that are produced are included in official statistics and where the workers engaged in the production of those goods and services receive a wage that is subject to tax. However, in addition to this formal work activity, there is a range of other work taking place that lies outside the formal work sector. We examine two major facets of this separately in our discussions of domestic work and voluntary work. However, in addition to these unpaid elements of informal work, another important area requireing consideration is paid work that is concealed, either because it involves illegal activities or it is employment hidden from the tax authorities (undeclared work). It is the latter which is the focus of our discussion here.

MEASURING INFORMAL WORK

One of the initial difficulties in examining undeclared work is that its purposely hidden nature means that accurate measurement is highly problematic. This not only means that estimates of the scale of undeclared work are difficult to arrive at but also that related discussions – such as what trends are occurring in relation to undeclared work – lack precision. No single measurement method fully overcomes the problem. Hence, in practice a number of methods are used, including aggregating the findings of individual investigations by tax and other authorities and the examination of national accounts to identify discrepancies between levels of national income and expenditure. However, whatever method is employed, it remains the case that a significant margin of error is likely to characterize estimates of the scale of undeclared working.

A second measurement (and broader definitional) problem arises from the array of activities that comprise undeclared work. These range from small-scale activities undertaken by individuals (such as paid work being performed for neighbours and the income not declared) to larger-scale groups of undeclared workers being hired to undertake labouring and other tasks. Further, these measurement problems are compounded by the inter-related nature of formal and informal work activity, with individuals being involved to a greater or lesser (and a varying) extent in both and the distinction between the two spheres often clearer to draw in principle than in practice.

Despite the extent of such measurement problems, however, various estimates of the extent of undeclared working have been made. The European Commission in the late 1990s estimated the level of undeclared work in the EU as somewhere between 7 and 16 per cent of Gross Domestic Product (European Commission, 1998). However, it is evident that there is considerable country-by-country variation in the amount of undeclared working both within the EU and outside. The OECD, for example, has reported that, in some of its member countries, informal employment represents at least 30 per cent of total employment activity and, in many developing economies, the proportion is much higher still (OECD, 2004). Indeed, part of the process of economic development involves a long-term transition from informal to more formal employment arrangements and the growth of more regulated work environments (Williams and Windebank, 1999). At the same time, even in highly developed economies, it is clear that a substantial informal employment sector continues to operate.

LOCATION OF UNDECLARED WORK

All sectors of the economy activity contain an element of undeclared work that is hidden or 'cash-in-hand' activity. In certain sectors, however, the incidence of undeclared work appears to be more prevalent; these include paid domestic work, home improvement and repair services, parts of the retailing sector such as street trading and parts of the transport sector such as part-time taxi driving. In addition, those sectors traditionally reliant on subcontractors to provide labour – sectors such as construction, agriculture and office cleaning – would seem to have a relatively high incidence of undeclared working, with workers hired on a casual basis (OECD, 2004).

At different times the question has been raised: is it unemployed individuals who are more likely to engage in undeclared work than their employed counterparts? However, it is now widely agreed that rates of undeclared working among recipients of unemployment benefit are likely to be similar to, or possibly lower, than those among workers employed in the visible work sector. Potentially, those who are unemployed have more time available for undertaking undeclared work than their employed counterparts. However, the low income levels of most who are unemployed means that any undeclared working is more likely to be restricted to those activities requiring little or no capital expenditure (such as labouring for others). For those in paid work on the other hand, not only may their formal work activity provide greater access to contacts, information and opportunities for additional, undeclared work but also their employment income allows a greater accumulation of resources (transport, tools and so on), which in turn facilitates, access to higher-paid undeclared work (see Pahl, 1984, 1988). This link between formal employment and increased access to undeclared work further underlines the interrelated nature of formal and informal work.

A LACK OF REGULATION

Clearly for the national exchequer, an important issue arising from undeclared work is the income lost to the tax and other public authorities that would be collected if the work undertaken was declared. Perhaps more significant, however, are the implications for many of those performing undeclared work, that their activities are unregulated and unprotected. The hidden nature of the work means that potentially not only are those involved vulnerable to exploitation (such as long work hours and payments below the legal minimum wage) but also they could be exposed to hazardous working environments unregulated by health and safety standards. Groups that figure in undeclared working include illegal immigrants with no visas or work permits and asylum seekers whose applications are pending. For these groups, the only employment opportunity open to them to gain income is by undeclared working. However, the dangerous and unregulated nature of work that may be undertaken by such groups was vividly illustrated by the deaths in 2004 of 21 Chinese cockle pickers drowned off the Lancashire coast, when the gangmaster who had hired the workers ignored any requirement to protect them from the highly dangerous working conditions (see Noon and Blyton, 2007: 340–1).

Informal work is likely to remain a significant part of economic activity, irrespective of any efforts by the public authorities to eradicate it.

This partly reflects the apparent social tolerance shown to cash-in-hand activities. The opportunities for customers to pay less for goods and services will continue to act as an encouragement to undeclared working. What is more likely to reduce over time, however, is large-scale undeclared work, as legislation strengthens in relation to the operation of subcontractors (exemplified in the UK by the Gangmasters Licensing Act, 2005; see Forshaw and Pilgerstorfer, 2005) and workplaces become increasingly liable for ensuring that all those on their site are subject to statutory employment regulations covering health and safety and other working conditions.

See also: employment patterns, flexibility, unemployment and underemployment.

REFERENCES

European Commission (1998) *On Undeclared Work*, COM (1998) 219, Brussels: Commission of the European Communities.

Forshaw, S. and Pilgerstorfer, M. (2005) 'Illegally formed contracts of employment and equal treatment at work', *Industrial Law Journal*, 34 (2): 158–77.

Noon, M. and Blyton, P. (2007) *The Realities of Work*, 3rd edn. Basingstoke: Palgrave Macmillan.

OECD (Organisation for Economic Cooperation and Development) (2004) 'Informal employment and promoting the transition to a salaried economy', *Employment Outlook*, Paris: OECD, pp. 225–90.

Pahl, R. (1984) *Divisions of Labour*. Oxford: Blackwell.

Pahl, R. (1988) 'Some remarks on informal work, social polarization and the social structure', *International Journal of Urban and Regional Research*, 12: 247–67.

Williams, C.C. and Windebank, J. (1999) 'The formalisation of work thesis: a critical evaluation', *Futures*, 31: 547–58.

informal work

Job Design

A job is typically composed of distinct tasks. Job design is concerned with the way such tasks are organized and connected with one another.

We begin this Key Concept by discussing general principles of job design and go on to consider the pressures generating the need for job redesign and the issues of job enrichment, rotation and enlargement.

JOB DESIGN

It is generally accepted that, where jobs are composed of monotonous, repetitive tasks, there is a risk of workers becoming increasingly alienated and disaffected. For example, when the principles of scientific management were applied to work and later developed into Fordism, output increased but workers performing atomized tasks had a much-reduced sense of purpose and meaning in their work (see **Fordism** and **Scientific Management**). In this case, job design is focused on output, but neglects human needs for socialization and personal 'growth' or job satisfaction in relation to work. However, it became increasingly apparent that 'one of the major influences on organisational productivity [is] *the quality of the relationship between people who do the work and the jobs they perform*' (Hackman and Oldham, 1980: 4, emphasis in original). For the employer, therefore, monotonous and repetitive work may initially produce higher-volume production but, in the longer term, it also risks highlighting the conflict in the employment relationship and requires close supervision of workers in order to maintain output. Where jobs are designed in such a way that tasks have little meaning, the workers feel scant responsibility for the overall outcome. If not given feedback on how well they are performing, 'motivational problems' are likely to ensue (ibid.: 76). To this end, the principles of effective job design take account of workers' need for autonomy, variety and gaining meaning from their work, with a view to guarding against boredom and frustration, and generating job satisfaction in the interests of good standards of productivity and service (see **Job Satisfaction**). The managerial challenge of achieving good job design is how to organize work into tasks 'that are small enough to be within the competence of individual job holders, but also challenging enough to motivate performance' (Sparrow, 1998: 123).

The 'Job Diagnostic Survey' developed by Hackman and Oldham (1980: 103–5) suggested that the job characteristics most associated with the personal motivation of workers were task variety, task identity, task significance autonomy and feedback. Their research related these job characteristics to levels of individual job satisfaction and the meaningfulness of the work and also considered the influence of contextual factors, such as supervision, job security and pay, on the potential for motivating workers through principles of good job design. Of these five elements, task variety is self-explanatory and relates to avoidance of monotonous, repetitive tasks. Task identity relates to the ability to complete a whole task from start to finish, while task significance concerns the impact of that task on others. Autonomy refers to the degree of control the workers feel able to exercise over their performance and methods of work; and, finally, feedback to the individual workers on the effectiveness of their performance enables them to feel their contribution is valued. All these factors have a part to play in job design, where the objective is to maximize the workers' sense of motivation and job satisfaction and 'match' the right person to the right job (ibid.: 260).

THE NEED FOR JOB REDESIGN

We now turn to the issue of the changing organizational and technological context for job design (see **Technology**). In the past, the elements that comprised a job might be assumed to be a comparatively stable collection of tasks, but in today's environment a worker's profile of job tasks may be subject to frequent reappraisal. When considering job design, therefore, we need to bear in mind the impact of factors such as the rapidity of organizational and technological change, which may profoundly alter the content of jobs. Technological change, for example, may mean traditional skills are made obsolete while new skills are demanded and workers are required to work in a completely different way (Wall and Kemp, 1987: 8–11).

In addition to changes in automation and computerization, there have been other influences on the content of jobs associated with, for example, organizations removing managerial layers from the hierarchy, sometimes referred to as de-layering. Such restructuring will normally require a decentralization of decision-making and a delegation of control. This will generally involve new responsibilities being devolved to workers. In this case, appropriate training, supervision and compensation are essential if workers are to feel supported, well prepared and fairly rewarded for their redesigned jobs.

In addition, individual jobs show an increased tendency to be less discrete and self-contained and to display more interdependence and interaction with other jobs within the same organization (see **Teamworking**). In no small part, this is related to the increased tendency for jobs to be 'closer' to the customer in that job holders either have more direct contact with external customers, are measured by external customer response or their jobs have been restructured to focus on 'internal' customers within the organization (see **Customers**). Further, new structures make new demands on the personal attributes of job holders: the ability to take decisions, exercise judgement, display a 'good attitude' and be able to deal with stress appear to be an increasing part of daily working life for many (Sparrow, 1998: 117–28).

JOB ENRICHMENT, JOB ROTATION AND JOB ENLARGEMENT

It may be difficult to organize jobs so as to incorporate the job characteristics that Hackman and Oldham (1980) associated with personal motivation and job satisfaction. Instead, employers and managers may draw on related techniques such as job enrichment and job rotation to improve the worker's experience. In addition to being relevant for relieving the monotony of mundane jobs, such interventions are also pertinent to more senior jobs and managerial positions, particularly in the context of flatter organizational structures characteristic of present- day organizations, where there may be fewer opportunities for upward promotion.

Job enrichment aims to increase the variety of tasks undertaken by workers, by introducing elements of work or extra tasks that demand higher skill and offer 'increased opportunities for responsibility, decision-making, and challenge' (Cummings and Blumberg, 1987: 45). Thus job enrichment may mean the workers acquiring new skills and taking on different or higher levels of responsibility for at least some portion of their working time. Job rotation, on the other hand, involves the workers 'rotating' from one set of tasks to another at different times during their working period, for example, working in different sections of the same organization for periods of time or simply moving between different tasks in the same work area. While job enrichment involves workers undertaking tasks at higher levels of skill, job rotation does not necessarily require this; workers may rotate around different types of task but at the same skill level, or sometimes higher skill levels, as the situation demands. Thus, job rotation *may* include elements of job enrichment, but this need not be the case.

An example of how work may be enriched would be the inclusion of workers in processes of quality management and continuous improvement of work processes, perhaps in self-managed work groups. Group working, team structures, quality circles and the like can have a considerable impact on the design of individual jobs and the experience of workers who perform them. Where decision-making is truly devolved, team responsibility may influence the individual workers' responses to the significance of their own job. For example, a set of comparatively mundane tasks may be given new significance by group autonomy over how they are performed, processes improved or quality of output ensured. But the impact of group working on issues of job design will largely depend on the wider organizational context and the extent to which the group can be described as being 'self-regulated', in the sense that members 'are given the necessary autonomy, skills, and information to regulate task behaviours' and actually manage their environment by being involved in higher-level decision-making about their work (ibid.: 45). More typical in the UK and elsewhere, however, is that self-managed work groups have not been much in evidence. Rather, teamworking is often characterized more by groups of workers performing 'routine yet related tasks', regulated by 'external control devices such as supervision and schedules' (ibid.: 45; see also **Teamworking**).

In this context, as organizations restructure and the composition of jobs changes, there is a strong view, based on research evidence, that while employers may say they are devolving responsibility to workers in the interests of good job design and job enrichment, in fact what is happening is a process of job 'enlargement' and work intensification. By job enlargement, we mean the process whereby workers are given a wider range of tasks, but at the same level of skill and with little real benefit in terms of relieving monotony or improving job design. This links with the debates over the effects of flexibility and the evidence of work intensification at the workplace (see **Flexibility** and **Effort and Intensity**). In the 1980s, there were claims that increased flexibility in working methods, and improved technology, would herald the era of the 'flexible specialist' – a highly skilled, adaptable worker – who would experience the benefits of job enrichment in this environment. But evidence suggests that this ideal has not frequently been realized and job enlargement has been the more typical outcome in 'flexible' de-layered, restructured organizations (Legge, 1995: 139–73).

See also: *alienation, conflict, consent, labour process, motivation and commitment.*

job design

REFERENCES

Cummings, T. and Blumberg, M. (1987) 'Advanced manufacturing technology and work design', in T.D. Wall, C.W. Clegg and N. Kemp (eds), *The Human Side of Manufacturing Technology*. Chichester: John Wiley, pp. 37–60.

Hackman, J.R. and Oldham, G.R. (1980) *Work Redesign*. Reading, MA: Addison-Wesley.

Legge, K. (1995) *Human Resource Management: Rhetorics and Realities*. Basingstoke: Macmillan.

Sparrow, P. (1998), 'New organisational forms, processes, jobs and psychological contracts' in P. Sparrow and M. Marchington (eds), *Human Resource Management: The New Agenda*. London: Financial Times and Pitman, pp. 117–41.

Wall, T. and Kemp, N. (1987) 'The nature and implications of advanced manufacturing technology: introduction', in T.D. Wall, C.W. Clegg and N. Kemp (eds), *The Human Side of Manufacturing Technology*. Chichester: John Wiley, pp. 1–14.

Job Satisfaction

> *Job satisfaction refers to 'a pleasant or positive emotional state resulting from the appraisal of one's job or job experiences' (Locke, 1976: 1300).*

Job satisfaction remains one of the most-researched topics in the study of work. Thousands of academic articles have been written on almost every conceivable aspect of the subject. This research attention forms three broad clusters: (1) what elements comprise job satisfaction; (2) what are the factors that influence job satisfaction, both inside and outside the workplace; and (3) what are the consequences of job satisfaction for individuals and the organizations they work for?

Yet, despite all the research undertaken and the many journal articles written on each of these subjects, not all the important questions about job satisfaction have yet been fully answered. Indeed, some very fundamental issues remain controversial or poorly understood. These include, first, whether job satisfaction is better envisaged as an overall 'scorecard' of satisfaction with the various different elements that make up a job or it is a distinct over-arching assessment. Second, if, and to what extent, the factors that give rise to satisfaction by their presence also create dissatisfaction by their absence. Third, what is the significance of individual factors (personality or even genetics, for example) in predisposing people to experience satisfaction or dissatisfaction at work? Fourth, what is the relationship between satisfaction and different work outcomes, such as performance? And, finally, to what extent do aspects of life outside work influence experienced levels of satisfaction within work (and vice versa)? On several of these questions, a continuing issue relates to the direction of causality between the factors: whether, for example, any link between satisfaction and performance is due to the fact that more satisfied people work harder or those people who work harder gain greater levels of satisfaction. In practice, a number of such associations are likely to contain elements of causality in both directions.

THE NATURE AND SOURCES OF JOB SATISFACTION

In the discussion on what job satisfaction is, many writers locate the source of satisfaction (and dissatisfaction) in the extent of discrepancy or distance between the amount of an aspect of work that a person desires or expects from a job at any given time and what they actually experience in their job. Put another way, job satisfaction may be seen as the extent to which a job fulfils a person's desires or expectations. Some, such as Locke (1976) also emphasize the importance of values in this association and the extent to which a person's job reflects those values. What this inclusion of values does is identify the relative importance of the employee's different expectations: that is, it focuses attention not only on the discrepancy between expectations and experience but also the importance of that discrepancy in different areas. For example, some may experience a variation between their views that their work organization should behave ethically and whether or not it actually does so, but this is likely to have a greater impact on the job satisfaction of those who value ethical behaviour particularly highly. In all of this discussion, however, the important point is that the smaller the gap between expectations, desires, values and experience, the higher the expected level of job satisfaction.

What many studies of job satisfaction show is that the majority of people (between six and eight out of every ten) normally report that overall they are satisfied with their job. Warr and Wall (1975: 14) comment: 'Such an outcome is not too surprising since strong dissatisfaction would in normal circumstances lead to a change of job and since habit and rationalisation over the years are likely to produce some kind of personal adjustment to a work situation.' What *is* surprising, however, is that, given the vast range of work situations and the wide variation that exists on virtually all dimensions of jobs (ranging from pay, security, job variety and autonomy to whether the job is safe or dangerous and conducted in pleasant or unpleasant working conditions), the majority of people not only in the most interesting and well-paid jobs but also in what from the outside may look relatively poor-quality and uninteresting jobs, find sources of satisfaction in their work. We return to this below.

FACTORS AFFECTING JOB SATISFACTION

Various aspects of jobs and the terms under which those jobs are carried out have been identified as important influences on job satisfaction. A key early contributor to the study of job satisfaction was Abraham Maslow, who linked job satisfaction with a five-fold hierarchy of human needs, ranging from basic physiological and safety needs to higher-order needs of self-expression and personal fulfilment (what he termed 'self-actualization'). Thus, for Maslow, the more satisfying jobs fulfilled more higher-order needs. Later, Herzberg's 'two-factor' theory of satisfaction became influential, based on the premise that the factors giving rise to satisfaction at work (factors relating to the work itself such as achievement recognition and creativity) are distinct from those that can create dissatisfaction (such as salary and working conditions). The former, Herzberg linked to psychological needs (with echoes of Maslow's notion of self-actualization), the latter he linked more to physical needs.

While both Maslow and Herzberg have been subject to both theoretical and empirical criticism, the lasting contribution of Herzberg (and before him, Maslow) has been to emphasize the psychological growth that a job allows as an important factor in creating job satisfaction. In line with this, later researchers have identified the importance for job satisfaction of work attributes such as the opportunity to use one's abilities and skills; the variety and meaningfulness offered by the job; a sense of achievement experienced; a recognition for work accomplished; a control over work pace and work methods; and the quality of relations with other organizational members. These factors Locke (1976: 1319) sums up as jobs that are both interesting and have an element of mental challenge. The opposite of this picture are boring, repetitive and unchallenging jobs in which the worker is able to exercise little choice or discretion.

In addition to these various intrinsic aspects of work are a number of extrinsic factors that also relate to job satisfaction, including the degree of security in a job, the opportunities for promotion, the length and arrangement of working hours and, especially, the amount of pay. Of these, most has been written on pay satisfaction. This has highlighted not only the importance of pay discrepancy (the extent to which pay expectations are matched by obtained pay) but also the importance of equity: how an individual's pay compares with that of others. In making comparisons on pay, it is clear that most people define their reference group very narrowly: it is how their pay compares with others immediately around them or doing identical jobs elsewhere that is important, rather than more broad-based pay comparisons (see **Pay and Performance**).

In terms of the overall distribution of job satisfaction, large surveys (such as by Clark, 1996) have identified that job satisfaction is associated with a number of individual and organizational variables. These include gender, age, education, hours of work, and size of establishment. Women tend to report higher levels of job satisfaction than men overall. Workers in their thirties, the well-educated, those working longer hours and workers in larger establishments, on the other hand, tend to report lower average levels of job satisfaction. Looking at two of these in a little more detail – age and education – first, age appears to have a 'U'-shaped relationship with satisfaction. Younger (under 25 years) and particularly older (over 45) workers record higher levels of job satisfaction than their intermediate-age counterparts; one study found that, in age terms, lowest levels of satisfaction were reported by 36-year-olds. One explanation for the higher satisfaction among older workers is that greater job experience may have enabled a closer matching of expectations and experiences. Further, in those occupations characterized by a significant degree of seniority (that is, those workers with longer service disproportionately occupying more senior positions), these jobs are more likely to be ones with greater autonomy, variety and financial reward compared to lower-level positions.

The inverse relationship between job satisfaction and education will be a particular interest (and perhaps surprise) to many readers: more educated employees tend to report lower average levels of job satisfaction. This may reflect a relationship between education and higher expectations (which, if not fulfilled, may generate dissatisfaction). A study of three industries in which many of the staff held relatively low-level jobs, found that high levels of educational qualifications were a disadvantage to job satisfaction (Brown and McIntosh, 2003). As the authors comment:

> If a company is going to hire well-qualified individuals, it is important to provide them with both the immediate rewards and the career prospects that they feel their skills merit, otherwise they will become dissatisfied and demotivated ... Hiring well-qualified individuals into jobs demanding lower skill levels is a surefire route for creating job dissatisfaction. (ibid.: 1253)

Clearly, educational qualifications may be a route to higher-level jobs in organizations, bringing greater autonomy, discretion, variety, challenge – and job satisfaction. However, the route to those jobs may be characterized by lower average satisfaction as employee expectations outstrip the quality of the positions available.

ORGANIZATIONAL OUTCOMES

As regards the organizational outcomes from job satisfaction, most has been written on the relationship between satisfaction and performance (sometimes known as the 'happiness–productivity debate'). Most commentators agree that at best the strength of the relationship between these two variables is a modest one and also that the potential exists for causality to run in both directions and even for it to be not only a positive but also a negative association. For instance, several individual studies show that the most productive people are not necessarily the ones who report the highest levels of job satisfaction. For example, employees on short-term contracts (and remembering that job insecurity is often a source of dissatisfaction) are often found to be more productive than their counterparts on permanent contracts. One explanation for this is that the former group may strive harder to improve their position in the organization or increase their employability elsewhere. Similarly, having a pressing deadline may make a person work hard, but the pressure of deadlines is rarely a source of job satisfaction.

Beyond the satisfaction–performance question, other organizational outcomes from job satisfaction have been more clearly established. Job satisfaction is associated with both intentions to quit and lower absence levels. More surprisingly, perhaps, a number of studies – several conducted in hospital settings – have found that more satisfied employees tend to work more safely and have fewer occupational injuries than their less satisfied colleagues. This relationship between satisfaction and safety has been identified in both small-scale and larger studies (see, for example, Barling et al., 2003). One explanation offered to account for this finding is that those employees reporting job dissatisfaction may be less likely to be motivated to gain safety knowledge and, as a consequence may maintain lower levels of safety compliance. Those with higher job satisfaction on the other hand are likely to demonstrate greater involvement in their job, including heightened levels of safety knowledge and awareness.

Finally, one of the most important long-term associations is that between job satisfaction and overall life quality, including physical and mental health. The clearest aspect of this relationship is evidenced by the finding that those with more job satisfaction appear to live longer than their more dissatisfied counterparts (Locke, 1976: 1328–9). To date, however, the discussion of the links between work and outside life has tended to neglect the significance of satisfying jobs for work–life balance and, more generally, for creating more satisfying and healthier lives overall (see **Work–life Balance**).

See also: *absence and turnover, career, job design, motivation and commitment, psychological contracts.*

REFERENCES

Barling, J., Kelloway, E.K. and Iverson, R.D. (2003) 'High-quality work, job satisfaction and occupational injuries', *Journal of Applied Psychology*, 88 (2): 276–83.
Brown, D. and McIntosh, S. (2003) 'Job satisfaction in the low wage service sector', *Applied Economics*, 35: 1241–54.
Clark, A.E. (1996) 'Job satisfaction in Britain', *British Journal of Industrial Relations*, 34 (2): 189–217.
Locke, E. (1976) 'The nature and causes of job satisfaction', in M.D. Dunnette (ed.), *Handbook of Industrial and Organizational Psychology*. Chicago: Rand McNally, pp. 1297–348.
Warr, P. and Wall, T. (1975) *Work and Well-Being*. Harmondsworth: Penguin.

job satisfaction

Job Security

> *Job security refers to the likelihood of a job remaining available to the current job holder.*

In a rapidly changing business environment, where competitive pressures have intensified and employees are expected to be increasingly flexible in responding to employers' and customers' demands, one of the attributes of a job that many employees say they value most is job security (Burchell, 2002: 61; Geary, 2003: 354). Having said this, we face a dilemma when determining the precise meaning of job security: do we consider 'facts' or feelings and perceptions? While undoubtedly we need to consider concrete factors such as the length of job tenure, redundancy and unemployment rates and the nature of work contracts, if we rely on 'objective', statistical evidence alone, we are likely to gain only a partial picture of exactly what job security means to employees and what implications this has for their employers.

In addition to objective measures, a number of studies have used employees' 'subjective feelings about the risk of job loss' to explore the issue of job *in*security (Burchell, 2002: 62). This approach focuses on job insecurity as an individual employee's sense of powerlessness to maintain his or her current position within the working environment (see Greenhalgh and Rosenblatt, 1984: 444). It is evident too that some researchers adopting this approach take a wider view of job security than the central concern of holding on to a particular job; it can also involve retaining the status and the terms and conditions that accrue to that job.

In practice, a thorough analysis of job security is likely to take account of both objective and subjective measures (Heery and Salmon, 2000). Before examining the changing nature of job security in contemporary society, however, we begin by clarifying the distinction between job stability and job security and between employment security and job security. Having considered the terminology, we examine the implications of job insecurity in the employment relationship.

JOB STABILITY AND JOB SECURITY

Job stability refers to the length of an employee's tenure with one employer. Thus, analysis of job tenure leads to a measurement of job stability in the labour market. But, while long periods of job tenure may indicate high job stability, we cannot assume from this that job stability equates with employees' sense of their job *security*. In order to explore this distinction, we need to consider examples of the interaction of findings on job stability with those for job insecurity.

In the 1970s, the 'average' worker in the UK had 6–7 jobs in his or her working lifetime; by the 1990s, this average had risen to 11–12 jobs. However, long-term employment with one employer is still the experience of a substantial minority. In 2000, for example, approaching half of employees in the UK had at least 5 years' service with their employer and 1 in 10 had worked for the same employer for 20 years or longer (ONS, 2001: 88; see also Doogan, 2001). Thus for some, their job stability is high. 'For others, however, work is a much more precarious affair, with insecurity, redundancy, temporary contracts and unemployment contributing to an overall experience of a fragmented, rather than unified working life' (Noon and Blyton, 2007: 46).

Indeed, attitude surveys reveal that there was a rise in feelings of job insecurity for all groups of workers between the late 1970s and 1980s and since that time some groups (though not all) have continued to report heightened levels of job insecurity. This latter feature is reflected among professional workers, for example, who in earlier decades might have felt themselves among the most secure within the employing organization (Burchell, 2002: 61–8). It would seem that even among groups of workers with a comparatively high 'objective' level of job security, for many their subjective *feelings* of insecurity have increased.

At least part of the answer to the apparent disjuncture between statistical 'facts' of job stability and feelings about job insecurity may lie in a complex interaction of labour market pressures, managerial actions and the individual and collective responses of employees. It is important to recognize that employees may also have sincerely held but inaccurate perceptions of their job security or insecurity. For example, feelings of security may relate to employees' assessment of the stability of their employer. In this they may be correct or wide of the mark but a sense of job security, or more specifically the lack of it, has been shown to influence employee behaviour, though reactions to insecurity will vary depending on the circumstances of the individual employee

(Greenhalgh and Rosenblatt, 1984: 444). For example, where a labour market is characterized by uncertainty, employees may cling to jobs they would otherwise seek to leave, in the interests of holding on to whatever security they feel they have established by length of service. But this does not necessarily mean that they feel 'secure' in the true sense of the word – in fact, the opposite may be closer to the truth (Burchell, 2002: 61). Conversely, earlier studies in the United States found job insecurity can increase the propensity of people to leave and also that it can make people resistant to change (Greenhalgh and Rosenblatt, 1984: 443). But in certain circumstances, might employers actually use employees' fears of job insecurity as a means of implementing change?

Research in the UK suggests that the threat of job loss has in many contexts been an important catalyst in the restructuring of work and for redrawing collective relationships between management and unions along more cooperative, partnership lines (see **Trade Unions, Collective Bargaining** and **Redundancy**). In addition to straightforward threats of job loss, the introduction of large numbers of temporary workers to an organization, possibly on less favourable terms and conditions, may also act to influence workers' attitudes towards changes in the organization of work. However, any use of job insecurity as a way of gaining acceptance of change and compliance with managerial demands involves a difficult balance for managers to strike: the negative effects of job insecurity can also give rise to demotivation and demoralization of workforces (Geary, 2003: 355). Nevertheless, the prospect of greater job security has acted as a powerful lever in securing significant changes in the organization of work and employment relations over the past two decades.

Commentators in the United States have warned of the risks to employee commitment posed by managerial work reorganization strategies that regard labour mainly as a cost to be minimized. They also point to a widespread weakening of broader aspects of job security and highlight reductions in retirement benefits as an example (Kochan, 2006: 16). These broader job-related aspects are of fundamental importance to job security, but are often not given sufficient attention. In concentrating on the issue of job tenure and overall job stability, the impact of the 'loss of valued job features is ... often overlooked' (Greenhalgh and Rosenblatt, 1984: 441). Yet this loss can have a profound effect on individual employees and their sense of worth and status in their work.

The issue of changing or reducing conditions of employment while maintaining job tenure brings us to the distinction between employment security and job security. While in the present discussion we are using the term job security to cover the topic of security of employment in its broadest sense, it is important to note that many employing organizations increasingly differentiate 'employment security' from 'job security'. Very few contemporary organizations will guarantee their employees long-term security in the same 'job'. Rather, where they make guarantees of security, employers tend to couch their assurances in broader terms, under the heading of 'employment security'. By this they mean that employees may be required to undertake new or different jobs according to the changing needs of the organization, but this adaptability will give them greater chances of employment security (that is, continuity of employment) as long as they continue to meet required standards of performance.

Finally, it is important to note the influence of the national context for employment in understanding employees' reactions to secure work and to look beyond blanket terms such as 'temporary' and 'permanent' workers and place these in their institutional framework. For example, the laws protecting employment in the USA are weak, so for many US employers, classifying a job as 'permanent' is unproblematic (that is, it does not prevent employers from re-classifying a job as redundant). In contrast, throughout much of Europe, there is more law surrounding the nature of employment and employee rights. Thus, for example, a temporary worker in a European Union member state may have a greater sense of their employment rights, and of job security, than many permanent workers in the United States (Burchell, 2002: 62).

In conclusion, job security for employees can be as much a feeling as a fact. It should be seen as a phenomenon in its broadest sense, encompassing terms and conditions of employment as well as length of employment. To equate job security with job tenure is to neglect many important factors that make employees feel secure or insecure at work. We have seen that raising a question mark over job security can potentially be used by managers to introduce uncertainty into the employment relationship in order to intensify employees' effort. Yet, as a strategy, this may rebound and result in demotivation, resistance and demoralization, since for many job security is one of the most prized features of their work.

See also: *career, flexibility, the law and contract of employment, unemployment and underemployment.*

REFERENCES

Bacon, N. and Blyton, P. (2006) 'Union co-operation in a context of job insecurity: negotiated outcomes from teamworking', *British Journal of Industrial Relations*, 44 (2): 215–37.

Burchell, B. (2002) 'The prevalence and redistribution of job insecurity and work intensification', in B. Burchell, D. Lapido and F. Wilkinson (eds), *Job Insecurity and Work Intensification*. London: Routledge, pp. 61–76.

Doogan, K. (2001) 'Insecurity and long-term unemployment', *Work, Employment and Society*, 15 (3): 419–41.

Geary, J.F. (2003) 'New forms of work organization', in P. Edwards (ed.), *Industrial Relations: Theory and Practice*, 2nd edn. Oxford: Blackwell, pp. 338–67.

Greenhalgh, L. and Rosenblatt, Z. (1984) 'Job insecurity: toward conceptual clarity', *Academy of Management Review*, 9 (3): 438–48.

Heery, E. and Salmon, J. (eds) *The Insecure Workforce*. London: Routledge.

Kochan, T. (2006) 'Taking the high road', *MIT Sloan Management Review*, Summer: 16–19.

Noon, M. and Blyton, P. (2007) *The Realities of Work*, 3rd edn. Basingstoke: Palgrave Macmillan.

ONS (Office for National Statistics) (2001) *Social Trends 31*, London: The Stationery Office.

Oxenbridge, S. and Brown, W. (2002) 'The two faces of partnership? An assessment of partnership and co-operative employer/trade union relationships', *Employee Relations*, 24 (3): 262–76.

key concepts in work

Knowledge Work

116

Knowledge work refers to the use of expert knowledge in problem-solving activities. Frenkel et al. (1995: 780) comment that 'knowledge workers rely predominantly on theoretical knowledge, and their work requires a high level of creativity for which they mainly use intellective skills'.

As the service sector continues to expand, those working in that sector perform a very wide range of tasks. For many, their work largely involves undertaking low-skilled activities in industries such as retailing, catering and cleaning. For others, work largely entails routine information-processing activities in low-discretion environments, such as characterize many call centre operations. However, a growing number of employees in service-sector contexts (and a proportion in manufacturing settings) are engaged in work that involves the creative application of knowledge of one form or another. This latter activity has come increasingly to be known as 'knowledge work' and the people who perform it as 'knowledge workers'. In essence, knowledge work entails the deployment of complex and technical skills in areas such as consulting, scientific research, computing and strategic planning, where expert knowledge is used to undertake relatively complex problem-solving work and thereby enhance the final output.

DEFINING KNOWLEDGE WORK

Advanced capitalism is increasingly seen as being 'knowledge-driven'. The implication behind much of this discussion is that, to secure competitive advantage, an economy needs not only to be at the forefront of developments in knowledge-based technologies but also that knowledge work and knowledge-intensive activities are critical to innovation and economic success. One outcome of this is that, as increased emphasis is placed on the importance of creating and utilizing knowledge, this in turn encourages higher levels of educational and skill attainment, as more job opportunities open up in knowledge-intensive industries.

Studying knowledge work and knowledge workers, however, has proved far from straightforward. Partly the problem is a definitional one. As Morris (1995) points out, the occupational categories covered by knowledge work are often so wide – ranging from managers and software engineers to consultants and scientists – as to make any detailed discussion and analysis of knowledge work (including a measure of the overall size of this category of worker) extremely difficult in practice. In recognition of this, some writers have sought to narrow the definition of knowledge work, for example, by distinguishing between knowledge workers and traditional professionals. In this distinction, knowledge work is seen to be more embedded within organizations, and knowledge workers are more likely to have less independence than their counterparts in traditional professions (such as doctors, architects and lawyers), who gain power by the ability of their profession to monopolize occupation-specific knowledge. For other writers in this field, however, the distinction between knowledge worker and professional is far less clear-cut. This partly reflects uncertainties over what constitutes a pro-fession (thereby giving rise to additional confusing categories such as 'semi-profession' and 'quasi-profession'). In addition, there is the problem that for the professional and the knowledge worker, the creation and application of knowledge are clearly central to the activities of both.

DIFFERENT FORMS OF KNOWLEDGE

One particularly useful contribution to the discussion of the growth of knowledge work has been that of Blackler (1995) who, in a wide-ranging review of the subject, sought to add clarity by distinguishing several different types of knowledge held within a workforce. Blackler argues that the recent period has seen a shift in the value placed on dif-ferent forms of knowledge – in particular, a reduction in the importance of knowledge derived from experience and learned routines and an increase in value placed on more abstract, conceptual forms of knowl-edge. A similar view, that more abstract knowledge lies at the heart of contemporary knowledge work, is also evident in the definition of knowledge workers by Frenkel and colleagues, quoted in the definition. For Morris (1995), one of the implications of this increased importance attached to knowledge work – and the expertise held by particular employees – is that the value of a firm can no longer be adequately mea-sured by its financial assets (such as its fixed capital), but in addition needs to take much greater account of its knowledge assets – the value of its human capital.

Despite attempts at clarification, a number of important shortcom-ings remain regarding the way that knowledge work has been depicted (for a fuller discussion, see Noon and Blyton, 2007). In some respects these stem from knowledge work being seen as something that is new to contemporary capitalism and the preserve of only a relatively restricted group of employees. As a result, the current emphasis on knowledge work as key to gaining competitive advantage underplays the fact that the holding of particular knowledge, and its creative deploy-ment, have always been critical to economic success. Further, the way that knowledge work has been depicted in many recent accounts has acted to discount the important knowledge held by workers at lower levels within organizations. As a result, the knowledge required to undertake 'routine' tasks, for example, has become even more invisible. Yet, what at first sight may appear to be highly routine activities are often in practice significantly enhanced by the knowledge and experience that the individual workers bring to the job – be that serving meals in an old people's home, tending the garden in the local park or answering queries in the tourist information office. The importance of workers' tacit knowledge – based on their skills and experience – has always been critical to employers, giving rise to a constant need for employers to secure the productivity embedded within the knowledge of its workforce.

By giving prominence to specialist knowledge work – the work of consultants, IT specialists, scientists and so on – for the economic success of a society, what this also does is highlight a growing polarization in contemporary society: those with access to knowledge (or, more specifically, with access to those aspects of knowledge recognized as important and valued accordingly) and those without. Taken to its logical extreme, this view depicts society as increasingly characterized by a cadre of high-status knowledge specialists in finance, engineering, IT and similar fields, purchasing an increasingly wide array of services supplied by relatively low-paid service workers.

One issue in the discussion has concerned the structures that best suit the development of knowledge work and how to manage knowledge workers and nurture the creation of 'intellectual capital'. In terms of structures, bureaucratic forms are generally seen to be less suitable for the nurturing of knowledge work than others (see **Bureaucracy**). Knowledge workers are judged to operate best as members of teams and in general within organizations that emphasize the importance of networks and multi-functional project groups (see **Teamworking**). Such structures contrast with a bureaucratic emphasis on working within hierarchies, which are more rigid structures than networks and are judged to be less favourable to harnessing the creative problem-solving powers of knowledge workers or to encouraging teams of complementary skills of knowledge workers.

In relation to appropriate styles of management, for Davenport, Thomas and Cantrell (2002), a key factor in the effective management of knowledge workers is the degree of choice given over where and how they work. This is consistent with other research findings that knowledge workers place a high value on autonomy and discretion in relation to their work. One aspect of this is the ability of some employees to work partly from home. This is typically reported to assist concentration on a particular problem by staying away from the noise, distractions and interruptions of the office (see **Teleworking**). At the same time, the fact that it tends to be disproportionately those in senior positions in organizations that have some discretion to work partly or occasionally from home, this is one more aspect of the polarization of privilege widespread within organizations between valued higher-grade knowledge workers and their less valued lower-grade counterparts.

CONCLUSION

Several factors, most notably the growing complexity of both economic activity and computer-based technologies, together with the speed of technological change, will increasingly place knowledge work (as it is currently conceived) at the forefront of developments in contemporary society and make experience-based knowledge less valued than hitherto. This trajectory for knowledge work will potentially have far-reaching implications for future social cohesion, given the prospect of a widening gulf between a so-called 'knowledge elite' and those working to provide the goods and services for consumption by that elite.

See also: career, employment patterns, skill, technology.

REFERENCES

Blackler, F. (1995) 'Knowledge, knowledge work and organizations: an overview and interpretation', *Organization Studies*, 16 (6): 1021–46.

Davenport, T.H., Thomas, R.J. and Cantrell, S. (2002) 'The mysterious art and science of knowledge-worker performance', *Sloan Management Review*, Fall: 23–30.

Frenkel, S., Korczynski, M., Donoghue, L. and Shire, K. (1995) 'Re-constituting work: trends towards knowledge work and info-normative control', *Work, Employment and Society*, 9 (4): 773–96.

Morris, T. (1995) 'Knowledge workers', in N. Nicholson (ed.), *The Blackwell Encyclopedic Dictionary of Organizational Behavior*, Oxford: Blackwell, pp. 280–1.

Noon, M. and Blyton, P. (2007) *The Realities of Work*, 3rd edn. Basingstoke: Palgrave Macmillan.

key concepts in work

Labour Process

Labour process refers to the process by which 'workers' capacity to labour
is translated into actual work' (Edwards, 1986: 1). The labour process
debate takes this further and examines the factors involved in the production of surplus value through work and the effects of technology and managerial control on the skill and autonomy of the worker.

MARX AND THE CAPITALIST LABOUR PROCESS

Karl Marx's critique of the capitalist labour process is an appropriate
starting point for the present discussion. Under capitalism, the pursuit
of surplus value, that is value which is greater than the actual cost of
producing a product, is pursued within a framework of employment
that pays the workers a wage for their part in this process. Marx rea-
soned that what is being sold in this transaction is the workers' 'labour
power' – what we refer to above as the 'capacity to labour'. Each worker
possesses the power to work – labour power – which may be defined as 'the
energies and faculties the worker uses when labouring' (Cohen, 1988:
211). However, only when this labour power is incorporated within a
labour process, does it have the potential to generate surplus value. Thus
the individuals' capacity to work is to be found in their skills and experience, but this power needs to be integrated within a system of work
organization – a labour process – in order to be productive. It follows
that the origin of the quest for managerial control over the way work is
allocated to workers and processes are organized is founded in the drive
to maximize the creation of surplus value (Braverman, 1974: 56).

A key issue in all of this is that, under capitalism, workers do not
receive the full value of the wealth created by their work as their wage.
Thus, they labour in order to create surplus value, but in return they are
not awarded a share of that surplus which is equivalent to their contribution. Hence Marx's evaluation of the capitalist labour process was
that it is one which is exploitative, that is in the objective, economic

sense, and one in which there is an inherent conflict of interest between employers and workers (Grint, 2005: 90–2).

BRAVERMAN'S LABOUR PROCESS THEORY

Moving on from Marx's analysis of the capitalist labour process in its widest sense, we turn to the work of Braverman, who stimulated the more recent labour process debate with his influential book *Labor and Monopoly Capital*, published in 1974. In this text, Braverman set out to examine 'the evolution of management as well as of technology, of the modern corporation as well as of changes in social life...[in]...the development of the capitalist mode of production during the last one hundred years' (Braverman, 1974: 4). Central features of Braverman's study were scientific management (see **Scientific Management**), the division of labour and the effects of technology (see **Technology**). He focused on the effects of technology and of managerial control systems founded on the Tayloristic principle that the planning of work should rest in the hands of management, while workers were confined to performing tasks assigned to them, such that there was a separation of the 'conception and execution' of work (ibid.: 124). Braverman concluded that, within the capitalist labour process, the continuing quest for surplus value leads managers to seek a means of maximizing their control in the interests of reducing their costs.

Human labour may be creative and adaptable, but it is also unpredictable. Hence, Braverman argued, managers will attempt to seize control of the process of work to ensure that workers provide optimum standards of performance for their employing organization. This may be accomplished in part by means of organizational procedures and disciplinary sanctions, but, where the work process is capable of being automated, technology facilitates greater managerial control over the pace and organization of work and, hence, allows for the maximization of worker productivity (ibid.: 1974: 194–5). Mechanization and automation are recognized as means by which traditional skills are undercut, 'a process reflected in the decline of pre-job training times' (Gallie, 1991: 320). New technology, particularly computerization, may require a worker to be trained, perhaps for some weeks or months, in order to be competent. However, maintains Braverman (1974: 443) this does not compare with a traditional craft apprenticeship in terms of duration or detail. It cannot be assumed to give the worker what Braverman called 'mastery', that is depth of knowledge combined with autonomy, over the process being executed. These combined factors result in the reduction of workers' control and 'mastery' over the labour process, in comparison with that enjoyed by the craft worker of earlier days, and contributes to the overall intensification of their work. This he described as the 'degradation' of work in the twentieth century (ibid.: 444–5).

Braverman's labour process theory was highly influential and remains of 'abiding relevance' (Noon and Blyton, 2007: 154), but his argument has been criticized on several grounds, with the main focus being his analysis of the deskilling processes associated with new technology. Critics of his position have accused him of failing to consider the heterogeneous nature of skills that workers develop within the new systems of work; also that he idealized the supposed autonomy of the craft worker. He is further accused of failing to consider variations in managerial techniques (see **Management**); ignoring the influence of the gender of workers on skill (see **Discrimination** and **Skill**); for underestimating workers' capacity to consent to the capitalist labour process (see **Consent**) and also, perhaps paradoxically, for largely ignoring the capacity of workers to respond and resist aspects of managerial control (see **Conflict**) (Grint, 2005: 182–3; Noon and Blyton, 2007: 157–9). In addition, it has been argued that in the current era, Fordism, identified with the principles of Taylorism and characterized by the mass production of standardized goods for mass markets, has been overtaken by a more flexible production of niche goods and where flexibility, new skills and greater autonomy characterize workers' experience of work (see **Fordism**). Thus, the criticism of Braverman maintains the labour process debate is less relevant because the world of work has changed, being for many 'upskilled', rather than 'deskilled' (see Noon and Blyton, 2007: 161–9).

While these points of criticism have some validity, a strong argument can be mounted in Braverman's defence, that many of his critics have become overly focused on, and have misinterpreted, his analysis of the 'deskilling' associated with new technology. Defenders of Braverman argue that this narrow focus misses the wider-ranging analytical scope of his critique, which was never simply restricted to a 'deskilling thesis' centred on a consideration of the specifics of workers' skills, but, rather, addressed the fundamental features of the capitalist labour process. If, in the present day, we wonder what relevance Braverman's thesis has, perhaps the answer lies in understanding the balance of continuity and change that exists within contemporary working environments. The current emphasis on leaner methods of production, for example, by prioritizing the elimination of 'waste' by minimizing the use of resources such as time, inventory and labour, gives new significance to the principles of scientific management. It was not simply 'skill' that Braverman was considering, but 'the crucial control element' – that is, the level of control the individual has over the *exercise* of his or her skill, in the wider processes of work organization (Armstrong, 1988: 157). This is what Braverman was pointing to: that managerial control systems and technology come together to maximize control over the workers, within a capitalist labour process that exploits their capacity to work. This is the essence of Braverman's labour process debate. So, in this context, labour process theorists would argue that their critique remains relevant in changing circumstances. For, while we may witness different variants of managerial control of work with the passage of time, in terms of basic principles, its aim remains the same: to maximize workers' productivity and the creation of surplus value.

See also: *alienation, power and authority.*

REFERENCES

Armstrong, P. (1988) 'Labour and monopoly capital', in R. Hyman and W. Streeck (eds), *New Technology and Industrial Relations*. Oxford: Basil Blackwell, pp. 143–59.

Braverman, H. (1974) *Labor and Monopoly Capital*. New York: Monthly Review Press.

Cohen, G.A. (1988) *History, Labour, and Freedom: Themes from Marx*, (reprinted 2003). Oxford: Oxford University Press.

Edwards, P.K. (1986) *Conflict at Work: A Materialist Analysis of Workplace Relations*. Oxford: Basil Blackwell.

Gallie, D. (1991) 'Patterns of skill change: upskilling, deskilling or the polarisation of skills?', *Work, Employment and Society*, 5 (3): 319–51.

Grint, K. (2005) *The Sociology of Work*, 3rd edn. Oxford: Blackwell.

Noon, M. and Blyton, P. (2007) *The Realities of Work*, 3rd edn. Basingstoke: Palgrave Macmillan.

key concepts
in work

The Law and Contract of Employment

> *The contract of employment is a contract of service where an individual undertakes to do work for an employer in return for a wage or salary.*

It has been written that 'most workers want nothing more of the law than that it should leave them alone' (Wedderburn, 1986: 1). This is probably true in the majority of cases; most people simply want to go to work and, get paid and rarely consider their employment 'rights' until something happens to force it upon them. But 'there can be no employment relationship without a power to command and a duty to obey' (Kahn-Freund, 1977: 7) and the circumstances in which people are drawn to examine the nature of their employment contract are often ones in which this relationship has broken down: where there is a dispute over the terms and conditions of work or where the contract has been breached by one or other of the parties. It can often be at this point that the importance of having an understanding of the 'contract of employment' becomes apparent.

We will consider the definition of the contract, its significance for legal rights, the form it takes and the nature of its performance. For the sake of clarity we occasionally explain specific details of the contract of employment with reference to principles founded in UK law; this is particularly the case in the section dealing with contractual status and the enforcement of legal rights. This does not mean, however, that this review of the employment contract is not relevant to other national contexts. First, the UK's legal system is increasingly influenced by its status as a member of the European Union (EU), particularly in the field of employment. Second, we use the UK example to highlight the contract's position within a framework and context of law and examine its relevance for rights and obligations. These are themes that may be considered and applied to different national contexts and legal frameworks.

There are several different parties involved in the employment relationship: the primary parties are the employer and employee; the secondary parties are employers' organizations, managers and trade unions; and the third party to the employment relationship is the state, as law maker, and its agencies, such as the courts. The contract of service, or contract of employment, gives an employer the right to the services of the employee, while the employee gains rights to his or her wages and terms and conditions; these rights are legally enforceable in each case, though there may be qualifications attached to the employee's rights, as we will discuss later.

Some contractual terms and conditions of an employee's employment will be clearly specified, such as the rate of pay, hours of work and holiday entitlements. Other matters may not be specifically referred to in the contract, but will nevertheless be implied into it – for example, the law of the land is 'implied' into every contract of employment. We will return to examine these issues in more detail later, but it begins to be clear why the contract of employment has been described as the 'cornerstone' of the employment relationship, because in relation to the law and contractual rights, 'everything hinges' upon what it contains (Kahn-Freund, 1954: 45).

In British law, there is a general assumption that the contract of employment is like any other commercial contract. It is regarded in law as a contract that is entered into voluntarily by both parties and as a contract made between equals. This is a view of the employment relationship that typically rests on assumptions of the free market and the freedom of choice available to workers. But this assumption of freedom of choice ignores the reality of power relations in the employment relationship; rarely will the individual employee possess bargaining power equal to that of the employer (Wedderburn, 1986: 5). A trade union may redress some of this power imbalance by representing the interests of groups of employees and negotiating with the employer on their behalf (see **Perspectives on Work** and **Collective Bargaining**). Thus, wherever it appears, law surrounds the employment relationship for a purpose: it regulates the exercise of power between the parties (Kahn-Freund, 1977: 1–17).

CONTRACTUAL STATUS AND ENFORCEMENT OF LEGAL RIGHTS

It is also important to consider the significance of a worker's exact contractual status for their statutory employment rights. Perhaps it is best to begin by thinking in more general terms of the 'rights' afforded to individuals in society. If we take the example of the notion of 'freedom of speech', it is regarded as an unqualified universal 'right' that everyone should enjoy in a free, democratic society, regardless of their wealth or social status. If we turn from societal 'rights' to employment rights, we see in a similar fashion that, within specific national frameworks, there will be legal or statutory minimum standards of treatment for workers that allow for prosecution of employers if they are contravened. Some of the clearest examples of such standards may be found in regulations for the provision of a safe working environment. In addition, in relation to the UK, for example, there are some statutory employment rights that apply irrespective of contractual status – for example, the right not to be discriminated against on grounds of sex or race – that all workers enjoy.

However, in the UK, there are other legal rights – for example, the right to complain of unfair dismissal or to claim financial compensation for redundancy – that are dependent on the existence of a clear and unambiguous contractual relationship with an identifiable employer, for specified minimum periods of time. For a direct employment relationship to be established, an individual must have been engaged under the terms of a *contract of service*, or contract of employment, with an employer. This relationship is different from that of a *self-employed* worker who undertakes to perform work for someone else under a contract *for* services. Thus we can say that a worker is 'anyone who works for a living', but the definition of an *employee* is narrower than the definition of a *worker*: 'all employees are workers, but not all workers are employees' (Selwyn, 2002: 2.2–2.6). The determining factor is whether or not there exists a clear, direct and unambiguous contract of employment.

How does this fine verbal distinction, between contracts of service and contracts for services, have practical significance in today's work environment? It was often the case in the past that when employers have been sued for compensation by a worker, for example, for injury at work, one of the simplest forms of defence in denying liability was to say that the person was a subcontractor rather than an employee and was therefore responsible for ensuring his or her own safety. This practice was particularly prevalent, for example, in the building and construction industry. But this device, of denying employer status, has also been made use of in the current context for work, where we see more flexible forms of employment and workers frequently engaged on a temporary basis through an employment agency. In this case, the direct contractual relationship between a worker and employer may be distanced, allowing the status of the contract of employment to become confused. This may work to the employer's economic benefit. Let us take the example of an individual who is placed with a call centre organization by an employment agency. The host organization, which owns and runs the call centre, will disclaim an employment relationship with the individual worker, citing its *commercial* contract with the agency to supply temporary labour. The employment agency disclaims an employment relationship with the individual by contracting with him or her under a contract for services and undertaking only to 'place' him or her in work. If an individual then tries to enforce legal employment rights, for example, in relation to unfair dismissal, he or she may be unable to do so because the legal employer cannot be identified. Thus the worker may be distanced from access to legal redress or entitlements.

Thus, in the UK context, the distinction between a worker and an employee is significant and highlights the national idiosyncrasies that may be of importance in the operation of the contract. The British approach is also a useful source of comparison with European regulation on employment matters. The EU concerns itself with employment rights across the member states and European intervention has been characterized by regulation for minimum standards of employment rights for all workers. The better standards of legal protection afforded to employees in, for example, Germany and the Netherlands, have not been fully replicated across the EU, but it is nevertheless the case that EU standards for employment are being rolled out across borders. Hence, in the UK, we have seen the expansion of statutory rights that apply irrespective of contractual status, for example, the introduction of the National Minimum Wage and statutory maternity provisions.

THE FORM OF THE CONTRACT

The contract of employment may be oral or in writing. If there is a dispute over terms and conditions, it is easier to prove if these are written down and formally recorded. But the sources of the contract are many and varied and not everything will find full expression in writing. The contract may comprise what are known as *express terms* and *implied terms*. Express terms are those that are expressly stated in the contract; they may deal with, for example, the rate of pay; the number of days' holiday; and the number of hours to be worked. They may also include the provisions of collective agreements and company rules.

Implied terms, on the other hand, may not be explicitly stated, but are nevertheless vital to the working of the employment contract, for there will be some matters that seem so 'obvious' that they are not actually written down. For example, it is implied into British contracts of employment that 'every employee shall serve his employer faithfully' (Selwyn, 2002: 10.121) and that the employer has an implied duty to provide work (ibid.: 10.23). It is clear to see that, in practice, the absence of such implied terms would make most contracts unworkable. Other implied terms may not be so straightforward to determine or interpret, however. This is often the case with so-called 'custom and practice'. This describes a situation where there are working practices that have existed for so long they are argued to have become part of the contract, even though they have never been formally written down. An example would be where management has allowed employees to leave work an hour earlier than actually stipulated in the contract every Friday afternoon over a period of years. If there is a dispute over the status of a 'custom', it will normally be up to a court to decide whether or not it is, or has become, a term of the contract.

Whether express or implied, the function of a 'term' is to lay down a particular requirement of the contract of employment, while a 'condition' will specify how that requirement is to be put into effect. For example, a *term* of an employment contract might be that the employee is required to work 40 hours per week, while the related *condition* would be that those hours should be worked between 8.00 am and 5.00 pm from Monday to Friday. The terms of employment are, in theory, open to negotiation and agreement between the employer and the employee, while a condition of employment would normally be a unilateral instruction by the employer. As well as substantive terms and conditions on matters such as pay, holidays and hours of work, the contract will also deal with procedural issues, by laying down guidelines and policy statements, to govern the behaviour of the parties to the contract. For example, under UK employment law there must be a disciplinary procedure, to establish guidelines for reasonable and acceptable behaviour of management and employees in cases where an employee is accused of misconduct, and a grievance procedure to allow employees' complaints to be dealt with. Finally, once the contract is established, it is not 'set in stone'. By giving notice, the employer may vary the terms of the contract; similarly, either party may terminate it altogether.

THE PERFORMANCE OF THE CONTRACT

While the contract can specify many things, like terms, conditions and the duration of the contract, ironically, one of the things that is not common in a contract of employment is how much work the employee is being contracted to do. On the matter of the level of effort an employee will devote to the work or the managerial style that will be used at a workplace, the contract is usually silent and in this sense the contract of employment is *indeterminate*. In practice, specifying the effort side of the wage–effort bargain is fraught with difficulty. As a result, the amount of *time* an employee contracts to the company for is used as a proxy for the amount of work expected (see **Working Time**). That is, the contract of employment specifies how many hours an employee is required to work and then one of the tasks of management is to ensure that the employee's time is translated effectively into actual work performed. Hence the managerial preoccupation with different forms of control designed to elicit the most effort from employees (see **Effort and Intensity, Labour Process** and **Management**).

Thus, the contract of employment forms the basis of the contractual and legal rights and obligations of employers and employees. The legal framework will vary between different national contexts and the presence, or absence, of employment law will be an indicator of the degree to which the state regulates the power of the employer and organized labour and protects the individual rights of employees.

See also: *power and authority.*

REFERENCES

Kahn-Freund, O. (1954) 'Legal framework', in A. Flanders and H.A. Clegg (eds), *The System of Industrial Relations in Great Britain: Its History, Law and Institutions*. Oxford: Blackwell, pp. 42–127.

Kahn-Freund, O. (1977) *Labour and the Law*, 2nd edn. London: Stevens & Sons.

Selwyn, N.M. (2002) *Selwyn's Law of Employment*, 12th edn. London: Butterworths LexisNexis.

Wedderburn (Lord) (1986) *The Worker and the Law*, 3rd edn. Harmondsworth: Penguin.

Management

'Management' is a term that can be used in three distinct ways: (1) to describe the discipline of organizing and administering resources within an organization; (2) to describe the system and hierarchy of responsibility and authority that exist within an organization; and (3) to describe the 'elite social grouping' of people, which organizes and administers resources and maintains authority within an organization (see Child, 1969: 13–16).

Summarizing the above definition, 'management' is a term that can describe a technical function, a system of authority or a social group. Each aspect of management interrelates with the others and this Key Concept will discuss each in turn, but we begin by taking a brief look at the origins of what we have come to recognize as the modern discipline of management.

THE ORIGINS OF MODERN MANAGEMENT

In the contemporary world, it is taken as given that organizations require good management. But modern management is a comparatively recent phenomenon, a mere 200 or so years old and it originated with industrialization and the move from feudal to capitalist societies. As Britain is generally accepted to be the first country in the world to have undergone an industrial revolution, its experiences are significant for the emergence of managers and the modern discipline of management. Prior to the industrial revolution, large agricultural estates, sometimes with associated mining operations and small workshops, dominated Britain and, while these required organizing and administering, they were not generally in competition with one another. Working relationships were dominated by feudal ties of responsibility and obligation and the generation of 'profit' was not the objective of estate stewards and land agents who ran matters for the major landowners. With the onset of industrialization and capitalism, increasing technical and administrative complexity was associated with a new focus on entrepreneurship, but at the time of the early industrial revolution the 'typical entrepreneur was his own manager' (Pollard, 1965: 104). As markets expanded and wealth grew, the growth of mass factory-style production saw an increasing scale and division of labour and the task of organizing production and generating profit was increasingly delegated to 'managers'. Thus there was an increasing separation of the ownership of a business from its control.

The early managers were frequently relatives of the owners of enterprises. They concentrated mainly on recruiting and training labour, the imposition of discipline, control of production and accounting. As industry expanded, so did the ranks of managers, many of whom rose to their positions on the basis of their technical abilities. The focus on technical expertise as a route into management meant that early managers had skills that did not easily transfer between industries (ibid.: 61), but as automation advanced, the technical skills of managers became less essential for their effectiveness while their organizational skills became more important. In particular, as factory sizes expanded, the coordination of resources became more critical to organizational success, increasing the importance of the management and control of that coordination process. We will return to these issues as we move to consider the three aspects of management: (1) its technical function; (2) its role as a system of authority; and (3) its status as a social grouping.

MANAGEMENT AS TECHNICAL FUNCTION, SYSTEM OF AUTHORITY AND SOCIAL GROUPING

The 'technical' aspect of management is bound up in the processes of managing the resources of an organization in order that they may be used *efficiently*, that is within budget and producing a good return on investment, and *effectively*, that is providing a good standard of service or product. In addition to organizing and coordinating the processes of work, management is responsible for marketing, distributing and finally selling a product or providing a service. The technical function of management thus demands organizational skills and specific areas of expertise, but it cannot be separated from our understanding of management as a system of authority. Within an organization, a system, or hierarchy of authority, distributes power and accountability and has implications for the roles that individuals are required to fulfil (see **Power and Authority**). Managers will occupy the upper strata of such structures of authority and will use their power to establish formal organizational norms, enforce regulations, apply sanctions and communicate the organizational objectives to lower-ranking employees. Having identified management as part of a *system* of authority, it is of fundamental importance that the role of management in *exercising* authority is seen as legitimate in the eyes of those who have to obey managerial direction. We will return to this issue later in our discussion.

Just as the technical function of management cannot be separated from its meaning as a system of authority, the distinctive nature of management as a social group is inseparable from its technical role and its status within an organization. The changing nature of work, organizational restructuring and educational developments mean that 'management' as a social grouping may comprise an increasingly diverse social mix. But important common factors prevail and these continue to set management apart from other employees. First, those who occupy managerial positions are explicitly given responsibility for fulfilling the aims of the enterprise. Second, there will normally be more demanding selection criteria applied for entry to managerial positions, often related to educational qualifications or their job experience. Third, managers enforce systems of authority on behalf of their organizations and are separated from other employees by hierarchies of accountability and responsibility (Child, 1969: 14–15).

The increasing scope of managerial responsibilities has seen the technical function of management come to be supported by a body of theory. Whereas in the early days of industrialization management was characterized by *ad hoc* problem-solving, by the turn of the twentieth century management theory was emerging as a distinct field of study. In the USA, the pioneer of 'scientific management', F.W. Taylor was highly influential, founding the principles of management as a 'science' and recommending the separation of the 'planning' of work from the 'doing' of it; the former was to be the preserve of managers, the latter of workers (Taylor, 1947: 40–5; see **Scientific Management**). Other schools of managerial thought, notably the Human Relations School, subsequently developed and thus a body of management theory began to be established (see **Human Relations**). Professional societies of managers, focusing on the managerial skills relevant to their industry or occupation, and managerial 'theory' as a distinct area of study also began to appear in Britain at this time (Child, 1969: 13–16). The development of a distinct managerial approach and a body of management theory has continued since those early days and the ongoing growth of managerial education programmes and professional institutions supports the higher status of a managerial position. The higher earnings that accrue to managers in comparison with other employees further reinforces the distinction between 'management' and non-managerial employees. This distinction is not confined to the employing organization, but has wider social implications relating to income, wealth, status and opportunity.

However, it is important to recognize that as a social group 'management' is not homogeneous. There are different degrees of managerial responsibility within any organization, ranging from the most senior director to the first line supervisor and tensions frequently exist between different managerial grades and functions (see Blyton and Turnbull, 2004: 109). Further, on the wider, global stage, management has developed different characteristics in different national contexts. For example, research suggests that there are very real differences in the educational requirements, technical expertise and the general approach of German as opposed to British middle-ranking managers. The differences are interlinked and can be summarized as: British managers are less likely to be technically involved in the work processes they manage than their German counterparts; British managers appear to be more conscious of their status in relation to subordinate workers, whereas German managers are more likely to regard themselves as peers of the technical work group; and, finally, the British approach to management focuses on managerial skills rather than technical expertise, leading to a far greater mobility of managers between different functions, departments and industries in the UK than in Germany (Ganter and Walgenbach, 2003: 183–4).

THE PROBLEMS OF MANAGEMENT

Management is charged with fulfilling the aims and interests of the enterprise, which in the private sector are increasingly 'equated with those of the shareholders' (Blyton and Turnbull, 2004: 100). This creates a dilemma for management in that, by fulfilling their operational functions, managers may be brought into conflict with other employees and also with wider society. To take the potential for conflict with other employees first: the wage–effort bargain embodied by the contract of employment requires that employees consent to being controlled in the interests of organizational efficiency, as determined by management (see **The Law and Contract of Employment**). But there is no guarantee that employees will agree that managerial decisions are indeed in their best interests. For example, management may decide a pay increase is *not* in the interests of the company, but that redundancies *are* and neither judgement might be amenable to the employees affected. In general terms 'the "effort bargain" is conducive to conflict with management' (Child, 1969: 21) and this presents a managerial problem, as one of management's pivotal tasks is to generate employee co-operation and consent, in the interests of optimizing productivity and standards of service in uncertain and rapidly changing competitive environments (Blyton and Turnbull, 2004: 101–2; see also **Conflict** and **Consent**).

In addition to the potential conflict from within the organization, there is also the potential for management to be brought into conflict with wider groupings in society. There may indeed be a general consensus that good management is a valuable and necessary 'technical resource' for organizations, but the aims of such organizations may not receive universal approval from all quarters. For example, certain commercial enterprises may be judged by some to be flouting environmental interests, or exploiting their workers, in the interests of increasing shareholder profits. Similarly, as public-sector services are increasingly measured against private-sector values, there may be unease over whether or not managers are properly addressing the 'public interest'. We have also to consider that managers, as individuals, are employees and citizens who may also have interests that are distinct from those of the employing organization, despite their relatively privileged position within it.

In the process of resolving these problems and the demands of competing interests both within and outside the organization, and indeed to reassure themselves that they are behaving in the best interests of all, managers have to foster acceptance of the legitimacy of their authority (Fox, 1966). In this respect, management relies on ideology as a legitimizing mechanism (see **Perspectives on Work**). Thus, within the organization managers may try to cultivate and claim a 'community of interests', or unitary view of the enterprise, in order to secure employee consent, compliance and commitment to the organization's objectives. To the wider society, management may be keen to convey a sense of their social responsibility (Child, 1969: 20–1).

However, while conflict resolution, good public relations and good employee relations may be important tasks for management, organizations are most likely to judge their managers on the basis of their operational abilities: their ability to organize and coordinate cost-efficient or profitable production and distribution of goods and services.

See also: *labour process.*

REFERENCES

Blyton, P. and Turnbull, P. (2004) *The Dynamics of Employee Relations*, 3rd edn. Basingstoke: Palgrave Macmillan.

Child, J. (1969) *British Management Thought: A Critical Analysis*. London: George Allen & Unwin.

Fox, A. (1966) 'Managerial ideology and labour relations', *British Journal of Industrial Relations*, 4 (3): 366–78.

Fox, A. (1971) *A Sociology of Work in Industry*. London: Collier Macmillan.

Ganter, H-D. and Walgenbach, P. (2003) 'Middle managers: differences between Britain and Germany', in M. Geppert, D. Matten and K. Williams (eds), *Challenges for European Management in a Global Context: Experiences from Britain and Germany*. Basingstoke: Palgrave Macmillan, pp. 165–88.

Pollard, S. (1965) *The Genesis of Modern Management: A Study of the Industrial Revolution in Great Britain*, (reprinted 1993). Aldershot: Gregg Revivals.

Taylor, F.W. (1947) *Scientific Management*. New York: Harper & Bros.

Motivation and Commitment

key concepts in work

> *Motivation refers to the influences that govern choices over the direction and strength of actions. Organizational commitment refers to 'the relative strength of an individual's identification with and involvement in a particular organization' (Mowday et al., 1982: 27).*

The factors that motivate people to work have been of long-standing interest among psychologists and others researching the world of work. These factors are not as straightforward as might first appear. Part of the complexity of the subject lies in the fact that, as well as a range of individual variables influencing patterns of motivation, these are in turn influenced by a wide variety of contextual factors, both internal to, and outside, the work organization.

Views on what motivates people at work are relevant to a number of the Key Concepts discussed elsewhere in this volume. One of the bases of scientific management, for example, is an assumption that workers are motivated solely by financial rewards and have no interest in job discretion and control (see **Scientific Management**). The Human Relations arguments, in contrast, maintain that workers are motivated by social relationships and their membership of work groups and also by the quality of communications from management and the type of supervision they receive (see **Human Relations**). The debate on the work–life balance, on the other hand, holds that many employees are increasingly motivated to have jobs that also allow the successful pursuit of non-work activities (see **Work–life Balance**). Similarly, discussions over career, employee participation, job satisfaction and pay contain important assumptions about the factors that motivate people at work (see **Career, Job Satisfaction, Participation and Involvement** and **Pay and Performance**). And of course, any links between these aspects of work and motivation are further complicated by the fact that different people will be motivated by different goals and conditions and individuals may be motivated by different goals and conditions at different stages of their working lives.

THEORIES OF MOTIVATION

Given the breadth of possible influencing factors, it is perhaps not surprising that many theories of work motivation exist. Various writers, however, have categorized these into several broad types. First, there are those theories based on the idea that, as humans, we share a number of similar goals. The emphasis in these theories is thus on the general factors that motivate people. An early example of this approach is that of Maslow (1954) who described five levels or classes of human need, ranging from basic physiological and safety needs to more refined needs for social relations, self-esteem and the highest level of need that he termed self-actualization (not unlike the notion of self-expression). Maslow's argument was that these different levels of need are ordered hierarchically and that, while exceptions will exist, individuals in general become motivated to achieve higher-order needs only when the lower-order needs have been met. Despite a lack of research evidence supporting this view of needs and motivations being ordered hierarchically, with higher-order motivations triggered when lower-order needs have been fulfilled, what Maslow and his followers usefully did for the study of work behaviour is reinforce the view that motivation to work is not only about gaining financial reward but also about undertaking work that develops social relations and provides a source of self-esteem and the possibility for allowing creativity and self-expression.

A second type of motivation theory relates more to the bases on which people make decisions about their actions. The most prominent of these has been expectancy theories (initially associated with Vroom, 1964). These focus on motivation being the result of an individual's expectations of what outcomes will follow from particular efforts or actions and the individual's valuation (what Vroom termed 'valence') of those outcomes. In addition to expectancy theories, different commentators have also discussed the motivational aspects of perceived equity in organizations: whether people think that the outcomes achieved from their investment of time and energy is equitable compared to others around them. In this approach, a sense of equity is seen as being an important factor in motivation. In turn, this forms part of a broader issue of the importance to workers of perceived 'justice' within organizations. This covers employees' views of both 'procedural' justice (the fairness of procedures) and distributive justice (whether outcomes are fair).

Over time, motivation theories have become more complex as recognition has grown of the wide range of factors that can influence why people behave at work in the ways that they do. It is increasingly recognized that theories of work motivation need to take account of individual differences (such as how different personality types, people's life stage and their non-work circumstances will affect their work motivation patterns); organizational factors (such as the nature of the job, the work group, management style and so on); and broader variables such as economic conditions (for instance, motivation patterns are likely to be different at times of economic buoyancy and depression) and cultural differences. An example of the latter, is that patterns of motivation are likely to vary significantly between societies that are more individualistic in orientation compared to societies that have a more collectivist, group-orientated value system. Thus, when thinking about what motivates people at work, we need to take account not only of the individual within the workplace but also the broader context within which that individual and the work organization are situated. As Warr (1978: 261) comments, however, 'increasing complexity is both a strength and weakness of recent motivation theories'. In particular, for Warr and others, a key problem in this increased awareness of the complexity of work motivation lies in the large number of potentially influencing variables identified and the heightened scope these create for generating measurement errors and interaction effects.

COMMITMENT

Commitment in relation to work is mainly discussed in terms of the degree of attachment that employees show towards their work organization. It is closely associated with motivation, but, whereas motivation is focused mainly on the individual, commitment is more strongly associated with the individual's attachment to, and identification with, the work organization and the organization's goals. In this way, commitment is typically viewed as the organizational face of motivation: the way in which worker motivation translates into a closer alignment with the organization, a loyalty to the company and a willingness to work on behalf of the company's success. The issue of commitment has become more prominent in the recent period, partly as aresult of the debate on 'high commitment management': how managers might manage in a way that ensures a high level of worker commitment, that in turn will contribute to high performance from the workforce as a whole (Marchington and Wilkinson, 2005: 71–98).

Most research on the subject of commitment has treated it in attitudinal terms, focusing on such issues as how much individuals identify with the goals of the organization, wish to be associated with it and how much they are willing to exert themselves on behalf of the organization (Mowday et al., 1982). Other recent studies of commitment, however, have raised the idea that, rather than there being a single view of organizational commitment, there are different components to commitment. In this view, and following our earlier comment, preparedness to exert oneself on behalf of the organization is not the same as commitment to remaining with the organization. Overall, however, commitment is important for discussions of performance and in relation to management's control of the workforce (see **Labour Process**).

Turning to other questions of commitment, one broader question is how committed people are to work and working in general. As Noon and Blyton (2007) discuss, one of the main ways that this has been studied has been by the use of a 'lottery' question. This involves asking people, if they won the lottery, or inherited a large sum of money, would they continue working? In the various countries and at different times that this question has been asked, majorities in each country indicate they would continue working, either in the same job or a different one, with only minorities indicating that they would give up paid work altogether. In one eight-country study, for example (cited in Noon and Blyton, 2007: 56), between 4 and 31 per cent said they would stop working if such circumstances arose. For large majorities in each country, however, their commitment to continuing working was clear.

A further issue that has attracted considerable attention over a long period is the degree to which workers are able to maintain a 'dual commitment' to their company and union. In other words, is it possible for workers to show allegiance to both company and union simultaneously or is the relationship more of a 'zero-sum' one, with commitment to one being at the expense of commitment to the other? Though not all studies have pointed in the same direction, the majority indicate that workers are able to maintain dual commitment, particularly where the climate of industrial relations is mainly cooperative (for more detailed discussion on this question, see Noon and Blyton, 2007: 313–14).

More recently, the work–life balance debate is also in part a discussion about dual commitment: whether workers can maintain a balanced commitment to both work and non-work life. As discussed elsewhere, this dual commitment is partly sought by work arrangements such as part-time contracts and flexible work hours that improve the possibilities for scheduling both work and non-work activities (see **Work–life Balance**). In this way, the presence of work flexibility opportunities could positively contribute to increased levels of organizational commitment. In practice, however, it is evident that it is not simply the presence of formal flexibility policies that is important for workers, but whether or not they feel free to use those policies without detrimental effects (for instance, in relation to their careers). For example, in a study of biotechnology firms, Eaton (2003) found a positive association between employees feeling free to use available flexibility policies and their level of organizational commitment. This association was not present, however, between the formal existence of policies and levels of commitment.

In terms of the future development of organizational commitment, an important issue is the extent to which management will be able to secure commitment in environments that may be characterized by higher levels of job insecurity. In the past, the commitment of many workers has been based in part on their assumptions and expectations regarding security and advancement in the organization; for example, loyalty to the organization being rewarded by promotion (see **Psychological Contracts**). However, as discussed elsewhere (see **Career and Job Security**), if future economic conditions result in higher levels of risk and lower levels of predictability and job security for employees, their continued commitment may need to be secured by other means, such as a greater emphasis on financial reward.

See also: *alienation, consent.*

REFERENCES

Eaton, S. (2003) 'If you can use them: flexibility policies, organizational commitment and perceived performance', *Industrial Relations*, 42 (2): 145–67.

Marchington, M. and Wilkinson, A. (2005) *Human Resource Management at Work*, 3rd edn. London: Chartered Institute of Personnel and Development.

Maslow, A. (1954) *Motivation and Personality.* New York: Harper & Row.

Mowday, R., Porter, L. and Steers, R. (1982) *Employee-Organization Linkages: The Psychology of Commitment, Absenteeism and Turnover.* New York: Academic Press.

Noon, M. and Blyton, P. (2007) *The Realities of Work*, 3rd edn. Basingstoke: Palgrave Macmillan.

Vroom, V. (1964) *Work and Motivation.* Chichester: Wiley.

Warr, P.B. (1978) 'Attitudes, actions and motives', in P.B. Warr (ed.), *Psychology at Work.* Harmondsworth: Penguin, pp. 227–63.

Organizational Culture

The culture of an organization is represented in its basic values, beliefs, norms and assumptions.

An organization's culture is often seen as manifested in its policies and practices and the understandings, language, behaviour and attitudes of organizational members. The history of the organization and the influence of its founders and/or key position holders are widely judged to be important influences on shaping the organization's culture. In turn, this culture is reflected in the characteristic style that a company displays.

In the 1980s, the culture of work organizations became the focus of attention for many management theorists and consultants. The most visible form of this was Peters and Waterman's book *In Search of Excellence* (1982) in which they argued that the success of particular organizations could be attributed to the 'excellence' of their strong corporate cultures. The prescriptive element in Peters and Waterman, and many managerial consultants that followed them, was that cultures could be managed and modified: that the right leadership, holding the right values and beliefs, could change the culture and inculcate those values and beliefs throughout the organization. The outcome was portrayed as a positive effect on levels of employee commitment, productivity and performance. In this way, cultures were viewed as potential sources of enhanced management control, capable of being shaped and harnessed in pursuit of greater organizational effectiveness.

This view of organizational culture as both unified and amenable to modification has been reflected in a number of high-profile 'culture change' programmes. In the UK, for example, one of the most prominent of these involved British Airways, which sought to transform itself from a lack-lustre and loss-making state-owned airline to a profitable, customer-focused and market-sensitive private company, partly through a culture-change programme or, more accurately, a series of such programmes over two decades (see Grugulis and Wilkinson, 2002 and Höpfl, 1993). This way of viewing organizational culture is attractive partly because of its simplicity – the notion that underlying an organization's activities is an embedded set of values and beliefs that are reflected in the organization's policies and practices and surface in the attitudes and behaviour of its workforce.

However, this approach to organizational culture is based on a series of implicit assumptions and, since Peters and Waterman's contribution to this field, these assumptions have been subjected to more thorough interrogation. These assumptions include, first, that organizations are characterized by a single and enduring culture that underpins the organization's values and beliefs. Second, that, while being embedded in the organization and intrinsic to that organization, this culture is open to manipulation – that it can be managed and shaped with the goal of improving organizational success. Third, that the culture of the organization has a consistent effect on how people think and behave: that by altering the culture, employees can be motivated to deliver higher performance, improved customer service and so on.

As a result, other writers in this field have adopted perspectives very different to that of Peters and Waterman, critical in particular of the way organizational culture is portrayed as an integrated and common set of values and beliefs that permeate every level of the organization and these are open to manipulation by management.

DIFFERENT PERSPECTIVES ON ORGANIZATIONAL CULTURE

Joanne Martin (1992; Martin and Frost, 1996) identifies three schools of thought or alternative perspectives on organizational culture. The first – the 'integration' perspective – is the one outlined above: that organizations are characterized by single, common cultures created and sustained by key position holders during the history of the organization. The second perspective – termed the 'differentiation' perspective – is based on the notion that organizations are characterized by not one but by several sets of values and beliefs, each tied to particular subcultures within the organization. These subcultures may reflect different sources of differentiation within organizations, such as occupation, grade, gender, age, ethnicity or location. The argument here is that members of each of these subcultures share interests in common, but that these are not jointly held across all the subcultures. Thus, for example, lower-grade employees, by the nature of their location within the work hierarchy, are unlikely to be guided by exactly the same values, beliefs and views of the organization as those held by the senior management. Alternatively, in an organization such as a hospital, the values and beliefs of the professional medical staff are unlikely to be wholly consistent with the values and beliefs of the hospital's managerial staff. The values and beliefs of the former are more likely to give primacy to patient care, while the latter will place a relatively greater value on efficiency and cost.

This differentiation perspective continues a long-standing interest by organizational sociologists in the development and maintenance of occupational subcultures and the role played by factors such as socialization into the occupational group and how the values of the group are transmitted. For Turner (1971: 1):

A subculture is a distinctive set of meanings shared by a group of people … [that] … is maintained by ensuring the newcomers to a group undergo a process of learning or socialisation. This process links the individual to the values of the group and generates common motives, common reaction patterns and common perceptual habits.

Thus, the general argument for writers such as Turner, and later writers on culture that fall within the differentiation perspective, is that the organization comprises a number of subcultures that hold values and beliefs in common, but that these differ across subcultures. This perspective undermines both the view that organizations have a single embracing culture and the notion that the culture can be shaped by those in senior positions.

The third perspective identified by Martin – termed the 'fragmentation' perspective – takes issue with the idea of *any* values and beliefs being enduring and held in common either throughout the organization (the integration perspective) or separately by individual subcultures (the differentiation perspective). In this third perspective, any consensus that develops in regard to values and beliefs existing in an organization is seen to be much more transient and issue-specific. Organizational members may come to share similar values and beliefs about specific issues for a particular time, but overall no clear, consistent or enduring culture exists, either across the organization as a whole or within particular subcultures. Thus, this view maintains that no consensus exists or persists as to what the underlying values and beliefs of the organization consist of.

What makes Martin's analysis of the three perspectives even more interesting is her argument that, rather than representing mutually exclusive alternatives from which to view organizational culture, all three perspectives may be relevant to understanding organizational culture. By studying organizations extensively enough (partly by studying them at a number of different levels), she argues that elements and evidence consistent with all three perspectives could be identified: that is, the existence of certain organization-wide values and objectives; evidence of subcultures holding conflicting opinions about what is important; and some issues that are ambiguous and generate multiple interpretations.

ORGANIZATIONAL CULTURE AND NATIONAL VARIATION

Another important theme in the study of organizational culture concerns the effects of external influences, in particular, the impact of national variation. Research on this question is particularly associated with the work of Hofstede (2001) who explored national influences on organizational culture initially through a study of IBM subsidiaries located throughout the world. Hofstede identified distinct national differences in the subsidiaries, which he linked back to differences in the national cultures in which the subsidiaries were located. The main variations he identified were: the degree of willingness of members to accept hierarchy and an unequal distribution of power and prestige (a dimension that he termed 'power distance'); differences in requirements for rules and standardization (a dimension he termed 'uncertainty avoidance'); the degree of independence and individualism exhibited ('individualism v. collectivism'); and the degree of separation of gender roles ('masculinity v. femininity'). As Hatch and Cunliffe (2006: 185) discuss, in later research Hofstede identified a fifth dimension of national cultural difference, termed 'long-term v. short-term orientation', reflecting the finding that in some contexts, for example, there is a greater emphasis on the long-term rewards from effort invested and a greater emphasis on tradition and long-term commitments than in cultures characterized by a more short-term orientation.

CONCLUSION

Earlier portrayals of single, pervasive organizational cultures are now generally seen to have given insufficient recognition to the potential for different groups within organizations to generate their own distinct subcultures. Similarly, exhortations to managers to effect changes to the culture in order to encourage greater employee commitment made assumptions about the accessibility of the culture to modification, the homogeneity of that culture and the anticipated links between the underlying culture and employees' behaviour. In subsequent research, each of these assumptions has been questioned and judged to be problematic.

In practice, it appears more likely the case that organizational cultures are less consistent than first discussed, with some elements shared by different groups at particular points in time, while others are fragmented and held only partially by different subgroups or not at all. In addition, while dimensions of the culture may be open to influence and modification (for example, the 'safety culture' within an organization or a 'long work hours' culture – see **Presenteeism**), other aspects may be less accessible to change. Further, even those aspects that may be modifiable will not necessarily have a predictable or long-term effect on employees' behaviour.

145

See also: *labour process, management, motivation and commitment, organizations: networks and alliances, teamworking.*

REFERENCES

Grugulis, I. and Wilkinson, A. (2002) 'Managing culture at British Airways: hype, hope and reality', *Long Range Planning*, 35 (2): 179–94.

Hatch, M.J. with Cunliffe, A.L. (2006) *Organization Theory: Modern, Symbolic and Postmodern Perspectives*. Oxford: Oxford University Press.

Hofstede, G. (2001) *Culture's Consequences: Comparing Values, Behaviors, Institutions and Organizations Across Nations*, 2nd edn. Thousand Oaks, CA: Sage.

Höpfl, H. (1993) 'Culture and commitment: British Airways', in D. Gowler, K. Legge and C. Clegg (eds), *Case Studies in Organizational Behaviour and Human Resource Management*. London: Paul Chapman, pp. 117–38.

Martin, J. (1992) *Cultures in Organizations: Three Perspectives*. New York: Oxford University Press.

Martin, J. and Frost, P. (1996) 'The organizational culture war games: a struggle for intellectual dominance', in S.R. Clegg, C. Hardy and W.R. Nord (eds), *Handbook of Organization Studies*. London: Sage, pp. 599–621.

Peters, T. and Waterman, R. (1982) *In Search of Excellence: Lessons from America's Best-Run Companies*. New York: Harper & Row.

Turner, B.A. (1971) *Exploring the Industrial Subculture*. London: Macmillan.

Organizations: Networks and Alliances

In the study of work, organizations refer to structures or arrangements that are established to pursue certain work tasks (see Watson, 2003: 76–8).

In this Key Concept, we need to cover a lot of ground in a short space: there are entire bookshelves, if not small libraries, devoted to the changing nature of organizations. Much of this writing involves a questioning of the extent to which 'classical' forms of work organization, based on self-contained entities that are both vertically differentiated (hierarchy) and horizontally differentiated (separate functions or divisions) are giving way to different structures and ways of operating (see **Bureaucracy**).

At their broadest these changes are seen to require a fundamental rethinking of the nature of the work organization itself, both in terms of its internal structure and its relations with other organizations.

Central to the argument that traditional forms of organization are undergoing major change is the belief that various developments occurring in the organization's environment are necessitating that change. These developments include a fundamental transformation in the nature of technology and communications; the conditions being created by increased globalization; intensified levels of competition and market turbulence; the high costs of entry into many new markets; and the greater need for organizations to be both more cost-effective and more responsive to their customers (see **Customers, Globalization and Labour Migration**). Ashkenas et al. (2002) among others argue that, as a result of these and other factors, the basic paradigm for organizational success has altered: from one emphasizing size, role clarity, specialization and control as key elements for success to one championing the primacy of speed, flexibility and innovation. As a result, many organizations have instigated far-reaching changes, both *internal* changes in the way they are structured and *external* changes in the ways they relate to other organizations.

INTERNAL AND EXTERNAL CHANGES

In terms of internal changes, one way that organizations are responding to this heightened uncertainty and need for flexibility is to work more with task forces and multifunctional project teams rather than relying on traditional hierarchical structures (see **Flexibility** and **Teamworking**). Such project teams often cross-cut traditional horizontal and vertical divisions and functions within organizations. A second response is for organizations to adopt a clearer view on what are their 'core competencies' and to focus direct employees on those core activities, while purchasing non-core functions from external suppliers (agencies, independent contractors and so on). One outcome of this latter development is that, within the boundaries of a single workplace, those working there may be employed by several different organizations, with the management acting as the agent of not a single but several employers (Rubery et al., 2004; see also **The Law and Contract of Employment**).

A major focus of the external changes taking place is that many organizations are developing closer interconnections than was formerly the case. These developments in inter-organizational relations can take various forms, such as franchising arrangements, joint ventures and strategic alliances. As a result of such developments, the boundaries around individual organizations are seen to be becoming more fluid and less distinct. Some commentators have even talked of the growth of the 'boundaryless' organization (Hatch, 1997; Ashkenas et al., 2002). In practice, however, it is not so much that organizations as we know them are disappearing, more that it is becoming less realistic to consider organizations in isolation, without considering how their relations with others – through partnerships, joint ventures and so on – affect how they function, including how much independent control they enjoy.

The lowering of organizational boundaries increases the organization's permeability to customers, suppliers and others. Examples of this include supplier or customer companies who relocate some staff to work alongside the organization's own employees, acting, for example, as advisers or inspectors. More broadly, as part of the response to the changing economic environment, organizations are devoting increased attention to the nature and quality of inter-organizational relationships they enter into. For some organizations at least, these relationships are assuming a greater significance for capacity building and success than either internal features such as structure and technology, or internally focused strategies such as growth and consolidation (Clegg et al., 1996). As a result, considerable attention is now being paid to the evolving nature of inter-organizational collaborations. These include not only joint ventures, but also the development of 'virtual' corporations that enable resources to be brought together in a temporary collaboration and also the creation of network structures of one form or another.

NETWORKS AND ALLIANCES

Network organizations can vary from loosely coupled informal structures to more formal arrangements. A common feature, however, is that most network structures rely heavily on electronic technologies to maintain coordination and control across the network. Networks potentially offer several advantages over more traditional, bureaucratic, forms of organization in that they allow for both risk and resource sharing and may provide considerable opportunities for knowledge transfer. Networks are also potentially more flexible than other structures, such as mergers, that seek to integrate resources. At the same time, as well as these and other potential advantages, there are also risks attached for those participating, not least an increased dependence on – and thus, vulnerability to – the other members in the network.

Strategic alliances are a further way for organizations to enter or expand in markets, particularly where high levels of investment in technology are required. In recent years, many companies across a range of sectors have actively sought alliances with organizations that previously they viewed only as direct competitors. Some have termed this development of alliances between competitors, 'cooperative capitalism'.

The international airline industry is a good illustration of many of the organizational developments noted above. Following significant change in the industry over the past two decades – in particular, a reduction in national state regulation of civil aviation and the widespread privatization of former state-owned airlines – this has led, among other things, to a growth in new operators (particularly 'low-cost' airlines) and an increase in competition. In addition, among the bigger airlines there has been an intensified search for a global presence to take advantage of the greater profitability of long-haul, compared to short-haul, passenger traffic. Prominent in this latter search has been the development of strategic alliances between carriers situated in different geographical regions. For example, both of the current leading airline alliances, the Star Alliance and Oneworld alliance, include major carriers in the three main airline traffic regions of Europe, North America and Asia. The gains from strategic alliances potentially include increased passenger numbers (deriving from better connections and benefits to those remaining with alliance members, such as frequent flyer credit), stronger collective purchasing power among alliance members (for example, for fuel and new aircraft) and a greater scope for reducing and rationalizing duplicate activities such as check-in and other within-airport services. At the same time, several factors continue to inhibit the expansion of alliances within the industry, not least that airlines remain legally constrained in various ways by national regulation.

As well as their use of strategic alliances, airline companies also demonstrate several other developments in regard to their own boundaries and their relationships with other organizations. These include increased 'code-sharing' where two companies combine activities on a particular route, extensive franchising (particularly of lower-volume and feeder routes) and the subcontracting of former in-house activities (such as catering, ground transport and maintenance). Some commentators have predicted that in the future there may also be significant growth in 'virtual' airline companies that exist only as a marketing and branding activity, with all the actual operation of flying passengers and cargo being either contracted out (e.g. ticketing and check-in operations) or leased on a short-term basis from elsewhere, including aircraft and flight crew (for more discussion of developments in the airline industry, see Blyton et al., 2001).

PUBLIC-SECTOR DEVELOPMENTS

It is not only in the private sector that traditional organizational boundaries are blurring. The public sector too has undergone major changes in recent years, leading among other things to a less clear-cut distinction between the public and private sectors themselves. Motivations for the changes include political ideologies that stand opposed to a large-scale public sector, as well as more prosaic political concerns for reducing the costs of public-service provision. A long-standing political argument has also been that public-sector organizations are less efficient than they could be because they lack exposure to the competitive forces that exist within the private sector. As a result, in different countries a variety of changes in the size, shape and functioning of the public sector have been taking place. These changes include first the full privatization of a wide range of former state-owned activities, from railways to airlines and air traffic control, and from water distribution to telecommunications. Second, in other areas of the public sector the state has created separate, semi-independent agencies with responsibility for individual services and with a greater degree of transparency in their costs and revenues. Third, the state has entered into contracts with private companies to provide public services on a commercial basis. In the UK, these contractual arrangements cover a wide range of activities, from road building and repair to the construction and maintenance of schools, hospitals and prisons. In some respects, this development, currently known as Public Private Partnerships in the UK, is an extension of former contracting out activities whereby the state utilized a variety of private-sector organizations to provide elements of different services. Taken as a whole, however, the current changes occurring within the public sector represent a significant blurring of the boundary between state and private-sector operations and a closer integration of organizations formally located in the two sectors (Grimshaw and Hebson, 2004).

Overall, whether these developments in both private and public sectors represent the early stages of a fundamental shift in the nature of organization remains open to question. Many of the features noted above – collaboration between firms, franchising, subcontracting and the use of agency workers, for example – are established practices and have been incorporated into organizational structures in the past without necessitating reference to concepts such as the 'boundaryless' organization. But at the same time it is clear that organizations across a wider range of activities are increasingly involved in more extensive networks of relationships – alliances, supply chains, closer customer relations and so on – and that the growing use of agency, freelance and other forms of contracted workers is contributing to a growth in multi-employer contexts. Together, these offer a far different picture of the future than one characterized by the traditional pattern of single employer and standalone organizations.

See also: *flexibility, teamworking, technology.*

REFERENCES

Ashkenas, R., Ulrich, D., Jick, T. and Kerr, S. (2002) *The Boundaryless Organization: Breaking the Chains of Organizational Structures.* San Francisco, CA: Jossey-Bass.

Blyton, P., Martinez Lucio, M., McGurk, J. and Turnbull, P. (2001) 'Globalisation and trade union strategy: industrial restructuring and Human Resource Management in the international civil aviation industry', *International Journal of Human Resource Management,* 12 (3): 1–19.

Clegg, S., Hardy, C. and Nord, W. (eds) (1996) *Handbook of Organization Studies.* London: Sage.

Grimshaw, D. and Hebson, G. (2004) 'Public-private contracting: performance, power and change at work', in M. Marchington, D. Grimshaw, J. Rubery and H. Willmott (eds), *Fragmenting Work: Blurring Organizational Boundaries and Disordering Hierarchies.* Oxford: Oxford University Press, pp. 111–34.

Hatch, M.J. (1997) *Organization Theory: Modern, Symbolic and Postmodern Perspectives.* Oxford: Oxford University Press.

Rubery, J., Earnshaw, J. and Marchington, M. (2004) 'Blurring the boundaries to the employment relationship: from single to multi-employer relationships', in M. Marchington, D. Grimshaw, J. Rubery and H. Willmott (eds), *Fragmenting Work: Blurring Organizational Boundaries and Disordering Hierarchies.* Oxford: Oxford University Press, pp. 63–87.

Watson, T. (2003) *Sociology, Work and Industry,* 4th edn. London: Routledge.

Participation and Involvement

> *Participation refers to 'influence in decision-making exerted through a process of interaction between workers and managers' (Wall and Lischeron, 1977: 38).*

Having influence or a degree of autonomy and control in one's job is frequently identified as an important contributor to workers' job satisfaction (see **Job Satisfaction**). Likewise, for management, involving employees in decisions potentially has a number of benefits: acquiring worker ideas and suggestions for improving the work process, gaining acceptance for organizational changes and stimulating greater trust and commitment, for example. However, while both workers and management may support participation and involvement, where there is more disagreement is over the extent of that participation: how much actual influence is to be shared by managers with their workforce.

Employee participation, and the increasingly common expression 'employee involvement', cover a range of activities that vary considerably. Marked variations are possible, for example, in the degree of participation, the range or scope of decisions subject to participation, the form that participation structures take, the organizational level(s) at which participation occurs and the purpose and outcomes of such activity. We will look briefly at each of these before considering management and employee perspectives in a little more detail, current patterns and trends in participation, together with future prospects.

THE NATURE OF PARTICIPATION

The *degree* of participation refers to the extent to which employees, or their representatives, influence organizational decision-making. Participatory activity can vary considerably and includes, at a minimum, receiving information from management, with no active involvement in the decision-making process; employees and/or their representatives having advisory or consultative powers, with management retaining authority over the final decision-making; jointly taking decisions; and, finally, employees having full control over decisions. Where this last situation exists, in most enterprises it is likely to be confined to areas of task arrangement, for example, craft workers controlling the way their craft is practised.

These differences in the degree of participation are also reflected in the variety of *forms* that employee participation can take. These range from briefing meetings to board-level representation, suggestion schemes to autonomous work groups. These different forms can also be classified in terms of whether they involve employees participating *directly* in discussions or participation is achieved *indirectly* via the election of representatives. Typically, much of the involvement or participation activity that occurs at the lowest levels of the organization – for example, team meetings to discuss the organization of individual tasks – involve employees directly, while participation in decisions away from the immediate work context more often involves indirect, representative forms of participation.

Variation also exists in the different *levels* at which participation occurs: within the immediate work setting or at departmental, workplace or company-wide levels, for example. A further source of variation lies in the *scope* of different participatory mechanisms, that is the range of decisions that employees or their representatives participate in. This scope may vary between task-level decisions such as work allocation, intermediate-level decisions such as changes in work organization and more distant-level decisions such as investment plans or major product changes.

The amount of participation occurring will be influenced by a variety of factors. These include the attitudes of the parties involved (particularly management's predisposition to employee participation); the level of experience among employees and their representatives to engage in participation; the nature of ownership and different organizational characteristics, including size and the degree to which decision-making is a centralized or decentralized activity; and the extent to which participation is based on statutory requirement (as is the case, for example, in Germany and Scandinavia) or voluntary agreement. In a landmark, 12-country study in the 1970s, the Industrial Democracy in Europe research group highlighted the importance of two factors in particular – statutory requirement and managerial attitudes – as the key factors explaining variations in levels of participation or industrial democracy between countries (IDE, 1981). Participation tended to be more extensive in those countries where it was not only underpinned by legislation (such as the German and Swedish Co-determination Acts) but also where managerial attitudes were more supportive of cooperation and openness in decision-making. Yet even in these countries the extent of employee influence and involvement in decisions was found to be fairly restricted and raises important questions about possible obstacles to the development of employee participation. We can explore these questions further by examining managerial and worker perspectives on participation in a little more detail (for more discussion of this and other issues arising from this discussion, see Blyton and Turnbull, 2004).

PERSPECTIVES ON PARTICIPATION

For managers, support for worker 'involvement' stems largely from the principles of Human Relations management, which draws attention to the importance of the social aspects of organization in general and the connection between, on the one hand, communication and consultation between management and workforce and, on the other, increased worker commitment, higher levels of job satisfaction and motivation and reduced resistance to change (see **Job Satisfaction** and **Motivation and Commitment**).

Management's advocacy of certain types of participation is an acknowledgement that employee commitment needs to be actively secured rather than passively assumed and that involving employees in decision-making is a means of achieving this. Management's support for (some forms of) participation also underlines the potential contribution of employee knowledge to the management of the organization – in particular, tapping valuable worker experience and benefiting from their suggestions regarding the way work tasks should be organized and performed.

However, management support is typically expressed for restricted forms of participation – advisory arrangements rather than where joint decision-making is involved. As Poole and Mansfield (1992: 207) conclude from a large-scale study of managers, 'Managers appear to support most employee involvement practices so long as these do not radically affect their control function within the firm.' This pattern is repeated in studies conducted elsewhere. Writing on the United States, for example, Freeman and Rogers (1999: 7) argue that managers are unwilling to share power and 'Many oppose programs that would keep them from making the final decisions about workplace governance.'

Turning to studies of employee attitudes towards participation, these generally point to a predisposition for greater involvement and participation, particularly in decisions with a direct bearing on their own jobs and working environment. While more direct participation is most frequently desired over these immediate-level decisions, surveys have revealed a weaker desire for participating in higher-level decision-making (such as over planning and investment) and a greater preference that any participation at this level should be effected through representatives rather than involving employees directly. In the Freeman and Rogers (1999) study, reasons cited for wanting more say included not only to improve the quality of their working lives, but also because many felt that it would make their organization more productive and successful.

THE EXTENT OF INDIRECT AND DIRECT INVOLVEMENT AND PARTICIPATION

Looking at the UK evidence, from the various workplace surveys and other studies that have been undertaken since the early 1980s, two contrasting trends are evident in relation to indirect and direct forms of employee participation and involvement:

- a decline in the coverage of indirect participation, particularly consultation arrangements;
- a growth in direct forms of communication and involvement between management and employees.

The proportion of workplaces with a joint consultation committee, and the proportion of employees covered by joint consultation machinery, have fallen significantly in the UK since the mid-1980s. In 2004, around one in seven workplaces had a functioning consultative committee compared with one in three in 1984 (Kersley et al., 2006). Consultative committees remain most common in larger establishments and in public-compared with private-sector establishments and were more than twice as likely to be present in workplaces where a union is recognized, compared with non-union workplaces. In respect of the activities of workplace consultation committees, in 2004, the most common issues for discussion were work organization issues, future plans, health and safety and training (ibid.: 129).

Though there has been an overall decline in coverage of consultation committees over the past two decades, the number of higher-level (that is, multi-workplace) committees in the UK has been more stable, reflecting partly the introduction of the European Works Council (EWC) Directive in the 1990s. In 2004, over one-quarter of workplaces belonging to a larger organization reported the existence of a higher-level consultative committee in their organization.

We may anticipate some recovery of workplace consultative arrangements in the UK following the full implementation of the European Commission's Information and Communication Directive (ICD) in 2008. The ICD sets out minimum requirements for employers in EU member states to consult with or inform employees on a range of issues, including the firm's economic situation, employment developments and work organization changes. The ICD is particularly significant for the UK, given the absence of statutory requirement before this time for consulting with employees (other than over certain specific issues such as redundancy). In other countries, such as Germany, the participation system based on works councils has been effective precisely because it is embedded in a broader statutory framework of participation and collective representation; works councils have been given sufficient statutory rights to maintain an independence from management; and for at least three decades many employers have shown a willingness to actively engage in workplace-based participation.

Turning to direct forms of employee involvement, these have increased in recent years, not only in the UK but also elsewhere. Marchington and Wilkinson (2000: 345) distinguish between two forms of direct communication: 'downward communication', where management inform staff about particular issues through written documents or face-to-face interaction, and 'upward problem-solving', which 'incorporates a range of techniques which are designed to tap into employee knowledge and ideas' (ibid.: 346). Clearly, the latter contains much more scope for employee participation than the different forms of downward communication.

Both downward and upward forms of direct communication have increased since the 1980s. For example, in relation to regular meetings between senior managers and all sections of the workforce, these were reported to be taking place in just over one-third (34 per cent) of UK workplaces in 1984, but almost four-fifths (79 per cent) of UK workplaces in 2004, while 'briefing groups' or 'team briefings' demonstrated a similar rise from just over one-third (36 per cent) of workplaces in 1984 to well over two-thirds (71 per cent) by 2004 (Kersley et al., 2006: 135).

FUTURE PROSPECTS FOR INVOLVEMENT
AND PARTICIPATION

Over a two-decade period of change, a general weakening of collective labour power – in particular, a decline in influence of trade unions and collective bargaining (see **Trade Unions** and **Collective Bargaining**) – has enabled management to shift the focus of participation away from joint decision-making towards those forms that are more advisory in nature and match more closely managers' own attitudes and orientations. Yet, while diminished labour power may explain the particular direction that participation has taken, a factor that now appears to be driving much of the current interest in employee involvement is the intensified levels of competition prevailing and, in particular, a managerial emphasis on the importance of achieving greater employee commitment. Thus, in the latest period, while labour market pressures have diminished, product market pressures have brought about a managerial reassessment of both the potential contribution of employees to quality improvement and the significance of employee commitment for overall productivity.

The continuing management need to secure active cooperation and employee contribution, together with the growth of various forms of downward communication and upward problem-solving machinery, point to the likelihood of forms of employee involvement and participation continuing to develop in coming years. The introduction of the Information and Consultation Directive in Europe, and the continued spread of teamworking practices, will reinforce this.

At the same time, a number of significant obstacles remain in the path of the general development of participation. Above all, in the vast majority of cases, organizations maintain an overriding emphasis on individual responsibility and accountability, top-down decisions and a strict adherence to a hierarchically ordered chain of command. These hierarchical structures and control-orientated practices do not easily lend themselves to responding to bottom-up ideas. As a result, organizational decision-making processes are often ill equipped to incorporate participatory activity. If senior and middle management are not fully supportive, insufficient space is likely to be incorporated into decision-making processes to allow effective consultation and participation to take place. The result, in many cases, is consultation taking place after rather than before decisions have been made, the exercise then becoming one of management selling decisions rather than consulting over them. This unwillingness to modify organizational structures is an additional factor encouraging the development of consultative rather than more far-reaching, joint decision-making forms of participation: the former can be accommodated into existing decision-making processes far more easily than the latter.

See also: *job design, perspectives on work, teamworking.*

REFERENCES

Blyton, P. and Turnbull, P. (2004) *The Dynamics of Employee Relations*, 3rd edn. Basingstoke: Palgrave Macmillan.

Freeman, R.B. and Rogers, I. (1999) *What Workers Want*. Ithaca, NY: Cornell University Press.

IDE (1981) *Industrial Democracy in Europe*. Oxford: Clarendon Press.

Kersley, B., Alpin, C., Forth, J., Bryson, A., Bewley, H., Dix, G. and Oxenbridge, S. (2006) *Inside the Workplace: Findings from the 2004 Employment Relations Survey*. Abingdon: Routledge.

Marchington, M. and Wilkinson, I. (2000) 'Direct participation', in S. Bach and K. Sisson (eds), *Personnel Management*, 3rd edn. Oxford: Blackwell, pp. 340–64.

Poole, M. and Mansfield, R. (1992) 'Managers' attitudes to human resource management: rhetoric and reality', in P. Blyton and P. Turnbull (eds), *Reassessing Human Resource Management*. London: Sage, pp. 200–14.

Wall, T.D. and Lischeron, J.A. (1977) *Worker Participation: A Critique of the Literature and Some Fresh Evidence*. Maidenhead: McGraw-Hill.

Pay and Performance

Pay here refers to the financial rewards deriving from work. Performance refers to the worker's productive output.

At the heart of 'work' is the price of labour and the wage–effort bargain, whereby workers sell their labour power in return for a wage or salary.

Thus, workers are paid, or remunerated, for the work they undertake and pay is seen as a central factor in motivating workers to perform in compliance with organizational objectives. When one starts to consider pay in any detail, however, issues of fairness, equality and social value come to the fore, as does the matter of conflict. While the saying 'a fair day's pay for a fair day's work' is often heard, the meaning of exactly what constitutes 'fair pay' may be open to dispute and different interpretations by management and workers (Hyman and Brough, 1975: 29).

We begin this discussion by defining and explaining the meaning of terms such as payment systems, payment structures, pay dispersion and pay determination. We then move on to examine current themes relating to pay, performance and equality. It should be noted that it is usual for weekly payments to be termed 'wages' and for monthly pay to be termed a 'salary', but when discussing the subject of pay it is also common for the term 'wage' to be used in a generic sense, to cover both wages and salaries, and this is the way the term will be used here.

PAYMENT SYSTEMS

The term 'payment system' is used to describe two interrelated aspects of pay: first, the guiding principles for the determination of a pay scheme, for example, the general level of pay and whether or not it is performance-related; and second, the administrative mechanisms that enable the payment system to function efficiently and effectively. Thus a payment 'system' may be defined as 'a set of rules and procedures which determines the size and kind of reward which will be received by a worker or group of workers' (Burchill, 1976: 71). In the current working environment, remuneration may take many different forms and encompass a wide range of benefits. For example, in addition to a basic wage, employers may also provide transport allowances or company cars, health insurance, pensions and sick pay schemes. It is therefore important to recognize that various benefits can come together to form a remuneration package for individual employees.

In broad terms, payment systems can be divided into two types depending on the extent to which pay is related to workers' input or output. Some payment systems are constructed around a fixed basic wage, relating primarily to the inputs a worker brings to the job, for example, the input of time or a level of skill. In contrast, where payment systems are based on the principle of 'payment by results', such as performance-related payment systems, these reflect measurable worker outputs and are underpinned by the premise that increased levels of effort on the part of the worker will yield a higher wage. We return to the issue of performance-related pay later.

THE DISPERSION AND DETERMINATION OF PAY

Within organizations, pay grading structures form hierarchies of wages and salaries for different types of jobs; these will be likely to reflect employees' status within the organization and varying levels of qualifications, experience, authority and responsibility. Different grades of pay will be ranged along a 'pay spine' and the gaps between levels of pay are termed 'pay differentials'. It may be the case that different categories of employees, for example managers and manual workers, will be on different pay spines and attract different benefits as part of their total remuneration package. The existence of pay differentials within an organization's pay system, and more generally across the wider labour market, is what is known as the dispersion of pay (Brown et al., 2003: 190–1).

Pay differentials within an organization will have a certain logic, in relation to employees' position in the organization's hierarchy. But there will also be differentials between workers in the external labour market that do not necessarily conform to the logic of the internal differentials. Some workers earn a great deal more than others and it is not necessarily the case that pay differentials reflect a situation where the highest earnings go to workers whose jobs are of the greatest value to society (Hyman and Brough, 1975: 31). Narrow pay differentials between the highest and lowest earners indicate a more equal distribution of pay within society; wide earnings gaps in contrast contribute to greater social inequality (Druker and White, 2000: 3). This is of concern when, particularly since the 1980s, many economies around the world are seeing pay dispersion between the highest and lowest earners widen.

Thus, questions of equality, fairness and social values are at the core of pay dispersion. For example, in some professions, such as teaching in the UK, there are nationally determined grading structures that are applied by different employers. In other areas of work, however, people performing similar jobs, but employed by different employers, can receive wide variations in pay. Thus there may be considerable pay dispersion between different organizations that is not reflective of the skill or expertise of the workers. There are also differentials in the earnings of particular groups within the labour market, such as women and workers from ethnic minorities, who generally earn less than their white, male counterparts (see **Discrimination**). This indicates factors that may influence the determination of wages, but before we consider how wages may be set, we need to explore some of the theories about why pay might be dispersed in this way.

Economists have put forward several reasons to explain the dispersion of pay. In terms of orthodox economic theory, the forces of supply and demand should establish a 'competitive wage' and the eventual reduction of pay dispersion for similar work. According to this argument, organizations paying more than the average rate of pay for particular jobs will be likely to make a loss, and those paying lower than that rate will be unable to recruit or retain staff; thus a 'competitive wage rate' would be achieved in particular labour markets. Another way of expressing this classical economic approach would be to say that a 'going rate' for particular forms of work is produced by prevailing economic conditions and forces of supply and demand in the labour market (White, 2000: 39).

In terms of classical labour market theory, wages are somehow beyond the control of either employers or workers and it is assumed that market forces will create an efficient distribution and allocation of labour between different organizations. So how does classical economic theory account for the existence of widening pay dispersion? The wage premium for higher levels of worker skills and ability is one classical explanation for a gap between high and low earners. In terms of pay dispersion for like work, however, it is suggested that this may be due to workers' imperfect knowledge of the wages available to them within the labour market: they take jobs for less than the competitive wage because they are not fully informed of what that rate might be. Alternatively, it is suggested that workers might have knowledge of labour market conditions, but accept less than the competitive wage, or 'going rate', because the employer offers other types of benefits as part of the remuneration package. But, in practice none of these explanations offers an entirely satisfactory explanation for significant differences in pay for similar work between different employers (Brown et al., 2003: 190–1). Therefore, we need to look at other possible explanations and these relate to the interaction of the external labour market with the circumstances of particular employers and organizations. First, we will consider conditions of monopsony; second, the 'insider–outsider' explanation for pay dispersion between employers; and third, the existence of an 'efficiency wage' in some organizations.

Monopsony exists where a single employer, or group of employers, have a monopoly of control over the demand for a particular type of labour within a region or locality and as a result can exercise a high degree of discretion over wage levels. To take an historical example, in many industrial villages in the South Wales valleys, coal mining was the only male occupation. In such conditions a single employer, or a coalition of employers within the same industry, could afford to pay less than the competitive wage without losing their workforce to competitors.

The second explanation for pay dispersion focuses on wage determination as a product of the interaction between the 'outsider' effect of supply and demand in the external labour market and the bargaining power of workers 'inside' a particular organization. This has been termed the 'insider–outsider' model. For example, if there are two organizations drawing labour from similar labour markets but paying different rates of pay, it may be the case that one workforce has some specific attribute or bargaining leverage that allows it to succeed in extracting a higher rate. This leverage might reflect a range of factors, but one possible influence might be whether or not a trade union is present: unionized workers may be able to extract a wage premium from their employer that cannot be achieved by workers without union representation. We will return to the role of unions in pay determination later (see also **Trade Unions**). In terms of the third explanation we consider for pay dispersion, the 'efficiency-wage' proposition, it is suggested that some firms will base decisions on wage setting on their ability to pay and may elect to pay above the competitive wage in an attempt to gain greater productivity from their workers. Thus pay is raised in the search for efficiency (Brown et al., 2003: 191–3).

In exploring the reasons for pay dispersion, we can see that the determination of pay, that is the process of setting of pay rates, may be the product of a complex interaction of factors operating in variable labour market conditions. This discussion also highlights the fact that, while we refer to *the* labour market, what we are really describing is activity in a collection of *different* labour markets. These relate to, among other things, specific localities, organizations and employment opportunities for particular areas of expertise, skills and categories of worker. Depending on the interaction of these factors, employers may have rather more or less power over pay determination. In recognition that the need for work may drive workers to accept well below a competitive wage, and that labour market conditions may allow employers to drive down wages to unacceptable 'lows', many countries around the world have legislated for a minimum wage (the UK, for example, introduced a National Minimum Wage in 1999). A further, non-statutory influence on the determination of pay may be the presence of a trade union and the relative bargaining strength of workers and their representatives in relation to the employer.

TRADE UNIONS AND PAY

Trade unions have traditionally sought to influence pay determination through collective bargaining in order to secure higher levels of remuneration for their members (see **Collective Bargaining**). The level of union density and coverage of collective bargaining have fallen in the UK and in many other countries around the world since the 1980s, though union density figures seem to be stabilizing in recent years (see **Trade Unions**). If we take the UK as an example of the implications this has for pay, we can see that collective bargaining remains an influential method of pay determination in the public sector, but there has been a clear shift in favour of managerial discretion in the determination of pay in the private sector (White, 2000: 31–3). In addition, a significant change in collective bargaining both in the UK and elsewhere, has been the decentralization of bargaining, which has effectively meant the demise of national or industry level agreements (ibid.: 36). Industry-wide agreements had some attractions for employers in the same industry because they effectively 'take wages out of competition' and were attractive for unions because industry-wide bargaining helped to control pay dispersion for similar work and establish a 'rate for the job' (Brown et al., 2003: 198–9). But as international competition has intensified, employers are more keen to exploit the particular circumstances of their business. The net effect is that unions have to find some foundation for bargaining leverage at the level of the enterprise or workplace. This can be difficult, particularly when negotiating with transnational companies, which can use the potent threat that they can move production to different labour markets where costs are cheaper (see **Globalization and Labour Migration**). The decentralization of bargaining and pay determination also highlights the trend for pay to be more focused on the individual worker as well as the individual workplace. This leads us into the final section of our review of pay, as we consider the ways pay may be related to individual performance.

PERFORMANCE-RELATED PAY

It is important to see any incentive payment scheme as part of the 'apparatus of management control' (Druker, 2000: 114). Since Taylor introduced his ideas on the scientific management of work, there has been a focus on relating pay to levels of individual worker effort, output and performance (see **Scientific Management**). Taylor favoured piece-work, or payment by results, as a motivator, where the volume of output of the individual worker was directly related to the wage he or she received. Piecework and similar early payment by results schemes were typically based on 'effort rating' where there existed a definition of 'standard effort' for a qualified operator in completion of a task. Such schemes were generally applied to manual workers, whose incentive was being able to increase earnings by increasing effort. While they offer considerable opportunities for managerial control, such systems can also be the focus of conflict and disruption in employment relations.

If we take piecework as an example, as well as using work-study techniques for establishing targets, there was inevitably an element of subjectivity and intuitive judgement involved on the part of managers responsible for setting targets. This offered scope for informal bargaining between individual workers, trade union representatives and managers over what constituted 'fair' targets and 'fair' pay for various levels of effort. The enormous potential for conflict and disruption this presented was often accommodated by informal arrangements between managers and workers. As a result, the controls of the piecework system could 'drift', so that work targets became slack, payments did not accurately reflect effort and managers felt they had lost control of the payment system (see Brown, 1973: 83–122). For this reason, many manual working environments sought other pay systems and means of motivating workers: for example, by removing the immediacy of payment by results and replacing it with a single pay spine or single-status payment systems for all classes of workers within the organization and using tools such as appraisal to motivate and inform employees about their performance.

Though they have declined in usage, payment by results systems continue to be a common feature of manual work and there is a continuing employer focus on performance-related pay for other categories of workers (Druker, 2000: 115). The rise of human resource management (HRM) has been accompanied by an increased focus on generating commitment and high performance, with some form of performance-related pay as a key element for managers and other types of employees. HRM assumes a causal link between pay, motivation and good performance, but this can be questioned, for, even if increased pay does lead to higher motivation, there may be factors preventing that being transformed into improved performance. For example, if a worker is simply overloaded with work, a monetary incentive may be incapable of increasing his or her level of performance; similarly, if the organization of work is poor, a single motivated employee may be unable to influence overall organizational performance.

In conclusion, pay is a core issue in work. The way it is organized says much about managerial control systems and the assumptions that are made about how workers are motivated and brought into line with organizational objectives. Payment systems may change but the debate over what constitutes a fair day's pay for a fair day's work remains a contentious issue.

See also: conflict, effort and intensity, motivation and commitment, power and authority.

REFERENCES

Brown, W. (1973) *Piecework Bargaining*. London: Heinemann Educational Books.

Brown, W., Marginson, P. and Walsh, J. (2003) 'The management of pay as the influence of collective bargaining diminishes', in P. Edwards (ed.), *Industrial Relations: Theory and Practice*, 2nd edn. Oxford: Blackwell, pp. 189–213.

Burchill, F. (1976) *Introduction to Payment Systems and Pay Structures with a Note on Productivity*. Buckingham: Open University Press.

Druker, J. (2000) 'Wages systems', in G. White and J. Druker (eds), *Reward Management: A Critical Text*. London: Routledge, pp. 106–25.

Druker, J. and White, G. (2000) 'Introduction: the context of reward management', in G. White and J. Druker (eds), *Reward Management: A Critical Text*. London: Routledge, pp. 1–24.

Hyman, R. and Brough, I. (1975) *Social Values and Industrial Relations: A Study of Fairness and Inequality*. Oxford: Basil Blackwell.

White, G. (2000) 'Determining pay', in G. White and J. Druker (eds), *Reward Management: A Critical Text*. London: Routledge, pp. 25–53.

pay and performance

> **Perspectives on work refers here to how people regard the nature of different interests in the employment relationship.**

'Perspective' is a term that may be used interchangeably with 'frame of reference' or 'ideology'. It describes a set of underpinning ideas and beliefs that informs an individual's assumptions about how society operates and influences their attitudes and behaviour. In terms of perspectives on work, our main focus is how people regard the nature of different interests and the distribution of power and control within the employment relationship. Three perspectives on work will be discussed: (1) the pluralist perspective; (2) the unitary perspective; and (3) the radical perspective.

THE PLURALIST PERSPECTIVE ON WORK

The pluralist perspective originates in an acknowledgement that, within capitalist systems, economic power is unevenly distributed. It follows that within the associated social and political systems there will exist different interest groups, each with distinct goals, beliefs and aspirations that may conflict with one another. In the context of work, perhaps the most basic example of the conflicting interests of employers and employees is the wage–effort bargain itself. Employees' desire to earn as much as possible might conflict with the economic interests of the employer or the organization's shareholders, who are mainly interested in the highest returns for their investment; in this respect their interests might be best served by maintaining lower rates of pay for employees.

Once conflicting interests are acknowledged, the question becomes, how to manage them? At the societal level, the state can either try to repress these different interests and impose its own definitive authority or it can engage in continuous processes of negotiation, concession and compromise, with the aim of accommodating the differing interests as harmoniously as possible. From the pluralist perspective, the latter solution is the only tenable one. Hence we have so-called plural societies, such as the UK, where the government tries to accommodate different interests through parliamentary democracy. When we turn to pluralism at the workplace, the principles are the same, though the context is narrower.

key concepts in work

Pluralism has a significant place in the history of British employment relations. It became the dominant perspective in Britain, particularly in the 1960s (see in particular, Fox, 1966). The fundamental principles underlying pluralism are that: the interests of workers and employers will at least partially conflict; workers have less power in the employment relationship than employers but this can be offset to a degree by collectively organizing into trade unions; and that conflicts of interest can be temporarily reconciled through processes of negotiation, accommodation and concession. We will look at each of these in a little more detail.

First, the pluralist perspective on work acknowledges that the different interest groups at the workplace will have either more or less scope to further those interests depending on their relative bargaining strength. For example, in securing concessions from employers, workers will seek to exert influence in the bargaining process, but an individual employee has far less economic power than his or her employer. Further, workers' interests in keeping their employment and increasing their wage may not accord with the interests of employers and shareholders in maximizing returns on investments. Conflict of interest is seen as inherent to the workplace, along with an imbalance of power favouring one side of the employment relationship (employers) more than the other. Thus the collective organization of employees by trade unions is seen as a valid mechanism for redressing this imbalance of power, as we discuss below. In this context, part of the role of management is therefore judged to be a mediating one, drawing together the interests of all parties through negotiation, leading to compromise and stable working relationships. There is an underlying assumption here that managers will act in the best interests of all, which radical critics of the pluralist perspective would judge to be a naïvely optimistic view of the reality of work as will be discussed later.

The pluralist perspective also acknowledges that management's functions and responsibilities (particularly to its shareholders), sometimes oblige it to act against the interests of employees. Fox and Flanders (1969: 159) were clear that 'power [would be] the crucial variable determining the outcome' of negotiations over conflicting interests. Therefore, the pluralist assumption is that collective bargaining, involving trade unions and employers, rather than individual bargaining between employers and individual employees, is the best method of facilitating concessions and compromise and of accommodating the diverse interests existing in a plural society (Fox, 1966: 371). Collective bargaining and negotiation offer a means of joint decision-making, facilitating fair concessions and compromise on the part of employers and employees and ensuring a measure of industrial democracy by allowing employees views to be voiced by their representatives.

perspectives on work

Thus the pluralist perspective understands conflict of interest to be an inherent part of the employment relationship. It regards collective representation as a means of mitigating the imbalance of power within the employment relationship. Collective bargaining is seen as the means to secure workable compromises on regulating the employment relationship and both resolving conflicting interests and establishing mutually beneficial working relationships for employers and employees. The dominance of pluralist thinking in the wider political context of the post-1945 period influenced managerial perspectives, assumptions and behaviours and saw collective representation and collective bargaining widely accepted as the norm for the resolution of conflict. This was to change, with the 1980s heralding a change in the political climate and the unitary perspective on work becoming pre-eminent.

THE UNITARY PERSPECTIVE ON WORK

The unitary frame of reference also has a political significance beyond the workplace. In essence, the unitary approach harks back to classical 'liberal' economic policies of the nineteenth century, which proposed 'the market' as the best mechanism for distributing society's resources; any interference in the free operation of the market was seen as both unwelcome and unnecessary. We need only consider the social deprivation that afflicted large sections of the population in those times to see that markets do not always operate for the benefit of all. But the agenda was refashioned in the 1980s, into what has become known as the 'neo-liberal' agenda. On the premise that, in the market for labour, individual workers are 'free' to sell their labour to employers, and that they are therefore free to leave work that is unrewarding or unsatisfying, it is held that neither trade unions nor governments should intervene in market processes. In the 'market-focused' environment of the 1980s and beyond (epitomized in the leaderships of Ronald Reagan and Margaret Thatcher), the unitary perspective came to dominate managerial thinking. For example, this perspective underpins the assumptions of human resource management (HRM) and continues to characterize much managerial teaching on methods and motivational techniques.

The unitary perspective centres on the pre-eminence of the individual's relationship with the employer and management's 'right to manage' and make decisions in the best interests of the organization and its employees. In contrast to the pluralist perspective's acknowledgement of different interest groups within every organization, the unitary perspective portrays the enterprise as a 'unified team pulling together for the common good' where 'management is the only legitimate source of authority, control and leadership' (Fox, 1985: 31). Put differently, while pluralism emphasizes the distinct interests held by employers and employees, the unitary perspective emphasizes their overriding common interest.

The assumption within this perspective is that management should be trusted as leaders who will safeguard the interests of employees. If an employer fails to do so, it is assumed that the long-term operation of the free market will right any short-term wrongs. For example, if the employer is not caring and the employee is not paid enough, the individual is in theory free to go to work elsewhere. Both pluralist and radical critics would say that this is an unrealistic view, as the freedom to leave a bad employer will depend upon there being a reasonable and acceptable alternative (see Cohen, 1988: 245). But from the unitary perspective, the logic is that such freedom does indeed exist.

What does the unitary perspective mean in practical terms? Perhaps its primary significance is that it underpins an assumption that managers will safeguard employees' interests without any interference from governments or other parties such as trade unions. Thus trade unions, rather than being regarded as having any sort of valid role to play (as in the pluralist perspective), are perceived as potential 'agitators of dissent', that may engage in stirring up discord where none would otherwise exist. Therefore, from this perspective, trade union representation is neither necessary, nor desirable, because conflict is regarded as pathological rather than inevitable within the employment relationship. If employees resist managerial logic, or take up opposing positions, they are judged to be acting against the interests of the 'team' and are probably best excluded from it – in other words, they may not be the sort of employees the organization wishes to continue to employ.

In summary, from the unitary perspective, it is the manager's role to 'lead', 'inform', 'consult' and 'educate', on the assumption that any apparent conflict of interest will disappear once managers explain to employees the reasons for their decisions. The unitary frame of reference may therefore underpin considerable managerial attention to informing and consulting with employees. But it is important to distinguish this from the processes of negotiation discussed under the heading of pluralism: consultation is a process of two-way communication where the final decision rests with the employer; this is unlike negotiation, which results in bargaining and joint decision-making between the parties (see **Participation and Involvement**). While there are powerful academic critiques of the unitary perspective (in particular, that it fails to reflect the realities of workers' interests or experience), its focus on harmony of purpose and the leadership role of managers has achieved significant acceptance and attention in managerial teaching and thought. It would therefore be a mistake to see the unitary perspective as a managerial preserve; much employer effort is devoted, through training and communication schemes, to persuading employees of the unitary view of the enterprise. Depending on the quality of these managerial initiatives and the degree of consistency between employers' rhetoric and the reality of workers' experience of their work, they may be more, or less, successful in their ideological aims.

THE RADICAL PERSPECTIVE ON WORK

The radical perspective springs from a wider, Marxist political viewpoint. It assumes that the workplace mirrors society and incorporates all of its inequities, contradictions and potential for conflicts of interest. In this, it is in accord with the pluralist perspective, but, unlike the pluralist frame of reference, the radical perspective sees the conflict of interests between employer and employee as irreconcilable (without the replacement of capitalism). This key factor sets the radical perspective apart from both the unitary and pluralist perspectives, which, despite their differences, both assume that 'stable and orderly relationships between employers and workers are normal and self-evidently desirable' (Hyman, 1975: ix).

Clegg (1979: 455) has argued that differences between the radical and pluralist perspectives relate more to the *attitude* towards conflict rather than the fundamental acknowledgement that it exists. But from the radical perspective, the pluralist focus on negotiation and accommodation neglects the central issue of 'whether the existing structure of ownership and control in industry is an inevitable source of conflict' (Hyman, 1975: 11). This issue lies is at the heart of the divergence between the pluralist and radical frames of reference. It has been argued that, in assuming that the imbalance in economic power at the heart of the employment relationship can be altered by trade union representation and collective bargaining, pluralism fails to take full account of the scale of the various power imbalances throughout society (Fox, 1985: 26–43). From the radical perspective, therefore, collective bargaining may indeed redress *some* of the imbalance of power from time to time but can never eradicate it because, compared with the power of capital, the workers' power is inevitably far weaker. In practice, the radical frame of reference is unlikely to inform managerial assumptions and behaviour, though it may influence some employees' attitudes towards the employment relationship and, hence, their potential for resisting managerial control and rejecting managerial ideology.

Overall, perspectives on work do not fashion reality, but influence our understanding and interpretation of it. The wider political context may have a considerable effect on the dominant managerial ideology or perspective on work. In turn, perspectives on work inform the behaviours and responses of the parties to the employment relationship.

See also: *collective bargaining, conflict, consent, labour process, management, trade unions.*

REFERENCES

Clegg, H.A. (1979) *The Changing System of Industrial Relations in Great Britain.* Oxford: Blackwell.

Cohen, G.A. (1988) *History, Labour, and Freedom: Themes from Marx* (reprinted 2003). Oxford: Oxford University Press.

Fox, A. (1966) 'Managerial ideology and labour relations', *British Journal of Industrial Relations,* 4 (3): 366–78.

Fox, A. (1985) *Man Mismanagement,* 2nd edn. London: Hutchinson.

Fox, A. and Flanders, A. (1969) 'The reform of collective bargaining: from Donovan to Durkheim', *British Journal of Industrial Relations,* 7 (2): 151–81.

Hyman, R. (1975) *Industrial Relations: A Marxist Introduction.* London: Macmillan.

Hyman, R. (2001) *Understanding European Trade Unionism: Between Market, Class and Society.* London: Sage.

Power and Authority

> *Power refers here to 'the capacity to pursue one's own interests' (Edwards, 2003: 13). Authority refers to 'the right to make decisions which must be accepted as binding' (Fox, 1971: 34).*

In this Key Concept we are concerned with power, authority and legitimacy in the working relationship. This leads us first to a consideration of managerial authority, which we discuss in the context of management's position within the organization, but our scope then widens to consider managerial power and legitimacy to enforce that authority, and employees' power to select a response to managerial control.

Power, authority and legitimacy are related but distinct concepts and in explaining one it helps us to understand the others. Thus, in the workplace, managers derive their authority from their superordinate position in the hierarchy, as agents of the employer, and will use their authority to control subordinate employees and workers. A clear way of visualizing 'authority' is that it does not preclude discussion or argument, but represents 'the right of the last word' (Simon, cited in Fox, 1971: 34). This brings us to the matter of power. The above definition of power, as the capability to enforce one's will, highlights its distinctive nature, for while authority may be determined by organizational structure, power is contingent upon different circumstances (Martin, 1988: 119). Finally, the existence of 'legitimacy' implies that those in subordinate positions recognize and accept the right of those in superordinate positions to exercise authority over them. Thus, in a work situation, where there is a sense of legitimacy attached to managerial authority, an employee willingly and voluntarily accepts managerial direction. In the absence of legitimacy, however, employees may not accept managers' claims for obedience and compliance with their decisions and may challenge managerial authority in order to pursue their own interests, either by individual or collective means. Their ability to do so will be influenced by their relative power relations with management, which will in turn be contingent on many different factors in the environment of work.

AUTHORITY

We have already associated authority with the right to the 'last word', but it is important to see authority as part of an ongoing relationship rather than as some sort of abstract concept invoked only as and when needed. Early managers derived their authority from their relationship with employers, whose power over property gave them their rights of control over the people who worked for them. In Britain, the exact position of managers and their authority to make rules and control resources on behalf of owners and employers was enshrined in an Act of Parliament (the Truck Act) in 1831. Thus the 'right to the last word' originated in the rights of ownership of capital and the means of production (Selznick, 1969: 63–6). But our understanding of authority is distinct from that of power, for as Fox (1971: 35) has argued, the essence of an authority relationship is its *voluntary* nature, as found, for example, in a worker's unforced acceptance of managerial decision-making and control. Such voluntary obedience to managerial rules requires that their authority is seen as *legitimate*. This is distinct from a straightforward power relationship where obedience may be forced, rather than given voluntarily.

However, the voluntary nature of authority relationships does not mean that they will not also incorporate sanctions designed to enforce desired norms of behaviour. The key thing in an authority relationship is that, because the source of authority is seen as legitimate and ideally founded on shared values, then disciplinary sanctions to enforce that authority are similarly legitimized, providing of course they are proportionate to the offence or transgression (Fox, 1971: 35–8).

THE LEGITIMATION OF AUTHORITY

There may be a variety of ways by which managerial authority is legitimized. Legitimization of managerial authority is fundamental to gaining 'consent' in the employment relationship (see **Consent**). Managers seek to establish and enforce norms of behaviour that accord with organizational objectives. Such norms are more likely to be accepted as legitimate by workers if they are founded on shared values about work and the specifics relating to the way the work is organized. For example, agreement over the notion of a 'fair day's pay' for a 'fair day's work' would form an important set of shared values underpinning managerial authority to impose sanctions on individual workers for failing to abide by work rules and norms of behaviour. Such shared values may be constructed around values within the working environment, but do not stop there. Values may also be cultivated in society, a good example being the 'work ethic' where the 'rightness' of being a good and hard worker is given social value and status. Thus the influence of society is also brought to bear on workers' expectations of what is reasonable and legitimate within the employment relationship. We can see such influences at work at both an individual and collective level. The current focus on communication and leadership in organizations, for example, emphasizes the quest to build shared values between managers and their individual employees, while the moves to cultivate partnership-style relations between managers and unions is an example of the legitimation of managerial authority by trade unions (see **Participation and Involvement** and **Trade Unions**).

POWER

Though power may, at least initially, underpin authority, by now it should be clear that they are not identical concepts. We have said that power is related to the ability to pursue one's own interests and this may be put into practice by individual or collective means. The individual worker is considerably disadvantaged in relation to the economic power of the employer, hence the collective organization of many workers into trade unions. The ability to oppose the actions of others is defined as 'reactive power', while the ability to pursue one's own interests or objectives is referred to as 'proactive power' (Edwards, 2003: 13). But all this may not be straightforward. As we have seen in the discussions on **Conflict** and **Consent** elsewhere in this volume, interests in the working relationship are rarely clearly defined in absolute terms; the 'structured antagonisms' (Edwards, 1986: 5–6) that are integral to work in the capitalist system exist side by side with impulses to cooperation.

Thus, as regards individual workers, their interests vis-à-vis the employer and management may change depending on the circumstances and vice versa. For example, working relationships comprise complex and shifting interdependencies between individuals and groups; power will ebb and flow within these interdependent relationships. The sources and manifestation of power may be witnessed in the distribution of organizational resources, which may be tangible, such as wages, or intangible, such as skills and knowledge. A change in the distribution of such resources may be brought about by a change in any number of contingencies, but an example would be the introduction of new technology. Such an innovation alters the distribution of knowledge and skill and we can see that this may have profound effects on the power of individual and groups of workers within an enterprise, particularly where job boundaries have been skill-related (Martin, 1988: 118–20; see also **Technology**).

It follows that power is not 'fixed' and is itself subject to change and the fact that power exists does not necessarily mean that it can or will be used. Power is 'embedded in continuing relationships' (Edwards, 2003: 13). Thus, for example, management might possess the power to force compliance with new rules, but may decide not to use that power because of a perceived risk of undermining the consent and legitimacy that lie at the heart of their broader authority. Also, it may be the case that awareness of the possession of power is limited and this inhibits the capacity to mobilize power into action. For example, workers may be overwhelmed by a sense of being power*less* in the face of the economic power of an organization, particularly where the organization of work isolates workers from one another: workers may become 'individualized' and have limited awareness of their collective power to resist managerial control and press for their own objectives (see Kelly, 1998: 11). There may also be a fear that the consequences of the use of power could have long-term implications for the well-being of the parties to the employment relationship, as in the case where managers use their economic power to secure worker compliance through the threat of sanctions such as dismissal, redundancy or discipline.

POWER AND AUTHORITY IN PRACTICE

Where authority is legitimized and managers' rules are complied with by workers out of a sense of consent and shared values, the quality of that compliance is very different from that which may be coerced from them by the exercise of power. Crucially, in an employment relationship characterized by the use of managerial power rather than legitimized authority, the coercive nature of the relationship may legitimize, in the eyes of the subordinate, alternative action to oppose that management power. Forced compliance may thus result in collective protest in the form of strikes or individualized protest in the form of absence, turnover and the like. Inevitably, the use of coercive power undermines authority (Fox, 1971: 38), but much will depend on the labour market, the level of unemployment and the influence of collective organization. We have seen that trade union power has declined (see **Trade Unions**) and workers' capacity to resist may be limited. In certain circumstances managers may in any case decide that the exercise of coercive power meets the needs of their organization. This might particularly be the case where the nature of the work process requires relatively little commitment to shared values. An example would be where the employing organization is engaged in producing goods or services at the cheaper, high-volume end of the market, where high automation and limited employee autonomy mean that low-skilled workers can easily and cheaply be sourced from the external labour market. In this case, management might take the view that the conflictual relations that ordinarily ensue from gaining compliance by coercion can be accommodated because the power of the workforce to resist in any collective sense is limited and labour turnover may be mitigated by a relatively easily sourced supply of replacement workers.

In contrast, with a growing focus on quality and customer satisfaction (see **Customers**), many organizations are actively seeking legitimation of managerial authority through shared values, in the quest for 'committed' rather than 'compliant' workers (see **Motivation and Commitment**). But in practice, within organizations it is rarely a case of power *or* authority that achieves organizational objectives. As with power, authority, once established, is not fixed for all time. Authority may relate to a constantly shifting set of relationships and interdependencies and may be characterized by various kinds of managerial initiatives, which would typically encompass communication, participation and involvement (see **Participation and Involvement**). The betrayal of shared values may undermine trust between workers and managers and could lead to a weakening of managerial authority. Alternatively, managers may conclude that they have to exercise power where their authority has failed in order to elicit the required response.

In sum, power and authority are linked but not identical concepts. The power of management originates in the rights of ownership of employers and is vested in managers. In order to exercise power in the most effective manner, it needs to be channelled through a system of authority, where the rights of managers to 'command' are legitimized by some level of shared understandings with the workers who are expected to 'obey' managerial authority over the organization of work.

See also: *the law and contract of employment, management.*

REFERENCES

Edwards, P. (1986) *Conflict at Work: A Materialist Analysis of Workplace Relations.* Oxford: Basil Blackwell.

Edwards, P. (2003) 'The employment relationship', in P. Edwards (ed.), *Industrial Relations: Theory and Practice*, 2nd edn. Oxford: Blackwell, pp. 1–36.

Fox, A. (1971) *A Sociology of Work in Industry.* Toronto: Collier-Macmillan.

Kelly, J. (1998) *Rethinking Industrial Relations: Mobilization, Collectivism and Long Waves.* London: Routledge.

Martin, R. (1988) 'Technical change and manual work', in D. Gallie (ed.), *Employment in Britain.* Oxford: Blackwell, pp. 102–27.

Selznick, P. (1969) *Law, Society and Industrial Justice.* New York: Russell Sage Foundation.

key concepts in work

Presenteeism

> *Presenteeism refers to 'the tendency to stay at work beyond the time needed for the effective performance of the job' (Simpson, 1998: 537).*

The expression 'presenteeism' derives from its opposite, absenteeism, or absence from work. Presenteeism is widespread. Almost one in five managers in Britain, for example, say that in the previous year they have worked more than 48 hours every week, according to the latest Workplace Employee Relations Survey (Kersley et al., 2006: 267). Long hours working is a significant contributor to the overall pattern of working time in the UK, where the average hours for full-time workers are the highest in Western Europe (see **Working Time**). As well as long work hours among full-time workers, presenteeism can be reflected in part-time workers remaining at work for significantly longer than their official hours and also workers attending work on days when reporting sick would have been more appropriate – what Aronsson et al. (2000) term 'sickness presenteeism'.

One of the main reasons that managers and others give for working long hours is simply to get through their workload. In general, increased employer and customer expectations, intensified competition and the extent of organizational restructuring – particularly where this entails substantial redundancies – have become associated with widespread increases in individual workloads (Simpson, 1998; see also **Effort and Intensity**).

LONG HOURS CULTURES

In addition to workload pressures, however, a growing number of studies point to other factors stimulating long hours working, particularly among professional and managerial groups. Of these, the primary one relates to the 'long hours cultures' prevailing in many work organizations. Senior managers appear to play a key role in establishing and maintaining these long working hours norms. If the senior position holders work long hours themselves, or did so while they were advancing within the organization, they frequently expect those working immediately under them to follow a similar pattern. Once the norm of working long hours is established, it becomes difficult for individuals to break this cultural expectation without being perceived as being less committed or less enthusiastic than their colleagues. Overall, long hours spent at work appear to be taken by many senior managers both as an indication of commitment and as a requirement for advancement to more senior levels (see **Organizational Culture**).

In her study of software engineers, Perlow (1999) quotes many employees who saw being present for long hours in the organization as necessary for promotion. As this author sums it up, 'Engineers perceived that the longer they worked, the more they were given credit for contributing' (ibid.: 69). This pattern is maintained despite Perlow's own findings – and supported by other studies (see for example, Rutherford, 2001) – that show these long hours are often far from productive. Not only may working long hours create fatigue and a lack of freshness in thinking but also, as Rutherford notes, for some managers at least, the knowledge that they are going to be spending the next 10 or 12 hours at work engenders a slower pace of activity throughout the whole period, particularly after the 'normal' work time finish of 5.30 or 6 p.m. Thus for many managers and others, being present at work for long hours each day may represent a way of conforming to organizational norms and a means of demonstrating commitment, more than a necessity for getting through a heavy workload.

At the same time, it is important to recognize that, for some people, working long hours will reflect the high level of personal interest, satisfaction and enjoyment that they derive from their jobs. If, for some, work life is more fun, more exciting and more challenging than life outside work, it would not be surprising to find these people spending long periods in the setting that generates those positive feelings. But for the majority of managers and others, it appears that the attractiveness of the job is not the major explanation for the long hours many of them work. In her survey of managers in two service organizations (an airline and a merchant bank), Rutherford (2001: 270) found that four out of every five managers said that their workload infringed upon their personal life. For these managers, the size of their workload and organizational norms about the hours that they should work, coupled with the perceived damage to position and career prospects of not being seen to put in the extra hours, represented much more important influences on their work pattern than any inherent love of the job.

ISSUES ARISING FROM PRESENTEEISM

Three broader issues are raised by the widespread prevalence of presenteeism. First, long work hours in general appear to be detrimental to health. Sparks and colleagues (1997), for example, concluded from an analysis of 21 studies that a small but significant relationship can be identified between poor physical and psychological health and longer work hours. A separate study of several thousand adults by Ferrie and Smith (1996) also found that those working 60 hours a week or more were twice as likely to report a depressed mood, compared to those working fewer hours.

Second, a number of writers have highlighted how a culture of presenteeism can act unfairly against women in organizations. Both Simpson (1998) and Rutherford (2001) note, for example, the particular difficulties faced by women managers operating within a long hours work culture. At the heart of these difficulties lies the continuing unequal distribution of domestic work and child-care responsibilities (see **Domestic Work**). The persistent pattern of women shouldering a disproportionate share of domestic tasks acts both to restrict their opportunities to spend longer hours at their paid work and also to make time available for their male partners to engage in longer work hours, if they choose. The women in Rutherford's (2001) study largely accepted the expectation of long hours working for holders of managerial positions. The main ways in which these women accommodated this expectation was by limiting their contact with their family to the beginning and end of the day and/or working at home late evening or very early morning to keep up with the job demands. It can also be argued (following Simpson, 1998) that many women's reduced presence at work late in the evening (because of their care responsibilities) could damage their chances of advancement in the organization in other ways. By having less opportunity to develop the informal relationships, networks and interactions that may stem from late working hours, women may miss out disproportionately on any benefit for career progression arising from those networks, compared to those who do not have to leave work to fulfil domestic commitments. There is, however, little evidence to date that the growing proportion of managers who are women is substantially reducing levels of presenteeism. For the moment, it seems more the case of women managers fitting in to long work hours cultures in order to demonstrate a commitment to the organization equal to that of their male counterparts.

A third issue arising from a culture of presenteeism is that it sits uncomfortably with the increased attention being given to establishing and maintaining an improved balance between work and non-work life (see **Work–life Balance**). Following from the above, the gendered nature of the domestic division of labour, particularly in the past, allowed long hours norms to develop in managerial groups formerly (and in many cases still) dominated by men. The persistence of these norms, however, exacerbates not only the problems highlighted above for women in managerial positions, but also acts to perpetuate assumptions about the nature of responsibility for domestic activities.

Any reduction in presenteeism practices in organizations will depend importantly on senior management's willingness to judge the commitment and contribution of their subordinates by the quality of the latter's output, rather than the quantity (in the form of extended work hours) of their input. One factor that may assist this is the small but growing number of organizations that are recognizing the deleterious effects of long hours working and are encouraging their employees to use their normal hours more effectively, rather than staying late at their desks.

See also: career, discrimination.

REFERENCES

Aronsson, G., Gustafsson, K. and Dallnes, M. (2000) 'Sick but still at work – an empirical study of sickness presenteeism', *Journal of Epidemiology and Community Health*, 54 (7): 502–9.

Ferrie, E. and Smith, K. (1996) *Parenting in the 1990s*. London: Family Policy Studies Centre.

Kersley, B., Alpin, C., Forth, J., Bryson, A., Bewley, H., Dix, G. and Oxenbridge, S. (2006) *Inside the Workplace: Findings from the 2004 Employment Relations Survey*. Abingdon: Routledge.

Perlow, L.A. (1999) 'The time famine: toward a sociology of work time', *Administrative Science Quarterly*, 44: 57–81.

Rutherford, S. (2001) '"Are you going home already?" The long hours culture, women managers and patriarchal closure', *Time and Society*, 10 (2/3): 259–76.

Simpson, R. (1998) 'Presenteeism, power and organizational change: long hours as a career barrier and the impact on the working lives of women managers', *British Journal of Management*, 9, Special Issue: S37–S50.

Sparks, K., Cooper, C., Fried, Y. and Shirom, A. (1997) 'The effects of hours of work on health: a meta-analytic review', *Journal of Occupational and Organizational Psychology*, 70: 391–408.

key concepts in work

Psychological Contracts

> *A psychological contract refers to 'an individual's belief in mutual obligations between that person and another party such as an employer'* (Rousseau and Tijoriwala, 1998: 679).

The term psychological contract was first coined in the 1960s to refer to expectations regarding the reciprocal obligations that comprise the relationship between employees and work organizations. The term rose to greater prominence in the 1990s, however, notably through the writing and research of Denise Rousseau (see, for example, Rousseau, 1995). In part, this recent attention reflects a heightened interest in the changing nature of employment relationships and, in particular, a perceived decline in the prospects for long-term careers with a single employer (see **Career**).

The notion of a psychological contract reflects the fact that formal economic contracts – specifying the main terms and conditions of employment (pay, hours, holidays and so on) – together with the main elements of formal job descriptions, do not cover all aspects of the employment relationship (see **The Law and Contract of Employment**). These other aspects importantly include various (and often implicit) beliefs, expectations and understandings held by both employers and employees about the nature of the employment relationship. For example, many employees hold a general belief that loyalty, hard work and a willingness to accept responsibilities in the workplace will be rewarded in due course by advancement within the organization, higher pay and/or greater job security. Likewise, employers may hold expectations about appropriate levels of employee commitment, motivation and flexibility that go beyond anything written down in job descriptions and contracts of employment. Thus, psychological contracts are perceptual in nature and based on beliefs that a contribution by one party will yield a future return (for example, employee loyalty and commitment yielding career advancement). In this way, beliefs that make up psychological contracts can act to reduce uncertainty by extending understandings about the employment relationship beyond the formal contract. Over time, the expectations comprising psychological contracts are likely to develop greater detail and elaboration. While new recruits need to seek out signals regarding the broader nature of the employment relationship, experienced employees are likely to have a much more developed sense of the dimensions of the psychological contract (for further discussion of the content of psychological contracts, see Herriot et al., 1997).

THE PROBLEMATIC NATURE OF PSYCHOLOGICAL CONTRACTS

At one level the meaning of the psychological contract appears clear, relating to the implicit aspects of the employment contract that extend and amplify what is agreed explicitly. At another level, however, various aspects of the concept of a psychological contract are problematic, potentially undermining its conceptual value, notwithstanding its increasing use in everyday language. Two of these aspects are particularly problematic. The first centres on the appropriateness of the term 'contract'. Because psychological contracts are largely implicit and unwritten, they rely on each party believing that the other shares the same understandings of the nature of the 'contract'. The unwritten nature of the contracts means that in important part they are based on trust. The idea of the shared nature of beliefs and understandings does not necessarily hold in practice. Indeed, it is more likely that the parties will differ, to some extent at least, in their understanding of the psychological contract. Each party, for example, may evaluate the other's responsibilities within that contract as greater than their own. This raises the question of whether or not it is appropriate to use the term 'contract' (psychological or otherwise) if it is not unambiguously based on agreed and shared understandings.

A second and more general problem, however, is whether it is reasonable to think of the employing organization as being party to the psychological contract. Most attention in the development of the concept has been given to employees and their beliefs and understandings, rather than establishing a clear employer perspective. Indeed, some writers on this subject emphasize that only employees maintain a sense of a psychological contract. The argument here is that employing organizations as such (as opposed to individual managers within those organizations) are unable to hold beliefs and expectations and thus are unable to establish a psychological contract. If this is the case, then the question returns as to whether it is reasonable to think in terms of a contract, which implies an agreement (implicit or explicit) between at least two parties. This issue remains unresolved and, for the time being, discussion is focused mainly on employees, while the employing organization is generally taken to be senior managers within that organization.

Yet, despite these unresolved issues, as we discuss below, the term nevertheless has utility and psychological contracts are widely seen as important factors influencing employee attitudes and behaviour.

THE INFLUENCE OF PSYCHOLOGICAL CONTRACTS

The influence of psychological contracts has been investigated particularly in relation to the effects on employees where they perceive that their psychological contract has been breached or violated. While violation is viewed by Rousseau (1995) as one party wilfully breaching or reneging on the psychological contract, other writers have adopted a more general view, referring to breaches as involving perceptions of unmet expectations. In principle, violations could equally be perpetrated by employers or employees; however, in practice most attention has been paid to situations where employees feel that their employer has violated the psychological contract. For example, Robinson and Rousseau (1994) report a longitudinal study of early career managers in the United States that found over half of those taking part reporting that their employer had, at some time, violated their psychological contract. The areas of work where perceived violation was most common related to training, development, pay and promotion. Those employees who felt that a violation of their psychological contract had occurred were found to be less likely to trust their employer, less satisfied with their job and less likely to remain with their employer compared with those who did not perceive that any violation of their psychological contract had taken place. This decline in trust and possible loss of valuable employees underline the potential consequences for organizations of being perceived as breaching the employee's psychological contract. One possible reason why such breaches may occur is if employers initially 'oversell' a job to attract recruits, thereby creating expectations it then does not, or can not, meet.

PSYCHOLOGICAL CONTRACTS AND THE NEW EMPLOYMENT RELATIONS

This issue of breaching the psychological contract has also been discussed in relation to the 'new employment relationship'. A common assertion is that contemporary organizations, due to intensifying competition and need for increased levels of flexibility, are no longer able to offer long-term job security to their employees (see Cappelli, 1999; see also **Flexibility**). For some commentators, this equates to a shift in the 'terms of trade' of the employment relationship that formerly rewarded employee commitment with job security (Osterman, 2000). Contemporary organizations, however, are increasingly seen to demand commitment from employees in return for simply having a job, rather than also being rewarded in addition by future job security.

If long-term job security becomes increasingly scarce (a prediction held by some, but questioned by others; see **Job Security**), then a question arises as to how this alters the nature of the psychological contract. One outcome may be that if employees come to expect to move jobs a number of times rather than develop their career with a single employer, then other potential elements of the psychological contract – such as access to training to improve skills and future employability – may take the place, at least partially, of job security. Another outcome may be that, if job security is removed or markedly reduced in psychological contracts in the future, then the significance of those contracts to employees could considerably diminish. In this case, the terms of the formal contract of employment are likely to become more important, particularly in regard to the financial rewards attaching to particular jobs, along with the work hours and other conditions of employment.

See also: *pay and performance.*

REFERENCES

Cappelli, P. (1999) 'Career jobs are dead', *California Management Review*, 42: 146–67.
Herriot, P., Manning, W.E.G. and Kidd, J.M. (1997) 'The content of the psychological contract', *British Journal of Management*, 8: 151–62.
Osterman, P. (2000) 'Work reorganization in an era of restructuring: trends in diffusion and effects on employee welfare', *Industrial and Labor Relations Review*, 53: 179–96.
Robinson, S.L. and Rousseau, D.M. (1994) 'Violating the psychological contract: not the exception but the norm', *Journal of Organizational Behavior*, 15: 245–59.
Rousseau, D.M. (1995) *Psychological Contracts in Organizations: Understanding Written and Unwritten Agreements*. Thousand Oaks, CA: Sage.
Rousseau, D.M. and Tijoriwala, S.A. (1998) 'Assessing psychological contracts: issues, alternatives and measures', *Journal of Organizational Behavior*, 19 (Special Issue): 679–95.

Redundancy

Redundancy is one way in which employers terminate an employee's contract. It can be voluntary (where the employee voluntarily agrees to leave) or compulsory. It is an event that many employees experience during their working lives, sometimes several times. Between 1990 and 2004 in the UK, for example, approaching eight million redundancies were announced. While redundancy is a major contributor to the inflow on to unemployment registers, unemployment is not necessarily the outcome of redundancy – some redundant employees move directly into another job.

In the UK, where a proposed redundancy involves a group of employees rather than individuals, the employer has a duty to consult in advance and this consultation should include consideration of avoiding or minimizing the redundancies and alleviating the consequences for those affected (Willey and Morris, 2003: 327). However, this duty is a far weaker obligation than exists in many other European countries such as France, Germany, Italy, the Netherlands and Spain, where employers are required to make a much stronger case for redundancies, to undertake detailed negotiations over redundancy and to make extensive provision for funding to alleviate the consequences of redundancy (through compensation, retraining and the financing of other social measures). An overall effect of these requirements on employers is that the social partners place much greater emphasis on avoiding, and seeking alternatives to redundancy, through measures such as early retirement, changes to working hours and job transfers. In the UK, in contrast, the law on redundancy is much weaker. Indeed, the UK's employment protection laws in respect to both individual dismissal and redundancy are among the weakest in Europe. In the UK, the employer determines the scale of redundancies and, provided the employer can show that proposed redundancies meet 'the needs of the business', this is likely to go unchallenged (Turnbull and Wass, 2000).

Redundancies have always been part of the experience of waged work. Embedded in the work contract is an assumption that the employer continues to carry out the activity that the employee was engaged to perform. When this activity diminishes or ceases, redundancy is one means of reducing the size of the workforce. Less extreme measures, where employers judge the shortage of work to be a short-term rather than a long-term phenomenon, include short-time working (where employees attend work for only part of the week) and temporary lay-off, where employees cease work for a limited period.

REDUNDANCY AND RESTRUCTURING

While redundancy has been a periodic experience, particularly for unskilled and semi-skilled manual workers, what has altered more recently have been the causes and timing of redundancy announcements and the range of occupational groups affected. The principal factor behind these changes is that in former times redundancies were associated with severe economic conditions: they occurred during business downturns or other severe difficulties, but were rare at other times. However, since the 1980s workforce reductions have become a common feature of all types of organization and in all economic circumstances. Firms now make workforce cuts when their business is doing badly *and* when it is doing well. In these circumstances – what has increasingly coming to be known as 'downsizing' (or less commonly 'rightsizing') – redundancy represents only one way of reducing labour totals (others include early retirement schemes, non-renewal of temporary contracts and natural wastage or attrition), but it is an important element. The main difference then, in what occurs in the contemporary economy compared to what prevailed hitherto is that downsizing – and redundancy – take place independently of the firm's current market position. Those firms that make cuts during periods of prosperity can be seen to be engaging in what Cascio (2005: 175) terms 'pre-emptive' downsizing, using a profitable period to reduce overheads and thereby seek to prepare for more difficult economic conditions in the future. One important purpose of downsizing is an attempt to send signals to the stock market (and thereby positively influence the share price) that the company is not being complacent but is actively seeking ways to further boost profitability.

Such downsizing has become increasingly common in the past 20 years. One estimate is that around two million workers a year in the United States are affected and countries such as China and several Eastern European countries have gone (and are still going) through extensive downsizing programmes as jobs are shed in former state-owned enterprises. The redundancies that form a major element in many downsizing and restructuring programmes illustrate the fundamental precariousness of the employment contract for employees (see **Job Security** and **The Law and Contract of Employment**).

Further, an important feature of recent patterns of redundancies is that groups that were formerly relatively immune from redundancy are increasingly being affected. White-collar and managerial jobs, whose holders in the past generally expected a high degree of security and career-long engagements, are now experiencing greater exposure to redundancy. Indeed, 'de-layering' and the flattening of organizational hierarchies have had a particular impact on supervisory and managerial-level positions that previously had suffered less from periodic waves of redundancy. In his analysis of UK redundancies for the period 1999–2003, Heap (2004: 198) reports that managers and senior officials had one of the higher redundancy rates among different occupations; other high-redundancy occupations were those working in skilled trades and machine operatives. More generally, Heap shows that men in this period were more likely to be made redundant than women and those aged under 24 years and over 50 years were more likely to be made redundant than their 25–49-year-old counterparts.

THE ORGANIZATIONAL IMPACT OF REDUNDANCY

Two questions that have led to a considerable amount of research are whether or not downsizing works as a means of boosting firms' performance and the related question how do those who survive the workforce cuts subsequently behave? Overall, on the first question, the evidence shows that downsizing does not represent a successful means of increasing profits or even share price. Reviewing several studies, Cascio (2005: 174) concludes that it is 'not possible for firms to "save" or "shrink" their way to prosperity'. Such downsizing activity tends to be successful for firms only when it is linked to a broader business plan.

The general absence of such a linkage is demonstrated by the tendency for large numbers of firms to engage in multiple rounds of downsizing as they make continued efforts to cut costs. Similarly, announcements of major workforce reductions may have an immediate impact on share price, but any boost to the price tends to be sustained only in those cases where there is clear evidence that the workforce cuts are part of a broader programme of organizational restructuring.

In terms of the second question, for downsizing to be a successful employer strategy, those remaining need to be both committed and productive. For this to be the case, however, several studies have pointed to the importance of how those remaining view the downsizing process that has taken place. What is crucial is that the process is judged to have been fair and equitable – in other words, that it demonstrates 'procedural justice'. Those remaining in the organization will tend to feel more secure if they perceive the workforce-reduction process to have been conducted fairly. The perception of procedural justice has been found to have a significant impact on levels of morale, trust, loyalty and commitment among those remaining.

Despite the evidence that downsizing activity has rarely resulted in the sought-after benefit of greater organizational success, its use is likely to continue, affecting a broadening range of employees, occupations and organizations. Downsizing and redundancy remain a relatively straightforward way of cutting costs as a response to more competitive conditions, at least outside those countries where strong legislation to circumscribe such employer activity exists. In the latter countries, limits on job cutting can be seen to force employers to consider longer-term strategic decisions about their competitive strategy and rely less on shorter-term, cost-reduction tactics. For an example of how this is illustrated in the international airline industry, with some companies responding to market changes by introducing cost-cutting measures such as redundancies, while others used more far-reaching organizational changes including the development of strategic alliances, see Turnbull et al. (2004).

More generally, however, as the scope for global production of goods and services expands, redundancies and downsizing in developed economies may become even more evident as firms locate more activities in lower-cost areas and outsource more activities in efforts to reduce their cost base. If downsizing activity increases in this way, it is likely that the scope for reductions by voluntary means is likely to diminish, making the experience of compulsory redundancy a more prominent feature of workforce-reduction measures in the future, and a growing experience for a widening range of employees.

See also: *flexibility, globalization and labour migration, psychological contracts, unemployment and underemployment.*

REFERENCES

Cascio, W.F. (2005) 'HRM and downsizing', in R.J. Burke and C.L. Cooper (eds), *Reinventing HRM: Challenges and New Directions*. London: Routledge, pp. 171–86.

Heap, D. (2004) 'Redundancies in the UK', *Labour Market Trends*, May: 195–201.

Turnbull, P. and Wass, V. (2000) 'Redundancy and the paradox of job insecurity', in E. Heery and J. Salmon (eds), *The Insecure Workforce*. London: Routledge, pp. 57–77.

Turnbull, P., Blyton, P. and Harvey, G. (2004) 'Cleared for take-off? Management–labour partnership in the European civil aviation industry', *European Journal of Industrial Relations*, 10 (3): 281–301.

Willey, B. and Morris, H. (2003) 'Regulating the employment relationship', in G. Hollinshead, P. Nicholls and S. Tailby (eds), *Employee Relations*, 2nd edn. Harlow: Pearson Education, pp. 302–39.

Scientific Management

> *Scientific management refers to the ideas developed by the engineer F.W. Taylor that centre on the notion that to raise the efficiency of work, tasks can be 'scientifically' analysed to establish the 'one best way' of performing them efficiently.*

Like many engineers before and since, Frederick Winslow Taylor (1856–1915) held a highly rationalistic view of work. At the heart of his approach to the organization of work was a view that contemporary management lacked control over the work process principally because it had not acquired the knowledge of how work could be organized 'scientifically'. Once this knowledge had been acquired and effectively applied, and other elements established to ensure that workers precisely carried out the tasks exactly as prescribed, Taylor saw the outcome in terms of substantial gains in efficiency and cost. His emphasis on applying scientific principles to the organization of work (what he termed 'scientific management' or sometimes 'task management') coincided with a period of substantial growth in the scale of industrial production, the degree of mechanization and the level of technical complexity in industrial firms. Each of these developments gave added significance to ideas promoting a more rational and managerially controlled organization of work (Rose, 1988).

Developing and promoting his ideas as a consultant and in a series of books (most notably, *The Principles of Scientific Management*, first published in 1911), Taylor had a substantial and lasting impact on the design of work, both in terms of influencing ideas about rational organization (an influence that can still be seen in many routinized operations today, on which more below) and in terms of stimulating alternative views about the effective organization of production and the motivation of employees. Together with Adam Smith, Henry Ford, Elton Mayo and only a handful of others, F.W. Taylor's name remains centrally associated with the analysis and development of work in industrial society.

TAYLOR'S STARTING POINT

Taylor's approach – or more accurately, his lifelong obsession – stemmed from his criticism of 'the defective systems of management' (Taylor, 1911: 15): his perception that management lacked both competence and control over the workforce to perform work efficiently. Skilled workers in particular were seen to enjoy considerable discretion over the pattern and speed of their work. Given Taylor's view that, left to their own devices, individual workers were inclined to be lazy and that work groups tended to establish easy-paced group norms over work effort and thereby restrict their output (practices of slow working he referred to respectively as individual and systematic 'soldiering'), this resulted in levels of output far below what Taylor judged to be achievable. This situation was seen to be particularly common where groups of workers were engaged in similar work and at a standard daily rate of pay (ibid.: 9). He estimated that the ending of soldiering would lead to a 'nearly doubling [of] the output of each man and each machine' (ibid.: 14).

His solution comprised a number of elements, centred on management acquiring detailed knowledge of the most 'scientific' way of organizing and performing tasks. This was to be achieved by the systematic analysis of tasks, involving first a careful examination of current work methods as employed by the best workers in a particular work group, followed by precise measurement of the most efficient way of performing the movements required to complete individual task elements. Central to establishing this 'one best way' was Taylor's development of time study to calculate the amount of time required to complete individual tasks and thereby establish a basis for exerting greater control over the way workers perform their work. This approach was seen as the basis for replacing old 'rule-of-thumb' methods of working with more 'scientific' methods (ibid.: 36).

Management was exhorted by Taylor to divide tasks into their smallest possible components (resulting in a high degree of repetition for the workers performing them) to facilitate not only more accurate timing of tasks but also to minimize the amount of training required to perform those tasks efficiently. From the analysis and timing of tasks, precise and systematic ways of undertaking the work were established that left no room for (what was seen as 'inefficient') employee discretion over how the task should be carried out. In this way, the planning of work was separated from its execution. Management was charged to undertake the former, workers the latter. Coupled with careful selection and training to fit the person to the job; close supervision to ensure that the tasks were performed as per the scientific analysis; attention paid to the length and spacing of rest breaks to maintain optimum performance; and the establishment of a payment system that directly linked output and reward, Taylor saw this system as the means to achieve greater managerial control over work processes and a more efficient organization of work.

TAYLOR'S ASSUMPTIONS ABOUT THE WORKFORCE

In the development of these ideas, Taylor held a number of assumptions about the workers performing the tasks. Two of these are particularly important. First, as noted earlier, Taylor assumed that workers, unless prevented or motivated otherwise, would seek to perform less than the maximum they were capable of. This was seen by Taylor to reflect not only a desire to 'take it easy' but also that by working slower, this would ensure that more work remained unfinished, thus generating continued employment. Second, Taylor viewed workers as motivated primarily by the payment they received and were less concerned about other issues such as having interesting work to perform or some control over how they carried out their work. Stemming from this view is not only the importance given by Taylor to incentive payments to achieve desired levels of performance, but also his expectation that the workforce would find fragmented and repetitive jobs, with little or no scope for variation or discretion, acceptable.

Thus, Taylor promoted a highly economic view of the worker, which acted to reduce the emphasis on the employee as a social actor within the workplace (an emphasis that was subsequently to be reasserted – (see **Human Relations**). Yet, despite this overwhelmingly economistic emphasis, there are in fact some positive (and generally ignored) social aspects to Taylor's ideas. Nyland (1995) points out that early in his work Taylor recognized the counter-productive tendency of very long work hours and their deleterious effect on fatigue and worker performance. In *The Principles of Scientific Management*, for example, Taylor quotes the case of women workers in a ball-bearing factory, where working hours (10½ hours per day) were too long for effective performance. When these daily work hours were reduced to 8½, and 10-minute rest breaks introduced every 1¼ hours, output per worker rose (Taylor, 1911: 86–92). More generally, Taylor asserted that under scientific management principles, the worker should not be

> called upon to work at a pace which would be injurious to his health. The task is always so regulated that the man who is well-suited to his job will thrive while working at this rate during a long term of years and grow happier and more prosperous, instead of being overworked. (ibid.: 39)

Later, similar ideas of reducing work hours in order to boost workers' productivity were taken up by Henry Ford who introduced the 40-hour week in his automobile company in 1926 (see **Fordism**).

Overall, Taylor was concerned with promoting a system based on scientific knowledge, in which workers' 'natural' instincts to limit their work effort would be overcome not only by the close supervision of rigidly designed tasks but also by a financial incentive system that rewarded efficient performance. Because this was based on a view of the worker as primarily motivated by monetary reward, Taylor saw this as acceptable to both parties: workers would gain improved financial rewards from their efficient performance of work tasks and management would gain cost savings through more efficient output. Within this picture, supervision is viewed as much in terms of ensuring that work is performed by the appropriate method as it is about monitoring work effort.

RECENT DEVELOPMENTS

More recently, there has been growing interest in the relevance of Taylorism to many service-sector activities. Areas that have been particularly considered include the work performed by those working in fast-food restaurants (where many of the tasks are automated and workers have very little discretion either over the operation of machines or the relationship with the customers) and the nature of work in the rapidly expanded call centre sector. For authors such as Bain et al. (2002), call centre work can indeed be characterized as Taylorized, exemplified not only in the ability of management to monitor employee performance, thereby reducing employee discretion significantly (a surveillance much facilitated by the communications technology used in call centres) but also in the widespread use of targets by management to measure and reward performance. As Bain et al., show, in call centres, these targets can be both extensive and diverse and can include not only quantitative targets (such as the number of calls processed, the average length of calls or – in sales environments – the proportion of calls converted to sales or total sales revenue achieved) but in addition a range of qualitative targets, often based on supervisors' evaluations of the nature of interaction with customers and the extent to which employees display desired attitudes, manners, friendliness and so on (see **Customers** and **Technology**).

CONCLUSION

Though it is more than a century since F.W. Taylor began developing his ideas of scientific management, many of the themes underpinning his views on the optimum organization of work remain significant. In practice, it has been rare for his principles of scientific management to be adopted comprehensively; nonetheless many of the individual elements have had a continuing importance. His emphasis on the importance of the division of labour, for example, and his support for incentive payments can be seen as influencing both subsequent developments in the specialization of work processes and a variety of 'payment by results' systems (see **Pay and Performance**). Taylor's approach also contributed to the rise of time and motion study within organizations and bolstered the role of works study engineers in the analysis, design and timing jobs (for a first-hand account of working in a work study department, see Jones, 2000). More generally, the subsequent development of Fordism as a form of work organization owes much to Taylor's earlier work. More recently, many of the ideas behind lean production also echo a number of considerations regarding efficiency first raised by Taylor. The recent application of Taylorist ideas to the analysis of service-sector activities such as call centre operations further underlines the continuing relevance of his ideas for interpreting contemporary work settings.

See also: *effort and intensity, job design, labour process, management.*

REFERENCES

Bain, P., Watson, A., Mulvey, G., Taylor, P. and Gall, G. (2002) 'Taylorism, targets and the pursuit of quality by call centre management', *New Technology, Work and Employment*, 17 (3): 170–85.

Jones, O. (2000) 'Scientific management, culture and control: a first-hand account of Taylorism in practice', *Human Relations*, 53 (5): 631–53.

Nyland, C. (1995) 'Taylorism and hours of work', *Journal of Management History*, 1 (2): 8–25.

Rose, M. (1988) *Industrial Behaviour*, 2nd edn. Harmondsworth: Penguin.

Taylor, F.W. (1911) *The Principles of Scientific Management* (reprinted in 1993). London: Routledge/Thoemmes Press.

Skill

> *Skill is proficiency at a given task, usually acquired through learning and experience.*

A number of factors have led to much greater attention being paid to skill in recent years. Politicians have identified increased skills in the labour force as a key contributor to economic growth. Researchers concerned with the impact of technological change have continued to question whether the consequences of such change is an overall upskilling or a downskilling of the labour force. Managers and others concerned with the issue of labour market flexibility have identified the significance of multiskilling – that is, the extent to which those proficient at one skill can be trained in additional skills to perform a broader role within the work organization. Finally, those addressing continued gender inequality in the labour market have identified the extent to which some skills – disproportionately ones performed by men – have been categorized as valuable, and rewarded accordingly, while other skills – more often carried out by women – have failed to be recognized as skills and have tended to be ignored and poorly rewarded.

Yet, despite all this attention, basic questions relating to skill remain unresolved. For example, at one level 'skill' appears to be a relatively simple concept, one capable of being captured in a straightforward definition such as the one at the start of this discussion, but further examination reveals the reality to be otherwise. As Attewell (1990: 422) comments, 'like so many common-sense concepts, skill proves on reflection to be a complex and ambiguous idea'. Different understandings of skill co-exist, which in turn lead to different interpretations of what is happening to skill in contemporary society. For our present discussion we can consider the issues by posing three broad questions: what are the different ways of defining skill; how can we measure skill; and how are skill levels changing within society?

DEFINING SKILL

As we have seen, the 'How can we define skill?' question can be answered at one level simply in terms of a proficiency or competence at a task. This positions skill as a property of the individual, normally acquired through some form of training in a particular field (in many cases leading to a specific qualification) and by accumulating sufficient experience to reach a competent level at the task in question. This view of skill, located in the individual, probably represents the most commonly held view of skill. However, this is not the only interpretation and two further approaches need to be considered. First, many writers and researchers on this subject locate skill in the requirements of particular jobs. The degree of complexity that a job contains, coupled with the amount of control over the job that the worker performing it has, are both regarded as central to gauging the extent to which the job (and, by extension, the person carrying out that job) can be defined as skilled. In this view, then, skill is seen to be more an attribute of the job than the worker.

In addition, a third approach is to view skill as a social process, the result of which is that some occupations are marked out as more skilled (and therefore more rewarded and with higher prestige) than others. This is the 'social constructionist' approach to skill, emphasizing the way that social processes act to define skill – processes that incidentally are seen to have operated to the advantage of some groups more than others. Integral to this argument is the identification of certain structures and actions that protect the position of some skill groups. The most direct way this is achieved is through processes of exclusion or social closure, whereby entry into a skilled group (and thus the size of the group itself) is restricted. This gives those within that group an added (monopoly) power in the market, which both increases the price of that group's labour and enhances its status. Methods of restriction may include lengthy periods of apprenticeship or qualification. Often the group itself, through a professional association for example, may act to restrict the proportion who qualify and pass into its privileged ranks. Such associations also monitor the activities of non-qualified workers to ensure that the monopoly power of the qualified group is maintained. Attewell (1990: 435–6) notes that this entry restriction may be further reinforced by processes of 'mystification' or keeping occupational practices and knowledge hidden. One means of achieving this is through the use of impenetrable jargon and other linguistic devices (ranging from doctors using complicated medical terminology to systems consultants using different forms of 'tekkie-speak'), which act to reinforce the impression that the skills of the group are highly complex and difficult to penetrate.

This social closure can be seen to occur at different levels within occupational hierarchies. Commonly, professional associations have undertaken such gatekeeper and policing roles for occupations such as lawyers and doctors, while trade unions (more so in the past than today) have acted in a similar way for various craft groups. Unions have utilized controls over apprenticeship, for example, and 'closed shop' arrangements (no longer legal in the UK, but still existing elsewhere) that require employers to contract only with union members for particular skills and occupations, to restrict competition from other workers.

As well as acting to favour some groups, and some skills, over others, it has also been recognized that processes of social closure have given primacy to occupations dominated by men, with the result that skills embedded in occupations where women predominate are frequently less highly valued and less well rewarded than comparable occupations where male workers are in the majority. More generally, the argument regarding gender bias in skill definition holds that much of the work that women perform has not been defined as skilled. This has been particularly true where women deploy social and domestic skills in their work, for example, in caring occupations. It is argued that skills used in these types of occupations are regarded (particularly by men) as coming 'naturally' to women, therefore not requiring additional training or justifying significant reward. More recently, a similar argument has been made in relation to emotional labour; again this type of work has been widely regarded as coming 'naturally' to women and generally not acknowledged as a significant skill in reward systems or status hierarchies (see **Emotional Labour**).

In terms of the social construction of skilled status, women are widely judged to have been less successful than their male counterparts in using professional associations, trade unions and other forms of collective power to ring-fence certain skills and thereby increase their exclusivity and the price those skills can command in the labour market. To a degree, the standing of skills in female-dominated occupations also reflects the influence of a 'male breadwinner' ideology, which has in the past given a greater primacy in the labour market to men, who are viewed as supporters of families, with women seen as secondary earners (Steinberg, 1990: 458) – an ideology that prevailed throughout much of the twentieth century (see **Employment Patterns** and **Work–life Balance**). Steinberg argues that this bias in favour of occupations undertaken more by men is also reflected in job-evaluation systems used to measure skills and apportion rewards within organizations. In such systems, skills that women disproportionately deploy – skills in areas such as communication, emotion work and caring activities – have tended to be overlooked or graded lower than other skills frequently found in jobs undertaken more by male workers.

To sum up the discussion so far, the study of skill and skilled groups needs in practice to take account of all three views on skill – the degree of individual proficiency, the scope in the task to exercise proficiency and control and the extent to which occupational power and social closure have produced skilled status. Where the different researchers on skill vary is the relative weight they attach to each of these elements, with some giving greater significance to the social determination of skill, while others prioritize the importance of work complexity or individual competence.

MEASURING SKILL

These different approaches to defining skill have implications for its measurement. In general, two approaches can be adopted: direct or indirect measurement of skill. The latter is increasingly evident particularly because of the difficulties involved in direct measurement methods. These difficulties with direct measurement are discussed in detail by Noon and Blyton (2007) and some examples of the problems will be sufficient here for our present discussion. First, agreement has to be reached at the outset of any direct measurement on whether what is being measured are the skills that the individual possesses or the skills they are currently using to carry out their job. A second issue is that very skilled individuals may perform tasks apparently automatically and without thinking. As a result, the skills they use may not be fully evident to the observer and thus go under-recorded.

For these and other reasons, indirect or proxy measures of skill have come to be more commonly used. The most frequent of these indirect measures is qualification, but using qualifications to represent an accurate measure of skill relies on two important assumptions. The first is that qualifications are closely linked to practising skills. However, this is not necessarily the case. For example, there is widespread evidence in the UK that many millions of people possess qualifications but work in jobs that do not require the skills that their qualifications relate to. Felstead et al. (2002), for example, estimated that over six million jobs in the UK require no qualifications but fewer than half of this number in the labour force have no qualifications.

The second assumption when using qualification as a measure of skill is that the bases on which qualifications are awarded remain fairly stable, but this too may be far from the case. As Grugulis et al. (2004) discuss, the nature of qualifications has been changing, with a tendency in the recent period to accredit a much wider range of 'skills' including what are sometimes termed 'soft skills' such as 'communication' and 'leadership' that formerly would have been seen as general attributes and not attracted qualification. Thus, by labelling a much greater range of characteristics and attributes as skills and accrediting them by qualifications of one form or another, the level of qualification and accreditation has risen. But the question remains whether this equates to an overall increase in skills or simply the certification of skills not previously formally recognized. The outcome has been a substantial increase in qualification, but this does not necessarily equate to an increase in the overall stock of skills held in the society.

WHAT IS HAPPENING TO SKILL LEVELS?

In the past, the pattern of skill development was debated mainly in terms of a single trajectory (Grugulis et al., 2004). Some saw this in terms of an overall 'upskilling': technological advances progressively removing the need for routine activities and creating a demand for higher-level, technical skills. Others, however, saw the link between technological change and skill as leading in the opposite direction: that the trend would be towards a progressive 'deskilling', with former craft skills and worker knowledge being increasingly built into technical equipment. This latter argument is particularly associated with the writing of Braverman (1974) and his argument that deskilling takes place in order for management to gain greater control over the labour process and be less reliant on the skills held within the workforce (see **Labour Process**).

Subsequently, however, empirical studies have tended to identify a more complex relationship between technological change and skill: that those already in possession of considerable skills tend to experience an increase in the demand for their skills, which gradually become more developed still, while those holding much fewer skills experience a reduced demand for their skills as work processes are developed that are less reliant on relatively low-level skills. This view thus maintains that a polarization of skills is taking place (Penn et al., 1994).

In terms of the future, this third, mixed picture of skill development is perhaps the most likely continuing outcome, with both winners and losers in the overall development of skill. What remains unclear, however, is the extent to which any polarization will be skewed – that is, will the upskilling element be dominant or the deskilling element? Further, a temporal dimension may also become more apparent if technological changes initially require new skills for implementation and development phases, but then, as applications become widespread, decrease the need for highly skilled workers. Any evaluation of skill development, however, will be further complicated if the basis of qualifications continues to expand.

See also: *discrimination, knowledge work, power and authority, technology, trade unions.*

skill

REFERENCES

Attewell, P. (1990) 'What is skill?', *Work and Occupations*, 17 (4): 422–48.

Braverman, H. (1974) *Labor and Monopoly Capital.* New York: Monthly Review Press.

Felstead, A., Gallie, D. and Green, F. (2002) *Work Skills in Britain 1986–2001.* London: Department for Education and Skills.

Grugulis, I., Warhurst, C. and Keep, E. (2004) 'What's happening to "skill"?', in C. Warhurst, I. Grugulis and E. Keep (eds), *The Skills That Matter.* Basingstoke: Palgrave Macmillan, pp. 1–18.

Noon, M. and Blyton, P. (2007) *The Realities of Work*, 3rd edn. Basingstoke: Palgrave Macmillan.

Penn, R., Rose, M. and Rubery, J. (1994) *Skill and Occupational Change.* Oxford: Oxford University Press.

Steinberg, R.J. (1990) 'Social construction of skill', *Work and Occupations*, 17 (4): 449–82.

Surviving Work

key concepts in work

> **Surviving work refers to the strategies that workers adopt to cope with jobs that are monotonous, pressured and/or unfulfilling.**

Some people are fortunate enough to have paid jobs that are varied and enjoyable, afford them considerable autonomy, are well rewarded and represent a continuing source of satisfaction and fulfilment. For these people, paid work is an agreeable and stimulating activity, providing a sense of accomplishment and self-worth. For others, however, their paid job is anything but a source of these things. It is something to be endured, relentless and often boring, demanding little or no skill, offering little control or discretion and yielding no sense of personal satisfaction. For people in jobs such as these, their paid work is a means to making ends meet in their non-work lives, but it offers little else. Individuals in such positions may be trapped in such jobs as a result of a lack of qualifications, experience or training or because their labour market participation is restricted – perhaps geographically if they have caring responsibilities in the locality or temporally if they can only work at certain times because of child-care or other demands or perhaps restricted psychologically if they fear breaking away from the (albeit unsatisfying) known and stepping into the unknown of a new job. Further, the experience of monotony and boredom is not the sole preserve of bad jobs. Even relatively good jobs – ones that are reasonably well paid and provide variety, satisfaction and a sense of achievement – have their less fulfilling sides; comparatively few jobs are interesting and rewarding all the time.

For those people in highly monotonous jobs, many of which also involve considerable work pressures, a key issue that faces them is getting through the working day: coping with the boredom and making the hours pass until they reach the time they can leave. Thus, for many in paid work, their experience is not one of job satisfaction, commitment and motivation, but rather one of survival. Survival strategies are important for both those people in very tedious jobs and those in highly pressured work environments, required to cope with prolonged work intensity and work pressure.

There are various strategies that employees can follow to assist them in getting through a monotonous working day. Many of the individual strategies are in one way or another related to securing a degree of control over the work situation: either physical control by modifying the job or the work context in some way or mental control over their thoughts and feelings while performing the job. Through different behaviours and attitudes, employees can seek to limit the extent to which they are subject to prescribed organizational behaviours and routines and thereby distance themselves to some extent and make the work regime more palatable.

PHYSICAL CONTROLS

One of the issues facing workers in monotonous and pressured jobs is how to break up the work routine: how to secure a measure of control over the work period or the work process, either to reduce the monotony or to gain a break from the work intensity. Interruptions to the work pattern can take various forms. One means of achieving this, for example, is for workers to temporarily absent themselves from work or to arrive at work late (or leave early) to shorten the working day (see **Absence and Turnover**). In those workplaces where attendance is still monitored by clocking equipment, late arrival or early departure may involve individuals being clocked in or out by others – an activity that persists despite it being grounds for dismissal in many organizations.

Within the working day, another common interruption strategy is to go 'walkabout': using some pretext to spend time away from the job and thereby break the work routine. Some jobs also allow workers to create additional informal breaks in their work by speeding up the work task, thus creating time before the next spell of work needs to be started. Mars (1982) categorizes these as 'linear' jobs; for instance, a delivery driver completing a job faster than scheduled in order to create a break before the next delivery is due. Other jobs, however, are less amenable to generating such breaks. Mars identifies 'cyclical' activities involving short repetitive tasks (such as a check-out operator or box packer) where opportunities for informal breaks may be limited. In such contexts, an alternative way of exercising some time control may be for workers to surreptitiously reduce the pace at which they are completing the work routine.

Another means of creating pauses in the formal work process is to perform other, informal activities during the working day. Examples highlighted by studies in the past have typically included workers manufacturing personal items during work time or taking items into work that needed repairing and using the employer's equipment to undertake the work. More recently, a common way in which people engage in other activities is through personal use of their work computers to play games or search the Internet for information, products and services. Where their job requires workers to sit behind a computer screen for long periods, then in many instances this alternative activity can be undertaken relatively covertly, as it requires no movement away from the office or workstation. Further, it is not only those workers subject to the greatest routinization that pursue such activities. In a detailed study of 30 managers working across a range of sectors, D'Abate (2005) found that the vast majority of her respondents admitted to pursuing a large number of home- or leisure-related activities during work time. These ranged widely from Internet surfing to taking part in betting syndicates and included making personal phone calls, reading novels, paying bills and writing personal e-mails. Of the different reasons given for pursuing these activities, boredom, long work hours and the need for a break from work obligations were the most common explanations, as well as others such as the convenience of having the telephone/computer available and to free up time away from work.

A more extreme activity to gain a degree of control over the work process is represented by workers sabotaging tools and equipment. Sabotage can take many forms and these in turn may reflect a variety of factors and causes (see also **Conflict**). One explanation, however, is that, in some situations, disabling tools and equipment will create interruptions in the work routine (for example, while the equipment is being repaired) or at least slow the work rhythm down.

MENTAL CONTROLS

In some situations, the scope for imposing any physical control over the length of the working period, or the pace of the work process, may be highly restricted. For example, in supervised assembly-line activities, where the shift period and any breaks are controlled and signalled by bells or buzzers indicating the start and finish of work periods, workers may have little access to altering either the timing or pace of their work. In these situations, workers may be more likely to respond to monotony or work pressures by exercising a psychological or mental control over their work situation, pursuing thoughts and feelings not connected with the job that they are doing. Indeed, probably the most common survival strategy to cope with a boring work process is to escape into one's own thoughts – 'switching off' and performing the work in an automatic and unconscious way. Various studies report workers recounting the importance of switching off – for example, flight attendants on long-haul flights working on 'automatic' as a way of coping with a long and demanding work shift (see Hochschild, 1983). This involves performing the physical and emotional labour required but with reduced mental engagement with the activities (see **Emotional Labour**). Similarly, individuals working on assembly-line production may be able to hold prolonged conversations or daydream while continuing to perform repetitive jobs.

Another way of mentally switching off from the pressures of work is through the use of humour to create an alternative narrative in the workplace. Jokes and banter serve to diminish the immediacy of work demands. As we discuss elsewhere, such behaviours can also act to secure for management a broader compliance with the overall work process as they are means of 'letting off steam' while essentially consenting to the overall work process (see **Consent**; see also Noon and Blyton, 2007, for a more detailed examination of survival strategies).

Overall, survival strategies are widespread and represent important means by which workers get through their working day. They illustrate too the limits of managerial control: however tight the supervision or surveillance system, however much the importance of commitment, performance and customer service is emphasized, workers in monotonous or otherwise unsatisfactory work situations will find some scope for developing survival strategies. Many of these strategies are covert, making it more difficult for management to control effectively. Yet, at the same time, these strategies represent ways in which work routines are maintained and work pressures accommodated by those subject to them.

See also: *alienation, working time.*

REFERENCES

D'Abate, C.P. (2005) 'Working hard or hardly working: a study of individuals engaging in personal business on the job', *Human Relations*, 58 (8): 1009–32.

Hochschild, A.R. (1983) *The Managed Heart: Commercialization of Human Feeling.* Berkeley, CA: University of California Press.

Mars, G. (1982) *Cheats at Work: An Anthropology of Workplace Crime.* London: Allen & Unwin.

Noon, M. and Blyton, P. (2007) *The Realities of Work*, 3rd edn. Basingstoke: Palgrave Macmillan.

Teamworking

Teamworking refers to groups of workers working together in a recognized team, either engaged in activities producing goods or services or in specific problem-solving or decision-making tasks. Production or service teams are often headed by a team leader either selected by management or chosen by team members.

EARLY DEVELOPMENTS

Recognition of the importance of groups within work organizations dates back at least as far as the Hawthorne Studies in the United States in the 1930s; in many respects the current wave of interest in teamworking is the latest manifestation of that recognition (see **Human Relations**). In giving greater prominence to the importance of the work group, the human relations researchers highlighted the shortcomings of the purely economic view of the worker and gave greater recognition to the importance of social factors and social relations within the work-force. This recognition was developed further by researchers at the Tavistock Institute in the UK in the 1950s, who identified not only the significance of the work group to productive activity, but also the importance of combining social factors and technology in the creation of effective work organization. The influence of this 'sociotechnical' view of the Tavistock researchers gained greater purchase outside the UK, particularly in Scandinavia, where industry examples in the 1960s and 1970s, most notably in Volvo, underlined the potential for work teams to operate with a considerable degree of autonomy, which in turn contributed to higher levels of job satisfaction. The significance of group working or teamworking was seen to lie in its influence on the attitudes and experiences of individuals belonging to the team; the increased level of shared decision-making and autonomy; and engagement in tasks that offered greater variety and represented a more meaningful job than typifies many individualized work roles. The effects of this greater sense of involvement and fulfilment were seen to translate into higher levels of satisfaction, motivation and commitment.

TEAMWORKING AND PERFORMANCE

In the latest wave of interest in developing work teams, this form of organization is widely identified as contributing to enhanced worker performance. For some advocates of teamworking, this is seen to be an outcome of a more positive work experience; a result of improved coordination and communication within the team; a reflection of greater shared knowledge among team members; and/or a consequence of a closer identification with the outputs of the team. In general, the performance of the whole (the team) is seen to be greater than the sum of its parts (individual workers).

This is a plausible explanation of why teamworking should enhance performance but it is one that is challenged, particularly by some sociologists. This counter-argument maintains that, in reality, teamworking operates very differently from its portrayal as autonomous and knowledgeable group working. This alternative view contends that various aspects of team operations – team structures, team leaders, team targets and group bonuses, for example – act as both forms of control on worker behaviour and ways to increase worker output. Thus, any enhanced performance is seen to be more due to an intensification of work associated with teamworking than an outcome of autonomous working by more motivated and involved employees (Batt and Doellgast, 2005). This view emphasizes the pressures of both not being seen to let the team down and contributing to the team meeting its targets, achieving its bonus and so on.

In important respects, this critical view of teamworking is an extension of discussions on control and the labour process (see **Labour Process**). It focuses on management's need to not only exercise control but also secure additional, discretionary labour from its workforce. This discretionary labour is seen to be captured through teamworking – teams acting to increase the work effort of the team members. In this view, teams represent the latest means of controlling the worker, where peer pressure from fellow team members adds to other managerial controls to increase the level of work intensification. This perception of teamworking and peer pressure is expected to be the case particularly where reward structures and workloads are affected by individual activity levels within the teams. For this view, therefore, teamworking has a 'dark side' of surveillance, peer pressure and self-exploitation, which augments broader management controls of work behaviour.

So, is teamworking self-actualization or self-exploitation, autonomy or peer surveillance? In practice, the answer is not a simple or clear-cut one, for what is increasingly evident is that teams demonstrate enormous variation in their origins, role, structure and the contexts in which they operate. These in turn have important implications for both worker and managerial outcomes (Benders and Van Hootegem, 1999). It is structural and contextual factors such as these that need to be taken into account when assessing how working in a team influences both the individual's experience of work and their productive activity. We can explore these issues in more detail by examining the recent rise in the use of teamworking, the factors underpinning that rise and the evidence of the outcomes from different forms of teamworking.

THE SCALE OF TEAMWORKING

In recent workplace surveys, substantial numbers of organizations claim that some or all of their employees are organized into formally designated teams. The latest national survey of UK workplaces, for example, found that approaching three-quarters (72 per cent) reported the existence of work teams among core employees in their establishment (Kersley et al., 2006: 89). Similar surveys in North America have also underlined the widespread use of teamworking. On closer inspection, it is evident that what constitutes a work team is open to broad definition – in the UK survey, only a very small proportion (around 4 per cent) of workplaces were operating fully autonomous work teams (for example, teams in which the members were able to choose their own team leaders and could jointly decide how the work was to be done). Nevertheless, it is evident that the use of some form of team organization has become very widespread in both manufacturing and service sectors, especially in larger workplaces, with teams typically bearing responsibility for specific products or services, where team members' jobs are interdependent and where tasks are rotated among members of the team.

The coincidence of several factors helps to account for this recent popularity of teamworking. First, group working or teamworking was identified in the 1980s as an important element in successful Japanese organizations such as Toyota. Both production work teams and particularly off-line teams concerned with quality issues were seen to be important for maximizing employee contribution to the continuous improvement of operating procedures (or *kaizen*). Second, teamworking fits well with other management priorities for more flexible working and the achievement of 'leaner' organizations through downsizing and reducing the number of hierarchical levels ('de-layering'). By devolving more responsibilities to production and service delivery teams, this potentially provides scope for reductions in supervisory and other first-line managerial levels; likewise job rotation in teams provides a vehicle for the further development of flexibility. Third, the emphasis on team structures fits well with management calls for greater partnership, commitment and identification with the organization – calls that have become more prominent in the recent period. The expression 'team' implicitly conveys a unitarist notion of collaboration and a sense of working together towards a common purpose (see **Perspectives on Work**). In this regard, teamworking has been identified as an essential component in the development of 'high-performance work systems', contributing to increased involvement of employees in work-related decisions that in turn is seen to encourage higher levels of trust and commitment and improved performance (Appelbaum et al., 2000; see also **Participation and Involvement**).

LIMITATIONS ON THE DEVELOPMENT OF TEAMWORKING

However, there are other factors that have acted to restrict the development of teamworking, particularly in its more extensive form. Fully developed teamworking, where team members enjoy considerable autonomy within their work area, requires not only a substantial investment by management in training to enable team members to operate interchangeably, but also a devolution of influence to shop-floor levels to give teams significant decision-making powers over areas such as work allocation, targets, recruitment and training requirements. What this devolution of authority challenges is the long-established practices of hierarchical control exercised by management. In practice, however, management has in general shown little willingness or commitment to devolving the powers necessary to allow teamworking to develop fully (see **Power and Authority**). Exceptions to this appear to be comparatively rare and, if present initially, appear rarely to be sustained.

What is more common is a significant devolution of *responsibilities* to teams for tasks such as production, monitoring, inspection and maintenance, but without any equivalent devolution of decision-making *powers*. This limitation on the development of teamworking is exacerbated in those situations where teamworking has been introduced within an employment relations context characterized by low trust. Claims for a new, high-trust, team-based relationship have fewer chances of succeeding in workplace contexts where trust has previously been largely absent. An additional problem for the further development of teamworking is that some work processes are less conducive to team organization than others. Where tasks are geographically dispersed, for example, or where there is a low level of interconnection between jobs, the scope for teamworking is reduced. Such factors help to account for the finding that, while work team structures have become widespread, fully developed teams remain comparatively rare (Procter and Mueller, 2000).

As regards the outcomes from teamworking and whether or not teams contribute to enhanced performance by jobs becoming more fulfilling or more intensified, in practice, both factors may help to explain the association between teamworking and performance. In a series of studies of teamworking in the iron and steel industry, for example, Bacon and Blyton found that workers moving from former work structures into teams reported an increase in variety in their jobs and a greater scope to influence decisions; but they also found themselves working harder, resulting in increased levels of physical and particularly mental fatigue (Bacon and Blyton, 2000). In terms of outcomes for organizations, these authors found that all forms of teamworking were associated with reported improvements in various aspects of performance (plant competitiveness, levels of customer care and product quality). However, this association was significantly stronger where more developed teamworking structures were in place (what these authors term 'high road' teamworking) than where more restricted, 'low road' teamworking was operating (ibid.).

In many ways, teamworking delivers a number of desired goals for management: providing a vehicle for the devolution of responsibilities, greater flexibility and a stronger identification among employees with their work activity. Yet, without sufficient management commitment to teamworking – a commitment that translates into adequate training and a devolving of power as well as responsibility to teams – the impact of teamworking on employees and their performance is likely to remain restricted. In many work settings this restricted impact is evident and in turn reflects a continuing dilemma for management in its relationship with employees: a desire to both exercise control over worker activity and yet at the same time secure the additional worker effort that is more likely to result from giving greater control to employee groups. For the time being, management's widespread unwillingness to cede significant influence to the shop-or office floor will continue to impede the full potential of teamworking from being realized.

See also: *effort and intensity, flexibility, job design.*

REFERENCES

Appelbaum, E., Bailey, T., Berg, P. and Kalleberg, A. (2000) *Manufacturing Advantage*. Ithaca, NY: Cornell University/ILR Press.

Bacon, N. and Blyton, P. (2000) 'High road and low road teamworking: perceptions of management rationales and organizational and human resource outcomes', *Human Relations*, 53 (11): 1425–58.

Batt, R. and Doellgast, V. (2005) 'Groups, teams and the division of labour: interdisciplinary perspectives on the organization of work', in S. Ackroyd, R. Batt, P. Thompson and P.S. Tolbert (eds), *The Oxford Handbook of Work and Organization*. Oxford: Oxford University Press, pp. 138–61.

Benders, J. and Van Hootegem, G. (1999) 'Teams and their context: moving the team discussion beyond existing dichotomies', *Journal of Management Studies*, 36 (5): 609–28.

Kersley, B., Alpin, C., Forth, J., Bryson, A., Bewley, H., Dix, G. and Oxenbridge, S. (2006) *Inside the Workplace: Findings from the 2004 Employment Relations Survey.* Abingdon: Routledge.

Procter, S. and Mueller, F. (eds) (2000) *Teamworking.* Basingstoke: Macmillan.

Technology

Technology can be defined in a narrower and a broader way. In its narrower use, technology refers to the equipment and techniques involved in the work process – the hardware and the software of different work systems. In its broader sense, technology can mean the overall 'way of doing things', encapsulating both the narrower definition and broader understandings of how work is organized: it can even refer to the overall pattern of social and economic development.

As the above definition indicates, the different usages and levels of definition of technology signify that the relationship between technology and work is a multilayered one. At its broadest, the character of the dominant technology contributes importantly to shaping the nature of society. The shift from an agrarian to an industrial, and a post-industrial, society is essentially a discussion about developments in technology. At each of these different stages of development, the nature of the prevailing technology impacts on most other aspects of life – what sectors are expanding or contracting, where work is located, what skills are required or becoming redundant (for a full discussion of perspectives on technology, see Grint and Woolgar, 1997).

Given this widespread impact, it is not surprising that issues relating to technology are pertinent to many of the discussions contained in this volume. The purpose of the present entry then is to give an overview of how technology is seen to impact on work and how the thinking on this has changed over time. In addition, one of the issues currently attracting much attention is the extent to which changes in technology have altered the amount that worker behaviour is monitored and how much it is subject to different forms of surveillance by management.

THE IMPACT OF TECHNOLOGY ON WORK

Over a long period, researchers have asked questions about the impact that technological change has had on jobs. Examples of this have included if some technologies are associated with greater levels of worker alienation than others and if technological change has positive or negative implications for the overall level of skills in society. The former is particularly linked with the arguments of Robert Blauner (1964) and is examined elsewhere (see **Alienation**). Two points from Blauner worth reiterating here, however, are, first, that some technologies – assembly-line technologies in particular – were seen to be more alienating than others (particularly craft-based technologies) and, second, that further technological development was viewed in a positive way, in particular that more automated technologies were potentially less alienating compared to machine-minding and assembly-line activities.

In terms of the impact of technology on skill, again this is dealt with in more detail elsewhere (see **Labour Process** and **Skill**). However, in summary, while some have viewed technological change as having a positive impact on skills – generating a demand for new skills – others (particularly, Braverman, 1974) have argued that technological change results in workers' skills being increasingly embedded in automated machinery, resulting in a reduced reliance on workers' skills and knowledge and an overall 'deskilling' of the labour force.

Other writers have focused more explicitly on intervening variables in the relationship between technology and jobs. An early example of this was the work of researchers at the Tavistock Institute concerned with the interrelationship of the social and technical aspects of work (Rose, 1988). This 'sociotechnical' approach emphasized the degree to which technological change would have different outcomes in different situations, as those outcomes would be influenced by different social factors, including the nature of the work groups affected. This view has developed further in more recent times, with greater recognition being given to the influences of different parties on the choice, development and implementation of new technologies. As Smith (1992: 753) puts it, 'technological change involves a process of choice and negotiation which, within certain constraints, offers scope for managers, unions and workforces to play a significant role in determining whether change occurs and, if it does, in its implementation and outcomes'.

In this way, the relationship between technology and work is increasingly recognized as being an indeterminate one: as much a political process within the organization as a technological one, involving choices, influence and decisions by managers and others. The upshot is that the introduction of identical equipment and processes can have very different implications in different contexts.

In the past generation the major technological developments have involved microelectronics. Quoting Smith (ibid.: 754) again on the distinctive characteristics of microelectronics, 'when incorporated into computing and information systems [microelectronic technology] radically increases their processing power, speed, reliability and flexibility, while decreasing both cost and size'. In practice, the range of applications for microelectronic technologies has proved enormous. Indeed, so great has been its versatility that from the outset a debate arose as to the long-term implications for levels of employment: whether this new technology would be associated with an overall growth or decline in employment. Many early predictions were that large numbers of jobs would be lost as a result of the labour-saving potential of new technology. In practice, many of these predictions have proved both over-pessimistic and over-determinist in nature. The impact of microelectronic technologies on jobs is influenced by various factors, including the prevailing economic climate, the economic conditions within the organization at the time of the change, the precise nature of the technology involved and the nature of the implementation process, including the role and influence of different parties within that process.

What is more apparent in some contexts is that new technology has had a significant impact on pre-existing job boundaries, with former discrete jobs becoming merged as a result of the power and range of the technological change. This is evident, for example, in various office environments where the introduction of computing and word-processing equipment acted to undermine previous job demarcations between typing, filing and other clerical activities. Likewise, in an industry such as newspaper production, the potential for journalists to word process their copy and then directly input this into electronically generated page composition, has undermined previous distinctions in the industry between journalists, compositors and printers.

Not only have some jobs been combined as a result of new technology, but there are indications that, for some, work may have become more intensified as a result. In his study of changes in reported work pressure for example, Green (2004) found that those more likely to report work pressure were disproportionately people whose jobs involved working with computers (for further discussion, see **Effort and Intensity**). In addition, developments in information and communications technology (laptops, mobile phones and so on) have increased the portability of many work activities, enabling workers to remain in contact with the employing organization and continue performing work tasks while physically away from the workplace. Among other issues this raises (and discussed in more detail elsewhere) is the continued – and in some cases growing – prevalence of long hours working among some groups and the implications for non-work life (see **Presenteeism, Working Time**, and **Work–life Balance**).

TECHNOLOGY AND CONTROL

One issue in this area that has generated considerable debate is if workers are subject to increased monitoring and surveillance as a consequence of new technology and whether or not this results in a reduced level of worker autonomy than was the case hitherto. It is certainly apparent that much new technology increases management's capacity for monitoring workers' behaviour. Centralized computer systems, for example, can record what time individual employees log on and off the system, how many key strokes are made by word-processing or data-entry workers, the level of usage of barcode readers, the amount of waste created or the time that particular machines are 'down' or off-line. Similarly, computerized telephone systems used in call centres and elsewhere can record various data on each workstation concerning, for example, the number and length of calls completed, speed of pick-up, length of breaks between calls and so on. The linked nature of the telephone systems also allows supervisors to listen in to calls between staff and customers as part of the monitoring activity.

For some commentators, these capabilities represent a much increased degree of surveillance and management control, on both the shop- and office floor. Several other perspectives need to be noted, however. For example, various researchers have focused not on increased surveillance but on the ability of workers to resist and cope with the level of control by adopting counter-strategies, such as call centre workers gaining short breaks by putting customers 'on hold'. Such studies further underline the point that employees are not simply

technology

the passive recipients of a technology but also capable of influencing how the technology is utilized.

Another perspective in the technology and control discussion is represented by those who identify technology as creating more, rather than less, discretion. One example here would be where technology allows workers the choice to conduct some of their work from home rather than needing to be always present at the workplace (for further discussion, see **Teleworking**). Finally, as Button et al. (2003) point out, those highlighting the surveillance capability of new technology may be overestimating its importance for the organizations investing in the technology. In many instances, they argue, this investment will be driven by market and other factors, rather than issues of labour control. The upshot, comment Button and colleagues, is that, while these technologies may embody greater potential for individual performance measurement, this will often be of such secondary importance as to not be utilized by management. Overall, this final perspective points to the potential dangers of assuming too great a significance for labour issues in overall managerial decision-making.

In summary, it is clear that technology plays a key role in influencing the nature and experience of work, as well as representing a central aspect of a society's overall pattern of economic development. As consideration of the relationship between technology and work has extended, the inadequacy of some of the arguments about the impact of technology on work have become more apparent. More suitable appear to be those that recognize the indeterminate and negotiated character of technological change and the potential influence of a range of variables affecting the nature of that change, its process of implementation and its outcomes.

See also: job design, knowledge work, redundancy.

REFERENCES

Blauner, R. (1964) *Alienation and Freedom*. Chicago: University of Chicago Press.

Braverman, H. (1974) *Labor and Monopoly Capital*. New York: Monthly Review Press.

Button, G., Mason, D. and Sharrock, W. (2003) 'Disempowerment and resistance in the print industry? Reactions to surveillance-capable technology', *New Technology, Work and Employment*, 18 (1): 50–61.

Green, F. (2004) 'Why has work effort become more intense?', *Industrial Relations*, 43 (4): 709–41.

Grint, K. and Woolgar, S. (1997) *The Machine at Work: Technology, Work and Organization*. Oxford: Polity Press.

Rose, M. (1988) *Industrial Behaviour*, 2nd edn. Harmondsworth: Penguin.

Smith, A.E. (1992) 'The nature of technological change: its implications for work and labour regulation', *Relations Industrielles*, 47 (4): 752–76.

Teleworking

> *Teleworking involves employment away from a central workplace, usually at home, and entails working and communicating via telephone and/or computer.*

ADVANTAGES AND DRAWBACKS OF TELEWORKING

Teleworking has attracted growing attention over the past two decades. Advances in computer and telecommunications technology have increased the potential for a widening range of functions to be conducted remotely. Work that is most suitable for teleworking includes tasks that involve analysing and communicating information; that can be conducted without extensive face-to-face interaction or require team-based activity; and where the work pace can be subject to individual control. Examples of tasks commonly carried out by teleworkers include word processing, accounting and software development. The term 'teleworking' has now generally superseded a variety of earlier expressions to denote this development in work arrangements, such as 'telecommuting' and the 'telecottage'.

Early on, a number of potential advantages of this practice were identified for individuals, organizations and society. For individuals, potential benefits include reduced time spent in commuting and greater flexibility over work and non-work time, as well greater job autonomy more generally. For organizations, the main potential benefits of teleworking were seen to be greater worker productivity as a consequence of lower levels of interruption and disturbance, as well as reduced costs of office overheads and accommodation. For society, teleworking was seen to offer potential benefits such as: reducing demand for office space; a means of contributing to greater work–life balance among its citizens; a way of reducing air pollution and traffic congestion from less commuting; a potential for increasing employment opportunities in rural areas; and a means to facilitate more employment opportunities for disabled and other groups who could find working from home easier than in many work environments.

At the same time, a number of possible drawbacks of teleworking have been noted. For individuals, potential disadvantages could include a greater sense of social isolation and increased levels of conflict between work and home spheres that are less clearly distinct under teleworking arrangements (see for example, Hill et al., 1998). There is the possibility too that a lower visibility within the work organization could hinder chances of advancement and contribute to the output of those working remotely being less recognized than that undertaken by their workplace-based colleagues. For organizations, several potential drawbacks of teleworking have been identified, including possible greater difficulties in supervising teleworking employees and in maintaining a corporate culture and organizational cohesion where some employees are working remotely. Overall, teleworking involves a greater degree of trust between employer and employee than is necessary when employer and employee are in direct physical contact (see Bailey and Kurland, 2002; and Daniels et al., 2001, for further review of possible advantages and disadvantages of teleworking for different interest groups).

Several factors have so far hindered a full assessment of these potential benefits and costs. These include a lack of precision over what constitutes telework (compared to more general forms of homeworking, for example) and the fact that, in practice, the teleworking community is highly diverse. In particular, while for some teleworking is a full-time arrangement, for others it represents something they practise occasionally, perhaps for a few days each month. Further, while a considerable amount of teleworking involves working at home, for some groups such as some maintenance engineers, who work mainly in different client organizations and are linked back to their employing organization via information and communication technologies, teleworking is a more mobile activity.

A series of more specific factors have also restricted a thorough assessment of the impact of teleworking on individuals and organizations. For example, while there is much anecdotal evidence that a move to teleworking is associated with increased productivity (see, for example,

Tietze et al., 2006), most of the findings reported on this are drawn from self-report data (that is, people reporting that they are more productive when working at home than in the office), rather than the result of more objective measurements of productivity. As Bailey and Kurlund (2002) point out, however, because the majority of teleworkers volunteer or request to work at home, their self-reports may be biased in favour of claiming productivity gains from the change.

An important factor in assessing the potential advantages and particularly disadvantages of teleworking is likely to be how frequently employees telework. Any negative impacts on individuals and organizations, for example, such as feelings of social isolation, organizational 'invisibility' and any issues of supervision and control, are likely to be significantly greater among those teleworking on a permanent basis compared with those who telework only occasionally. In studies so far conducted, however, the frequency of teleworking has not been adequately accounted for. If anything, the discussion has assumed that the norm of teleworking is a full-time arrangement, whereas for a substantial proportion, teleworking is a periodic activity.

THE SCALE OF TELEWORKING

In 2001, there were an estimated 2.2 million teleworkers in the UK, comprising over 7 per cent of the total in employment (Hotopp, 2002). This number increased rapidly in the late 1990s and is expected to continue growing. Overall, EU countries appear to have a lower level of teleworking than the United States, though precise comparisons are hindered by some variation in what activities are included in any measures of teleworking. Studies in North America and Europe both show, however, that teleworking is mainly concentrated in service-sector activities and is rare in manufacturing contexts.

In the UK, two-thirds of teleworkers are men and many are self-employed (in the UK, over two in five teleworkers are self-employed, compared to just over one in ten of the labour force as a whole). Around three-quarters of teleworkers are employed in the private sector, particularly in professional, managerial and technical occupations. While a proportion of teleworkers are engaged in clerical work, overall it appears it is occupations that have greater organizational power – such as specialized professionals – successfully securing the right to telework from home for part of their time to a greater extent than less powerful occupational groups such as clerical support staff.

THE FUTURE OF TELEWORKING

While teleworking is expected to grow further in coming years, the extent of this future growth is far from certain. On the one hand, there is evidence of a widespread reluctance among management to adopt teleworking. Many managers seem to perceive little need or advantage accruing to teleworking that would justify or outweigh any actual or perceived costs (Bailey and Kurlund, 2002: 388). Yet, on the other hand, continued increases in workload and work pressure may well mean that a greater proportion of employees seek to work away from the office for short periods in order to benefit from spells of reduced interruption. In our own case, for example, the reason why we worked on Key Concept entries such as this one on our computers at home, rather than in the office at work, was to try to achieve a better wording for the entries than would probably have been the case if we were working at the university and subject to a higher level of disturbance. At the same time, we have frequently to be in touch with the university because of normal student and other matters that arise daily.

If it proves to be the case that the general growth in workplace pressures and other factors mean that the scale of teleworking increases further, then a number of consequences may be foreseen. First, as a growing proportion of employees become absent from the workplace for short periods, those left in the office may find themselves dealing with a greater number of enquiries, due to the 'invisibility' of their teleworking colleagues (see Tietze et al., 2006). The upshot, for those who are able, may be a further increase in teleworking as more and more seek refuge from the pressures of the office. 'If office-bound colleagues, overburdened by teleworking peers, subsequently seek escape to the home to catch up with their own work, teleworking might prove a self-reinforcing phenomenon' (Bailey and Kurland, 2002: 393).

While the above quotation suggests a progressive spread of teleworking, as we noted above, to date, teleworking tends to have been available disproportionately to some groups in organizations more than others: to the more powerful occupational groups compared to the less powerful. The effect of a further growth of teleworking among some groups, therefore, may be an increasingly negative perception of teleworking among other groups of staff (those for whom teleworking is not available), with consequent potential implications for the latter group's work pressures, morale and overall levels of organizational cohesion. 'The practice of teleworking might cause mounting frustration among a support staff unable to relieve its stress with occasional days away from an ever more hectic office' (ibid.).

Thus, as in several other entries included in this volume, in some contexts at least, teleworking represents a further potential way in which work-related advantages – better pay and higher levels of autonomy and flexibility, for example – are unevenly distributed (and becoming more so) within the organizational hierarchy, further reinforcing and deepening the difference in the experience of work for different occupational groups.

See also: *domestic work, effort and intensity, flexibility, labour process, technology, work–life balance.*

REFERENCES

Bailey, D.E. and Kurlund, N.B. (2002) 'A review of telework research: findings, new directions and lessons for the study of modern work', *Journal of Organizational Behavior*, 23: 383–400.

Daniels, K., Lamond, D. and Standen, P. (2001) 'Teleworking: frameworks for organizational research', *Journal of Management Studies*, 38 (8): 1151–85.

Hill, E.J., Miller, B.C., Weiner, S.P. and Colihan, J. (1998) 'Influences of the virtual office on aspects of work and work–life balance', *Personnel Psychology*, 51: 667–83.

Hotopp, U. (2002) 'Teleworking in the UK', *Labour Market Trends*, 110 (6): 311–18.

Tietze, S., Musson, G. and Scurry, T. (2006) 'Improving services, balancing lives? A multiple stakeholder perspective on the work–life balance discourse', in P. Blyton, B. Blunsdon, K. Reed and A. Dastmalchian (eds), *Work-Life Integration: International Perspectives on the Balancing of Multiple Roles*. Basingstoke: Palgrave Macmillan, pp. 180–95.

teleworking

Trade Unions

> *A trade union is an independent, voluntary, collective association of workers whose purpose is to represent and advance its members' interests in relations with their employer.*

We begin this examination of trade unions with a brief review of union theory and structure and consider the methods and aspirations of trade unionism before moving on to explore current and future challenges facing unions.

TRADE UNIONS: THEORY AND STRUCTURE

The existence of trade unions constitutes a recognition that employees have interests that are distinct from those of the employer. If each party held all interests in common, there would be no need for employees to seek separate representation, for employer action would always be consistent with employee interests. However, as discussed elsewhere (see **Perspectives on Work**), it is evident that while in several areas the interests of employees and the employer broadly coincide (both parties, for example, are likely to value the organization surviving and prospering), in other areas, such as the distribution of rewards between shareholders, executives and the workforce, management and workforce are likely to hold distinctly different interests. There may also be differences in perspective on procedural issues such as how much influence employees should have in decision-making in the organization. Thus, in both substantive and procedural aspects of the employment relationship, trade unions act as a source of collective employee representation.

The formation of trade unions also signals a recognition that not only are the interests of employers and employees distinct, but that individual workers, in isolation, have fewer power resources than employers with which to defend and promote their interests, a lack that can be at least partially offset by combining with other workers into a trade union (see **Power and Authority**).

Trade union influence thus rests on its claim to represent large numbers of employees. More specifically, trade union power relies on either significant breadth or depth of its membership. On the former, some trade unions claim power by their sheer size, representing workers in a broad range of activities. These have traditionally been referred to as general unions (such as the Transport and General Workers' Union in the UK). In contrast, other unions seek influence on the basis of a much more specific membership, such as a single occupation. By seeking to organize everyone working in a particular occupation, this gives a union a distinct representational advantage in that the employer has no alternative source of labour other than those who are also members of the occupational union. In many countries, these more specific unions were the first types of union to become established, followed later by more general unions.

One of the key foundations of most trade union organization is that it is based fundamentally on democratic principles, such as members electing their local representatives and national elected officers and appointed officials being answerable to the membership (or their representatives) through regular national conferences where general union policies are determined. In this structure, the role of the local workplace representative is pivotal, particularly in terms of membership recruitment and communication between individual members and the union organization. Various studies have shown that presence of a trade union representative significantly influences an individual's willingness to join: one of the most common reasons given by non-members for not joining is 'I haven't been asked to join'. Studies in the UK, Australia and elsewhere have shown that where a union representative is present and where he or she devotes a significant amount of time to union activities, he or she is more likely to have recruited new members.

However, presence of a union representative is only one factor influencing employees' decision to join a union. Other factors include whether or not work colleagues are union members and if the employer accepts the union's representative role within the organization (known as granting union recognition). We will return to this latter issue in the final section, where we look to the future challenges for trade unionism. First, we consider the actual methods by which trade unions have sought to achieve their aims and objectives.

TRADE UNION METHODS

Trade unions were founded on aspirations for the betterment of the lives of working men and women, and in pursuit of these aspirations unions established certain methods. This subsection will explain these methods by reference back to a classic study of trade unionism written by two nineteenth-century British social historians – Sidney and Beatrice Webb (1897). In their work we find comprehensive accounts and explanations of the theory, structure and methods of trade unionism. Their analysis was based on Britain but the matters they discussed are applicable to trade unionism in the wider sense and, by looking back at this historical analysis, we can more easily locate the actions and aspirations of the trade unions of today.

In the earliest days of union organization, unions represented a threat that employers generally wished to eliminate or avoid, for they posed a challenge to the status quo in emerging capitalist society. The essence of this challenge was that trade unions sought to increase the price of labour and improve the working conditions of their members. In that sense, then, as now, unions aimed to secure better working conditions and a higher price for labour than a worker might be able to secure in a purely individual bargain with the employer. To accomplish this, early trade unions employed three main methods: mutual insurance, legal enactment and collective bargaining. We will look briefly at each of these methods in turn.

The labour market works on competition between workers for jobs; if there is a worker or a group of workers who will work for less money, or generally lower terms and conditions than the norm for an occupation, then it is likely that the employer will be able to progressively drive down the 'price' of labour. The essence of trade unionism is that workers unite in solidarity for the good of all, so that union members refused to undercut one another or take a lower rate of pay in order to gain employment. To this end, early British unions, which were organized in the main around crafts or 'trades', established a system of 'mutual insurance'. This constituted a fund, created from the contributions of members, to be used for two types of financial benefit: 'friendly' benefits and 'out of work' benefits. The former were paid out of the union funds to members in circumstances of injury, death or hardship. The latter were paid to members who were out of work in order to 'prevent [them] from accepting employment, under stress of starvation, on terms which in the common judgement of the trade, would be injurious to [their] interests' (Webb and Webb, 1897: 161). In this way, mutual insurance was a means of exerting control over the supply of labour and was a tactic in the establishment and preservation of a standard wage for a trade.

Unions still maintain such funds, which, for example, may be called on to give financial support to members in the event of a strike. Furthermore, the issue of competition between groups of workers for jobs has hardly been more relevant than it is today. As we discuss elsewhere, there is an increasing trend for transnational companies to search the globe for cheap labour markets and migrant labour is a feature of most economies (see **Globalization and Labour Migration**). The dispersal of the international labour market makes it more difficult for unions to overcome the competition between workers for work; in this context mutual insurance, as described here, has become a method of more limited utility.

In addition to mutual insurance, early trade unions sought to influence the laws governing employment and to lobby the political system to enact legislation to enforce minimum standards of treatment for workers in certain circumstances. The earliest combinations of workers had relatively modest hopes of the law; they aspired to obtain statutes regulating minimum rates of pay and the length of apprenticeships, but did not look for very much more. The unions of the later nineteenth and twentieth centuries, however, lobbied for laws on hours of work and safety, but faced an uphill battle in getting laws passed. The political environment of nineteenth-century Britain and elsewhere was dominated by economic advocacy of free trade and the doctrine of *laissez-faire* and Parliament and the courts were implacably opposed to intervention in the market. Thus trade unionists faced a 'prolonged and uncertain struggle' in pursuit of laws to protect workers and then had to rely on generally hostile law courts to enforce such regulations.

The pursuit of laws designed to improve the conditions of the working class highlights an important aspect of trade unionism – that of the union as a social and political movement. The desire for the redistribution of wealth and greater social justice lay at the heart of early trade unionism and continues as a feature of trade unionism around the globe today. With regard to legal legislation we now see a great deal more law in the employment relationship, particularly in Europe, but, interestingly, the evidence from the UK indicates that the presence of a trade union is necessary if the employer's compliance with the law is to be made more likely (Brown et al., 2000).

The final method of trade unionism to be considered is collective bargaining. This is examined in more detail elsewhere (see **Collective Bargaining**) and so it will be discussed only briefly here. In essence, the method relates to the trade union representing to the employer the 'collective will' of its members and settling 'the principles upon which ... all work[ers] of a particular group, or class, or grade, will be engaged' (ibid.: 173). The attraction of this method for strong trade unions was that they could exercise any local bargaining leverage they had established and in favourable bargaining conditions could exact more concessions from the employer than could ever be achieved on a wider scale through legal enactment (ibid.: 255). In the current context, however, as levels of union membership have declined over recent decades and competition has increased on an international scale, the incidence and influence of collective bargaining have fallen. Thus it is in the context of a weakened bargaining position that the legal regulation of minimum standards of employment has become increasingly attractive to modern-day unions.

CURRENT AND FUTURE CHALLENGES

Having considered the historical development of unions, their aspirations and the origins of their methods, is it the case that they remain relevant in today's environment or have they become anachronistic relics? In terms of whether trade unions are effective in achieving what their members seek from membership, on average, pay and conditions of employment remain higher in unionized than non-unionized establishments. Yet this has not been sufficient for trade unions to retain membership levels over the past two decades: many countries have recorded substantial falls in overall union numbers since the early 1980s. The restructuring of industry in Western developed economies has seen employment in many of the industries that were bastions of trade union membership, such as manufacturing, engineering and mining, drastically reduced. While unions have lost members in traditional areas of strength, they have been unable to achieve equivalent recruitment in newer areas of employment growth in the private service sector. In part, this reflects a greater unwillingness among employers in the latter to recognize trade unions. In part also, trade unions have been less successful in appealing to growing numbers of part-time and casual workers compared to full-time permanent employees. The orientation of trade unions is changing, however, and over recent years the decline in trade union numbers has stabilized in several countries, including the UK. But there is as yet little sign of a significant revival of union membership totals.

A considerable debate has arisen both within the trade union movement and beyond as to the best way to recover membership levels. This relates both to the way trade unions can appeal to potential members and to relations between trade unions and employers. In terms of appeal to new members, there has been a move to greater openness in recruitment as more trade unions have sought to counter membership losses by recruiting outside their traditional areas. This is in line with the 'organizing model' of trade unionism, which has been an international trend, originating in the USA. In essence, this model focuses on attracting into membership the types of workers who previously might have not naturally been drawn to trade unions and by emphasizing unionism as a social movement leading to better quality of working life (Heery, 2002). This move to greater openness in recruitment is particularly evident in unions the traditional membership base of which has dwindled as a result of changes in industrial structure. The main steelworkers union in the UK, for example, in the face of substantial decline in the number of workers employed in the industry, has sought to secure its future partly by merging with other unions and also by opening its recruitment to a much broader range of workers, including those who live within steel communities rather than just those who are employed in the industry directly. The union has also sought to reflect this change in membership by changing its name from the 'Iron and Steel Trades Confederation' to 'Community'.

In terms of union relationships with employers, different commentators have argued the merits of collaboration or partnership with employers rather than an 'arm's length' relationship (Ackers and Payne, 1998). One outcome of this is seen to be employers granting unions a greater role within the work organization, which could appeal to potential members as both more relevant and also seen to be accepted by employers. In contrast to this, critics of partnership argue that it leads inevitably to unions becoming incorporated by employers (the union given responsibilities but no real powers) and as a result are likely to appeal *less* to actual and potential members rather than more (Kelly, 1996). For these critics of partnership, a more independent role for the union is advocated as the basis for attracting members by negotiating improvements in terms and conditions of employment.

An important point to make about unions in the present day is that research suggests that people continue to join unions for the same reasons they always did (Waddington and Whitston, 1997). The commonest factors tend to be instrumental in character: the union being seen as a source of collective protection, representation, advice and a means to negotiate improvements in pay and conditions. These reasons for joining are also reflected in member attitudes regarding the priorities they think trade unions should have – to protect jobs, improve pay and conditions and act as representatives in disciplinary cases.

In conclusion, as trade unions face continuing challenges to their continued existence, we have to remember that their levels of membership have always fluctuated. Economic cycles, political change and industrial restructuring are just some of the factors that may influence their fortunes. The evidence does not appear to suggest that union membership has declined simply because workers no longer see collective organization as relevant (ibid.: 537). Current developments in work organizations, where many people feel under more pressure and lack a sense of security, also suggest that there will be ample issues for trade unions to address in the future (see **Effort and Intensity** and **Job Security**).

See also: *conflict, employment patterns, pay and performance.*

REFERENCES

Ackers, P. and Payne, J. (1998) 'British trade unions and social partnership: rhetoric, reality and strategy', *The International Journal of Human Resource Management*, 9 (3): 529–50.

Brown, W., Deakin, S., Nash, D., Oxenbridge, S. (2000) 'The employment contract: from collective procedures to individual rights', *British Journal of Industrial Relations*, 38 (4): 611–29.

Heery, E. (2002) 'Partnership versus organising: alternative futures for British trade unionism', *Industrial Relations Journal*, 33 (1): 20–35.

Kelly, J. (1996) 'Union militancy and social partnership', in P. Ackers, C. Smith and P. Smith (eds), *The New Workplace and Trade Unionism: Critical Perspectives on Work and Organization*. London, Routledge, pp. 77–109.

Waddington, J. and Whitston, C. (1997) 'Why do people join unions in a period of membership decline?', *British Journal of Industrial Relations*, 35 (4): 515–46.

Webb, S., and Webb, B. (1897) *Industrial Democracy*. London: Longmans, Green & Co.

key concepts in work

Unemployment and Underemployment

> *Definitions of unemployment vary, but typically included are those who are without a job and actively seeking employment. Underemployment refers to a situation where a person's employment is insufficient in some way.*

In a society where so much turns on paid work – its importance for feelings of self-worth and social standing, its role in income distribution, its significance as a source of satisfaction and fulfilment and its anchoring function in giving structure and purpose to people's daily lives – it is not surprising that for most individuals the experience of unemployment is a difficult and debilitating one. And it is an experience that affects not just individuals but entire households, in which both spouses and their working-age offspring are unemployed. These 'work-poor' households experience contemporary life in a dramatically different way from the dual-earner, 'work-rich' households discussed elsewhere in this volume (see **Work–Life Balance**; see also **Employment Patterns**).

MEASURING UNEMPLOYMENT

Examining trends in unemployment over time, and comparing unemployment patterns of different countries, are beset by three different types of measurement problem. First, within individual countries, the basis for unemployment statistics does not remain constant; in the UK, for example, the basis of these statistics (who is counted in the unemployment total and who is not) has altered over 30 times since 1979. Second, countries vary in their definitions of unemployment, for example, how those on sickness or invalidity benefit are treated or those following training courses or whether those who have reached 60 years of age are treated as unemployed or early retired. Finally, whichever definitions are used, they are unlikely to capture all who are jobless but would like to work. In particular, the ones most likely to be omitted are those who have become disillusioned with finding paid work and have ceased actively looking.

Yet, despite these definitional and measurement problems, some features of unemployment remain relatively clear. In terms of aggregate levels, it is evident that while unemployment fluctuates over time and also varies from country to country, in many societies there has been a gradual tendency for unemployment to rise over the past half century. In the UK, between 1945 and 1970 average annual unemployment stood at around 2 per cent of the labour force. The equivalent average for the 1970s was around twice this level, while in the 1980s and 1990s, the average level doubled in size again (Blyton and Turnbull, 2004: 74). Despite falls in unemployment in the current decade in the UK and elsewhere, average levels remain substantially above pre-1970 levels. One argument that this increase has given rise to concerns the notion of 'full employment' and if, in a more rapidly changing economy, the minimum level of unemployment will be higher (as a result of more economic turbulence as some sectors rapidly expand and others decline) than when the pace of economic change was less rapid. Whether or not this argument is valid, however – that 'full' employment may equate with an unemployment rate nearer 4 or 5 per cent than the earlier 2 per cent level – it remains the case that, in many countries and despite long periods of economic growth, those who are unemployed represent a significant proportion of the total labour force.

What is also clear about unemployment is that it affects some groups in society much more than others. In particular, unemployment rates in industrial countries tend to be significantly higher among both younger and older age groups, among unskilled workers, disabled groups and people from ethnic minorities; the unemployment rate for men is also generally higher than that for women. As regards youth unemployment (that is, those under 25 years of age), the average level is more or less double that of general unemployment. Across the OECD countries as a whole, the youth unemployment rate stood at 13.5 per cent in 2004, compared to an overall average unemployment rate of 6.8 per cent. However, in some countries the youth unemployment rate was far higher in that year: over 40 per cent in Poland for example and over 20 per cent in Italy.

The level of qualifications held is also an important factor affecting unemployment. Begum (2004) in an analysis of the characteristics of the unemployed in the UK, reports that the unemployment rate among those with no qualifications is over three times that for those with a degree or equivalent as their highest qualification. Those with no qualifications were also disproportionately represented in the long-term unemployed group (those out of work for over one year). However, the proportion of the working-age population with no qualifications is declining (see **Skill**).

EXPERIENCING UNEMPLOYMENT

Even among groups where the unemployment rate is much lower (men and women aged between 25 and 45 years), the experience of unemployment is much more widespread than the headline unemployment rate might suggest, for the unemployment rate reflects the difference between unemployment 'inflow' and 'outflow' – those becoming unemployed and those leaving unemployment in any given period. These 'flows' can be very large. In the third quarter of 2004 in the UK – a period chosen here for its unexceptional nature – the unemployment level fell by just over 60,000 (representing a fall of 0.2 per cent in the unemployment rate). However, in this period both the inflow and the outflow to and from the unemployment count were each *ten times* this level at over 600,000 people entering and leaving the unemployment count. This indicates the extent to which the experience of unemployment is much more common within a working population than average levels of unemployment might suggest.

For many who become unemployed, through redundancy, dismissal or the non-renewal of a short-term contract, for example, unemployment is a short-term experience that has a comparatively modest effect on their lives. For others, however, unemployment is a much longer-term and more profound experience. Across the 30 OECD industrial countries, almost a third of those unemployed in 2004 had been out of work for over a year and, in some countries (such as Germany, Italy and the Slovak Republic), this proportion was substantially higher. Groups who are disproportionately represented among the long-term unemployed include those over 50 years of age, those with disabilities and those with no qualifications (Begum, 2004).

Further, for those unemployed who are able to find a job, this is not necessarily the end of their problems. To a much greater extent than their counterparts moving from one job to another, those who are unemployed who find work are more likely to have a job that is temporary. This in turn contributes to the finding that around one in five of those who leave the unemployment register are unemployed again within a year (Blyton and Turnbull, 2004: 75). Further, even those who regain employment are likely to find jobs at lower levels of pay than they received prior to becoming unemployed (ibid.). In part, this reflects the temporary nature of many jobs that unemployed people secure and the greater willingness of those without work to accept jobs at lower rates of pay.

The poverty and financial problems associated with unemployment are substantial and accumulated debts often linger long after the period of unemployment is over. However, the loss of income is only one of the problems associated with unemployment. Reviewing a large number of studies on the unemployed, Warr (1987) concludes that unemployment is generally bad for people in terms of both their physical and psychological well-being, as well as their material position. Various studies point, for example, to poorer levels of mental health among the unemployed, lower levels of aspiration and increased apathy compared to their counterparts in employment (see also Jahoda, 1982). One factor that can make it more difficult for individuals to adjust to unemployment is if they have a strong work ethic; a strong orientation to work is likely to generate greater feelings of frustration from being unemployed compared to those whose work ethic is less pronounced. In general, studies of unemployed men and women ind cate the maintenance of a strong commitment to work (Edgell, 2006: 105–6).

At the same time, unemployment is not an undifferentiated aspect of contemporary society, but will be experienced differently by different people. Some who are unemployed are likely to take any job that becomes available, while others will seek a specific type of job or in a specific location; still others (perhaps many of those nearing retirement age, for example) may not be too anxious whether they have a job or not. Yet, these variations notwithstanding, it is clear that the vast majority of those who are unemployed (including many not officially counted as unemployed) wish to work if they can. A challenge for the societies in which they are located is to help improve the employability of those unemployed, endeavouring to reduce the likelihood of long-term unemployment and also seeking to intervene in the vicious cycle of unemployment being punctuated by periods of insecure and relatively low-paid work, followed again by further periods of unemployment.

UNDEREMPLOYMENT

In addition to the distinction between whether a person who is active in the labour market is employed or unemployed, a third, intermediate, category of employment status is 'underemployment'. There are different bases on which underemployment can be defined. These include people working in jobs where they do not utilize the skills or education that they possess (education or skill-based underemployment) or where jobs provide an inadequate level of income to maintain a reasonable standard of living (income-based underemployment). The most common definition of underemployment, however, is a time-based definition – job holders who are working fewer hours than they desire due to the non-availability of additional work. The largest source of underemployment is to be found in developing countries and this is often associated with large-scale migration from rural to urban areas and the inability of the developing urban economies to generate sufficient employment for the expanding labour supply. However, in developed economies, too, underemployment is evident within labour markets. Accurate figures on the overall level of underemployment in economies are difficult to establish. However, in the UK the Office for National Statistics collects data on reasons why people work part-time. In 2006, just under one in ten of the 7.2 million people working part-time reported that this was because they could not find a full-time job (ONS, 2006).

One of the main studies of underemployment, by Dooley and Prause (2004), concludes that for many the experience of being underemployed is more like that of being unemployed than being employed. In particular, these authors found that negative outcomes associated with unemployment – such as loss of self-esteem and an increased likelihood of suffering depression – were similarly identified among those who were underemployed.

The expansion of part-time working in general, and very short part-time schedules in particular, potentially increases levels of underemployment among those working part-time because they have been unable to find longer-hours jobs. One response to this is multiple job holding where individuals undertake several rather than a single part-time job in order to gain sufficient income For many in this position, however, even the holding of two or more limited-hours jobs does not resolve the income needs and other problems associated with underemployment.

See also: *absence and turnover, discrimination, flexibility, globalization and labour migration, job security, redundancy, working time.*

REFERENCES

Begum, N. (2004) 'Characteristics of the short-term and long-term unemployed', *Labour Market Trends*, April: 139–44.

Blyton, P. and Turnbull, P. (2004) *The Dynamics of Employee Relations*, 3rd edn. Basingstoke: Palgrave Macmillan.

Dooley, D. and Prause, J. (2004) *The Social Costs of Underemployment: Inadequate Employment as Disguised Unemployment*. Cambridge: Cambridge University Press.

Edgell, S. (2006) *The Sociology of Work: Continuity and Change in Paid and Unpaid Work*. London: Sage.

Jahoda, M. (1982) *Employment and Unemployment: A Social-Psychological Analysis*. Cambridge: Cambridge University Press.

Office for National Statistics (2006) 'Full-time, part-time and temporary workers, table B1', *Labour Market Trends*, 114 (12): S25.

Warr, P.W. (1987) *Work, Unemployment, and Mental Health*. Oxford: Oxford University Press.

Voluntary Work

> *Voluntary work entails giving unpaid help to an individual, group or organization.*

Like domestic work, voluntary work is often characterized as a form of hidden or informal work, reflecting the fact that it is unpaid (see **Domestic Work** and **Informal Work**). However, this should not be taken as an indication that voluntary work is not a significant element of the totality of work. Activities that constitute voluntary work vary enormously. One has only to think for a few moments of the different activities taking place in one's immediate surroundings to gain a sense of this. First, there exist a wide range of 'formal' voluntary activities: working in a charity shop, for example, or running a children's youth group, acting as a school governor or raising money for a good cause. In addition, there is an equally wide range of activities that make up informal voluntary work. These might include, for example, looking after a friend's child after school, driving an elderly neighbour to the doctor's, helping another neighbour mend his fence or being on the rota for cutting the grass in the local churchyard. A few minutes' reflection will generate a long list of activities that constitute voluntary work.

THE SCALE OF VOLUNTARY WORK

Just as the range of activities is very large, so too is the overall scale of voluntary work undertaken. A national survey in the UK in the 1990s found that just under half (48 per cent) of the adult population had engaged in some formal voluntary work during the previous year, while almost three-quarters (74 per cent) had undertaken some informal voluntary work (National Survey of Volunteering, 1997). On average, those undertaking some voluntary work were doing so for just over four hours a week; this translates into approximately 88 million hours per week being devoted to voluntary work in the UK. A subsequent survey undertaken in England and Wales has similarly highlighted the large scale of voluntary activity being undertaken (Office for National Statistics, 2005: 181).

Those performing voluntary work are not distributed evenly throughout the population. The first of the surveys referred to above, for example, found voluntary activity to be most common among those in paid employment, those with higher incomes and those in middle age, rather than older or younger age groups (National Survey of Volunteering, 1997). This same survey found men and women equally likely to be engaged in voluntary work, contrary to the conventional belief that voluntary work is undertaken mainly by women. The survey also found, however, that men and women tended to volunteer for different types of work. Women are more likely to undertake voluntary work in schools, with social welfare groups and to undertake fundraising activities, while men are disproportionately active in voluntary work involving sports groups and committee work.

In terms of the most common activities undertaken, most of the evidence available relates to formal voluntary activity. The most frequent of these activities are organizing events, raising money, leading a group, being a member of a committee, providing transport, undertaking administrative work and providing advice or information (National Survey for Volunteering, 1997; Office for National Statistics, 2005). These activities take place most frequently in connection with sports, social clubs, education, religion and health and social welfare.

The survey findings also identify a variety of factors motivating people to undertake voluntary work. These include altruistic reasons, such as a desire to contribute to the community or society and to accomplish something that would not otherwise be provided by public or private services, and more personal reasons such as to increase social contact and make friends and improve a personal sense of self-worth. Taylor's (2005) qualitative analysis of why people undertake voluntary work further underlines the range of motives involved. Prominent in her study, however, were such factors as socialization (for example, parental encouragement to undertake voluntary work) and economic factors, such as gaining experience to assist in securing paid employment (see also below). The overall picture from both survey and more in-depth enquiry is one of voluntary work fulfilling a variety of personal and social needs.

VOLUNTARY WORK AND PAID WORK

An important aspect of voluntary work is how it relates to paid work. Some people take part in voluntary work or perceive that activity as a way of enhancing their chances of securing paid work. This may be by acquiring skills, confidence and experience through voluntary work, finding out about employment or training available, building up contacts or facilitating a switch in direction into the work area of the voluntary activity. In a number of sectors, voluntary work operates alongside remunerated work – for example, in parts of the health service, social services and education – where voluntary experience may be highly relevant for employment in the corresponding paid work sphere. In addition, the voluntary sector itself is a significant employer of paid labour, such as paid administrators, field officers and managers of charities.

At the same time, as a means for individuals to move from unemployment to paid work, the significance of working voluntarily while unemployed should not be overstated. A study by Hirst (2002) found that, while a majority of volunteers believe that undertaking voluntary work improves their employability, in practice, there was little evidence that those undertaking voluntary work moved off unemployment registers more quickly than those who did not volunteer. Nonetheless, in some sectors and for some activities, the experience, skills and contacts gained through voluntary work could play an important role in helping secure particular types of paid work.

THE FUTURE OF VOLUNTARY WORK

In terms of the future, on the demand side it is clear that large areas of social life will continue to rely heavily on voluntary work, given the unlikelihood of substantially enhanced funding for those activities to be undertaken by paid labour. As Taylor (2005: 121) points out, 'successive governments have viewed voluntary work as a cost-effective weapon in the fight against particular social problems'. These 'problem' areas include aspects of health, social and care services, not least in rural communities where public and infrastructure services such as transport, are often inadequate.

Yet, on the supply side of voluntary work, a number of developments potentially threaten future levels of volunteering. The increased level of female participation in paid employment for example, together with increased work intensification and longer work hours being experienced by some groups, could act to reduce the overall level of engagement in formal and informal voluntary work (see **Effort and Intensity**, **Employment Patterns** and **Working Time**). A second threat to the level of engagement with voluntary activity is signalled by the work of

Putnam (2000) and others, who argue that people's 'social capital' – the extent to which they are engaged in community and civic life – is declining, reflecting the increasingly privatized and individualized character of contemporary society. If this continues to be the case, it potentially has far-reaching consequences for the extent to which people will be willing to take part in local voluntary activities.

On the other hand, the continued improvement in the health of older groups indicates a potential greater source for volunteering in the future as more active older men and women seek avenues to utilize their time fruitfully, following retirement from work. Further, in terms of their younger counterparts, should the current emphasis on achieving greater work–life balance continue to grow, this could contribute to a greater level of volunteering by providing both more opportunity (time) and motivation (increased recognition of the importance of activities other than paid work) that could enhance voluntary work in the future.

See also: *work–life balance.*

REFERENCES

Hirst, A. (2002) 'Links between volunteering and employability', *Labour Market Trends*, 110 (1): 45–6.
National Survey of Volunteering (1997) Available at: www.ivr.org.uk/nationalsurvey.htm
Office for National Statistics (2005) *Social Trends 35: 2005 Edition*. London: Office for National Statistics.
Putnam, R. (2000) *Bowling Alone: The Collapse and Revival of American Community*. New York: Simon & Schuster.
Taylor, R.F. (2005) 'Rethinking voluntary work', *Sociological Review*, 53 (s2): 119–35.

voluntary work

Working Time

Working time refers both to the duration and the arrangement of working hours.

The amount of time that people spend at work and what periods of the day and week they are at work represent key contributors to a person's overall experience of work. Our present discussion focuses primarily on these two aspects: the length of working time (its duration) and how this time is scheduled across the day, week or year (its arrangement). A third aspect, the utilization of working time concerning the amount of the individual's work time that is actually spent working, and the pace of that work, are examined elsewhere (see **Effort and Intensity**).

Weekly working hours, together with the length of paid holidays, are among the more clearly defined elements of the employment relationship, though a series of other factors influence the overall time spent at work, including the amount of paid or unpaid overtime worked and levels of absence and lateness. Despite the variability created by these other factors, however, the length of the working week is one of the more concrete aspects of the employment contract. When an employer purchases labour power by offering an employment contract, the exact amount of work an individual is expected to perform cannot normally be stipulated precisely in the contract. As a result, the amount of time that an individual is required to work is used as a proxy for the amount of work required. In this way, the majority of employment contracts purchase labour time rather than a specified amount of labour performance (see **The Law and Contract of Employment**). Once that time has been purchased, a key management objective is to ensure that the maximum amount of that time is used productively. This in turn gives rise to a series of measures, ranging from the monitoring and control of absence and the management of shift start and stop times, to the effective matching of available labour time with production schedules.

In securing employee discipline over working time, such that employees attend for work regularly, arrive at work punctually and utilize their working hours productively, employers are assisted in this task by the high degree of time consciousness and time discipline that most individuals in contemporary industrial society possess. Thompson (1967) identifies the growth in time consciousness as a crucial factor in the development of industrialization. A workforce with a high degree of time consciousness and time discipline is a necessary element in the synchronization of activities that a factory system requires, much more so than, for example, in small-scale cottage production activities. For Thompson, greater time discipline was instilled into individuals by such institutions as the early school system and non-conformist religion with its emphasis on time-thrift, together with the gradual spread of clocks and watches in the nineteenth century and the severe ways that factory bosses reinforced timekeeping by punishing lateness and absence. In combination, these factors created a growing time consciousness among an increasingly industrialized labour force, compared with their pre-industrial rural counterparts for whom a more general sense of clock time was adequate for their lives.

DAILY AND WEEKLY HOURS OF WORK

Over the past century, the development of working time is one mainly (though as we will see not wholly) characterized by a reduction in the duration of daily and weekly work hours and the introduction and extension of paid holidays. The early phases of industrial development in the UK and elsewhere were characterized by very long work hours, including for children, and became the focus of campaigns both by early trade union movements and social reformers. These campaigns eventually enjoyed significant success. Early reductions in daily hours for specific groups (notably young workers and women) were followed by more general reductions. Overall, the basic working week for full-time workers reduced from over 60 hours at the beginning of the twentieth century to 35–40 hours today, though, in many developing economies, the basic working week exceeds this level (OECD, 2006: 265).

In all societies, however, the picture of actual working time is far more complex than consideration of the basic working week suggests. Industrializing countries are typically characterized by high levels of underemployment (individuals wishing to work more hours than are available to them) as well as others working long hours (see **Unemployment and Underemployment**). Similarly, in industrial countries, there is much variation around the 'norm' of the basic full-time week. For example, significant proportions of workers work considerably more (48 hours+) than the basic week, while others work very short (8 hours or less) weekly schedules. In the UK, approaching 1 in 5 workers report that they usually work more than 48 hours each week. Long work hours are also a growing feature of employment notedparticularly in Australia,

Canada and the United States. At the other extreme, large numbers of people work very short weekly schedules of eight hours per week or less (for more discussion of part-time working, see **Employment Patterns**). This polarization of work hours is also highly gendered, with a disproportionate number of men spending long hours in paid work each week and large numbers of women working very short weekly schedules.

OVERTIME WORKING AND ANNUAL HOURS

Traditionally, for hours worked over and above contracted hours, and particularly those worked during weekends and holidays, employers paid for these 'overtime' hours at a premium rate (such as 'time-and-a-half' or 'double-time'). This represented an acknowledgement that there was a social cost to working these additional hours in terms of the disruption to domestic and other life outside work. Some groups receive time off rather than additional payment, while others, such as managers, typically do not receive specific additional payment for overtime hours. Moreover, even among those receiving overtime payments, the practice of a premium payment for unsocial hours working has diminished in recent years as employers have sought to contain labour costs, partly by introducing a wider definition of what constitutes 'normal' working hours. Thus, many of the shops, cafés, museums, libraries and so on that are opening later in the evening than they used to, increasingly define all opening hours as 'normal' for purposes of scheduling and payment. Elsewhere, notably in Germany, a growing number of workers can 'bank' hours worked in excess of the agreed work week and convert these hours into time off at a later stage. Some of these time banking arrangements allow the possibility of much longer periods away from work or even earlier retirement.

One means of broadening the definition of what constitutes normal working hours has been through the introduction of 'annualized hours' contracts. Under these contracts, employers and employees agree the length and scheduling of working time over a 12-month period; this contrasts with 'standard' contracts that normally define the length of weekly work hours. Annual hours contracts potentially provide management with several sources of temporal flexibility, as well as seeking to reduce their reliance on overtime working (see **Flexibility**). For example, in organizations that experience fluctuating seasonal demand (such as companies manufacturing Christmas crackers or outdoor barbecue equipment), annual hours contracts may include a seasonal hours variation whereby 'normal' work hours are longer in the busier period, offset by shorter weekly hours during the quieter months. A further source of flexibility is where a proportion of the agreed annual hours is held in reserve (that is, not rostered into the shift pattern), which can then be utilized by management to cover both planned activities (such as training) and unplanned circumstances such as absence and unforeseen fluctuations in demand (see Bell and Hart, 2003, for an analysis of annual hours contracts).

THE ARRANGEMENT OF WORKING TIME

At the same time as the average basic work week in industrial countries has been declining, employers' interest in increasing overall operating time has grown. As a result, it is increasingly likely that the operating hours of a goods- or service-provider exceeds that of an individual employee's hours, requiring one worker to replace another in some form of shift work system. The practice of shift working is long established in those activities involving continuous operations, such as a metal smelting, where furnaces need to be constantly lit to function effectively or a hospital where emergency and other services need to be available 24 hours a day. However, a feature of the recent period is that a growing number of commercial activities are being performed for progressively longer periods of time each day. These include shops, bars and restaurants, for example, together with public transport, entertainment, financial services and sports facilities. Often shift work systems incorporate both full-time and part-time elements, by some workers working full-time during the day time and others engaged on part-time evening (sometimes known as 'twilight') shifts.

Overall, the temporal restrictions on accessing goods and services are declining. Coupled with other factors, such as an employer's desire to maximize the utilization of plant and equipment by extending operating hours, this development has led to a growth of many different work schedules, both full- and part-time, to cover a greater proportion of the 24-hour day and 7-day period. One upshot of this is that a declining proportion of the workforce continues to work a traditional '9 to 5, Monday to Friday' pattern and a growing proportion of the labour force now undertakes work outside these hours during the evenings, nights and at weekends.

A broader issue in the arrangement of working time is whether, by reducing the work hours of those in employment, these unworked hours can be arranged in such a way as to create additional jobs and thereby reduce the level of unemployment. This work-sharing idea has periodically arisen during periods of high unemployment, though in practice it has been evident that shorter hours do not translate easily into new job vacancies (for various reasons but including the tendency for employers to introduce efficiencies to compensate for the shorter hours, thereby reducing the need for additional workers). However, a revatively recent nationwide attempt to link hours reductions to job creation occurred in France with the statutory reduction of the working week to 35 hours in 2000. This legislation, introduced despite strong employer opposition, resulted in a significant reduction in actual working time. However, the net effect on job creation is less clear, particularly the extent to which any new jobs created in the economy since that time can be attributed to the working time change. However, as with other work-sharing initiatives, a significant effect may be improved job retention – jobs remaining that would otherwise have been lost – rather than the creation of new jobs.

The recent pattern of working time developments has been characterized by a move away from standardized time arrangements to one exhibiting much greater diversity. This primarily reflects employers' objectives of covering longer operating and trading periods and gaining cost efficiencies from matching work hours more closely to demand. To a lesser extent, the more diversified and individualized working time patterns also reflect a labour supply in which a growing proportion of the workforce are seeking a better match of work and non-work demands on their time (see **Work–life Balance**). It seems likely that in the coming period this search for more effective work time scheduling, by both employers and employees, will gain further momentum.

See also: *absence and turnover, employment patterns, presenteeism.*

REFERENCES

Bell, D.N.F. and Hart, R.A. (2003) 'Annualised hours contracts: the way forward in labour market flexibility?', *National Institute Economic Review*, 185: 64–77.

OECD (Organisation for Economic Cooperation and Development) (2006) *Employment Outlook.* Paris: OECD.

Thompson, E.P. (1967) 'Time, work-discipline and industrial capitalism', *Past and Present*, 38: 56–97.

Work–life Balance

Work–life balance refers to the ability of individuals to pursue their work and non-work lives, without undue pressures from one undermining the satisfactory experience of the other.

The role of work within an individual's broader life is a long-standing area of interest and lies at the heart of much of the discussion of issues such as workers' orientations to work; their attitudes to work and leisure; and sources of satisfaction and commitment. The more general issue this area also relates to concerns the role and significance of work in society. In recent years, this relationship between work and non-work has received increased attention and much of this discussion has been centred on the notion of 'work–life balance'. On closer inspection this term is somewhat problematic; for example, though the expression juxtaposes work and life, in reality, work is clearly part of, rather than distinct from, life. Also, it is not automatically evident what 'balance' means in this context. Indeed, some would argue that for some groups at certain times within their life course, or others in particular economic situations, their spheres of work and non-work are, in the short term at least, not capable of being 'balanced'. Yet, despite any problems of terminology, the notion of work–life balance represents for many a sense of the importance of preventing the demands of one sphere of life dominating all other spheres.

It is evident that what comprises a satisfactory work–life balance will vary from person to person, reflecting individual circumstances and preferences. Thus, a central component of achieving a work–life balance is the degree of choice that individuals experience in their work and non-work lives to enable them to create and maintain their desired level of work and non-work activity. And for those studying work, the significance that people attribute to work–life balance indicates that it is not sufficient just to look inwards at the characteristics of work itself, but also that work needs to be viewed more broadly in terms of how well it allows individuals to fulfil their other social roles.

FACTORS INCREASING ATTENTION ON WORK–LIFE BALANCE

Several factors may help to explain the recent increase in attention being paid to the question of work–life balance. These range from a growing proportion of people reporting increases in workload and work pressure, to arguments that values in society may be shifting towards a greater emphasis on quality of life and less on material gain (what some characterize as a shift from a value of 'living to work' to one of 'working to live'). Yet, of these different factors, the most significant by far in shaping the work–life balance discussion has been the marked increase in female participation in paid work activity. Prior to this increase (evident from the 1950s, but accelerating from the 1980s onwards) employment systems in many industrial societies were more characterized by a 'male breadwinner–female homemaker' pattern, with men working full-time and their wives remaining at home and undertaking the domestic and child-care responsibilities. Under this system (and notwithstanding the different sex role issues it generated), a form of balance was created by the clear division of roles between men and women. However, the rise in women's paid work activity – and in particular the increase in dual-earner households – has given greater prominence to policies and practices that seek to reconcile the demands of work and family life (see also **Employment Patterns**).

For the employing organization, work–life balance issues to date have fallen mainly into one of three categories, often referred to as 'family-friendly' policies and practices:

- policies that provide time off for child-bearing and child-care;
- arrangements to create shorter and/or more flexible work schedules that allow work and non-work time demands to be reconciled more easily (for example, via part-time working, flexible work hours, term-time working, working at or from home or job sharing);
- workplace provisions to support parents, such as child-care facilities or subsidies (see Glass and Estes, 1997).

Of these three categories, the first is the most highly regulated (for example, through statutory maternity, paternity and parental leave) while the third is generally the least available. In the UK, in 2004, only around 3 per cent of all workplaces provided access to a workplace nursery (Kersley et al., 2006: 254). The extent of employer provision of the second category – shorter and/or more flexible work schedules – varies

key concepts in work

enormously from organization to organization and from country to country. In the UK, the latest Workplace Employment Relations Survey found that, while over a third (38 per cent) of employees indicated they had access to flexible working hours (or 'flexitime') if they needed it, much smaller proportions perceived that they had access to term-time only working (14 per cent) or the facility to work at or from home (14 per cent; ibid.: 252). Overall, flexible working hours are far less common in the UK than in several European countries such as Germany, where over 4 out of 5 larger organizations (those with over 500 employees) operate flexible working time systems for their staff (Croucher and Singe, 2004: 153).

Research shows that, whether or not formal provisions to promote a work–life balance such as flexible working are in place, a key factor in whether or not they contribute to a work–life balance is the organizational culture in which they are situated and managerial attitudes to work–life balance issues (Trinczek, 2006). Overall, it seems less important what formal policies exist in organizations in respect of flexible working, than what the organization's attitude is to those seeking greater flexibility – for example, whether those working shorter hours or seeking greater flexibility are regarded as less committed to the organization. If employees feel that they will be perceived less positively by their employer if they avail themselves of the flexibility or other work–life balance provisions, this will deter take-up. And it is evident that some employers clearly view requests to change or reduce hours as a sign that the employee's commitment to the job may be in question. One example quoted in the work–life balance literature, for example, concerns an investment bank that used employee enquiries and applications for flexibility or parental leave as a means of identifying those who were less committed to the organization and who thus should be next in line for redundancy.

Aside from the question of employer provision (or lack of provision), what is becoming more widely recognized is that the issue of work–life balance stretches far beyond the family-friendly provisions designed principally to allow women to maintain employment while fulfilling child-care roles. For example, there is a growing awareness of the different nature of work–life balance for different groups and for those in different stages of the life course. The work–life balance preferences of younger and older workers, for example, of single and married employees, those with and without children and the healthy and the not so healthy are likely to vary considerably. A point also being increasingly recognized is that work–life balance is an important issue for men as well as women.

Second, there is an increasing recognition that non-work is far broader than domestic activity and incorporates a range of community, voluntary and leisure spheres. Given the decline in civic participation over recent decades – reflected, for example, in reduced levels of local and national political and trade union participation and other voluntary association activity (see Putnam, 2000) – one question this raises is the extent to which the decline can be explained by greater demands being imposed by the work sphere, rather than by some other explanation, such as increased individualization in contemporary society.

Third, there is a need to take fuller account of the implications for work-life balance of changes occurring in the workplace, including: widespread increases in reported work pressure; a growth in average working hours in some countries in recent years; an increased blurring of work–non-work boundaries by more varied work patterns including the rise of evening and weekend working; and the ability of new communication technologies (e-mail, home computers, mobile phones) to allow work more easily to invade and disrupt non-work domains (see **Effort and Intensity, Teleworking** and **Working Time**).

Fourth, research on preferences over working time underlines that work–life balance issues cannot be reduced to a simple question of shorter and/or more flexible working hours. Indeed, for a number of groups (such as the unemployed and those on very short hours) work–life balance is about securing more, not less, work (see **Unemployment and Underemployment**). Overall, studies of employees' preferences on working time show that those working long hours would prefer to work fewer, whereas many of those working few hours would prefer to increase the amount of time they work.

Fifth, and related to the previous point, much greater recognition needs to be given to the critical importance of income level and job security for understanding employees' views on work–life balance. Balancing work and life means very different things in a professional, dual-earner household, enjoying high income (and high security regarding future income), good-quality jobs, considerable autonomy and working for employers who will be more inclined to accommodate requests for flexibility, than in a low-income family whose members are subject to low-paid and often less secure jobs, often in situations where there is less autonomy and flexibility and where employers are less likely to be sympathetic to family-friendly policies. In these different contexts, then, work arrangements such as part-time working are likely to have very different implications for work–life balance. In the higher-income household, one member working part-time may be the ideal way to balance household and other non-work activities with paid work. In a low-income family, however, one member working part-time may exacerbate the difficulties arising from a shortage of income, thereby undermining any potential of part-time work to contribute positively to work–life balance (Warren, 2004). Further, while a high-income household may create additional work–life balance for itself by buying in services (child-care, house cleaning, laundry services and so on), in a low-income household such purchasing of work–life balance will be unaffordable.

THE FUTURE

Work–life balance is a relevant issue for all working people and is likely to become more so as the demands for higher performance in the workplace continue to grow. A danger is, however, that work–life balance becomes (and in some respects has already become) one more characteristic that distinguishes good jobs from bad jobs. Already, some jobs and occupations enjoy far greater access than others to relatively high income, security, a career, a pension scheme, interesting work with a degree of autonomy and work that is performed in a healthy and safe working environment. It is likely that these same jobs and occupations are also the ones offering job holders greater access to work–life balance. In part, what will dictate this in the future will be the relative labour market power of some employee groups compared with others. Employers' desire to attract and retain certain skills means that inducements such as work–life balance features are more likely to be made available to some than others. In the light of this, it becomes all the more important that key provisions are underpinned by statutory regulation and also that employee representatives (trade unions and staff associations) work to ensure that measures aimed at achieving a greater work–life balance are operated without prejudice to those seeking access to them.

See also: *career, domestic work, flexibility.*

REFERENCES

Croucher, R. and Singe, I. (2004) 'Co-determination and working time accounts in the German finance industry', *Industrial Relations Journal*, 35 (2): 153–68.

work–life balance

Glass, J.L. and Estes, S.B. (1997) 'The family responsive workplace', *Annual Review of Sociology*, 23: 289–313.

Kersley, B., Alpin, C., Forth, J., Bryson, A., Bewley, H., Dix, G. and Oxenbridge, S. (2006) *Inside the Workplace: Findings from the 2004 Employment Relations Survey.* Abingdon: Routledge.

Putnam, R. (2000) *Bowling Alone: The Collapse and Revival of American Community.* New York: Simon & Schuster.

Trinczek, R. (2006) 'Work–life balance and flexible work hours – the German experience', in P. Blyton, B. Blunsdon, K. Reed and A. Dastmalchian (eds), *Work-Life Integration: International Perspectives on the Balancing of Multiple Roles.* Basingstoke: Palgrave Macmillan, pp. 113–34.

Warren, T. (2004) 'Working part-time: achieving a successful "work–life balance"?', *British Journal of Sociology*, 55 (1): 99–122.